REGULATING CONCEPTION

FAMILIES, LAW, AND SOCIETY SERIES

General Editor: Nancy E. Dowd and Robin A. Lenhardt

Masculinities and the Law: A Multidimensional Approach
Ann C. McGinley, Edited by Frank Rudy Cooper

Justice for Kids: Keeping Kids Out of the Juvenile Justice System
Edited by Nancy E. Dowd

The New Kinship: Constructing Donor-Conceived Families
Naomi R. Cahn

What Is Parenthood? Contemporary Debates about the Family
Edited by Linda C. McClain and Daniel Cere

The Marriage Buyout: The Troubled Trajectory of U.S. Alimony Law
Cynthia Lee Starnes

A New Juvenile Justice System: Total Reform for a Broken System
Edited by Nancy E. Dowd

Children, Sexuality, and the Law
Edited by Sacha M. Coupet and Ellen Marrus

Divorced from Reality: Rethinking Family Dispute Resolution
Jane C. Murphy and Jana B. Singer

In Our Hands: The Struggle for U.S. Child Care Policy
Elizabeth Palley and Corey S. Shdaimah

Ending Zero Tolerance: The Crisis of Absolute School Discipline
Derek W. Black

The Poverty Industry: The Exploitation of America's Most Vulnerable Citizens
Daniel L. Hatcher

The Politicization of Safety: Critical Perspectives on Domestic Violence Responses
Edited by Jane K. Stoever

Blaming Mothers: American Law and the Risks to Children's Health
Linda C. Fentiman

The Ecology of Childhood: How Our Changing World Threatens Children's Rights
Barbara Bennett Woodhouse

Living Apart Together: Legal Protections for a New Form of Family
Cynthia Grant Bowman

Social Parenthood in Comparative Perspective
Edited by Clare Huntington, Courtney G. Joslin, and Christiane von Bary

The End of Family Court: How Abolishing the Court Brings Justice to Children and Families
Jane M. Spinak

The Architecture of Desire: How the Law Shapes Interracial Intimacy and Perpetuates Inequality
Solangel Maldonado

Children's Rights and Children's Development: An Integrated Approach
Edited by Jonathan Todres and Ursula Kilkelly

Making the Best of Semen: Prospects for Law and Regulation
Anita Bernstein

Centering Families of Color: A Reimagination of Family Law
R. A. Lenhardt and Nancy E. Dowd

Accessing Abortion: Global and Comparative Perspectives
Edited by Rachel Rebouché and Mindy Jane Roseman

Regulating Conception: Science, Politics, and Reproductive Genetic Innovation
Myrisha S. Lewis

Regulating Conception

Science, Politics, and Reproductive Genetic Innovation

Myrisha S. Lewis

New York University Press

New York

NEW YORK UNIVERSITY PRESS
New York
www.nyupress.org

Library of Congress Cataloging-in-Publication Data
Names: Lewis, Myrisha S. author
Title: Regulating conception : science, politics, and reproductive genetic innovation / Myrisha S. Lewis.
Description: New York : New York University Press, 2026. | Series: Families, law, and society | Includes bibliographical references and index. | Summary: "Regulating Conception is an examination of controversy in medical, genetic, and reproductive genetic innovation and the uncovering of a hidden federal system for the (burdensome) regulation of reproduction and controversial innovations like abortifacients and contraception"— Provided by publisher.
Identifiers: LCCN 2025021767 (print) | LCCN 2025021768 (ebook) | ISBN 9781479831524 hardback | ISBN 9781479831531 ebook | ISBN 9781479831555 ebook other
Subjects: LCSH: Human reproductive technology—Law and legislation—United States | Genetic engineering—Law and legislation—United States | Reproductive technology—United States | Abortifacients—United States | Contraception—United States
Classification: LCC KF3830 .L49 2026 (print) | LCC KF3830 (ebook) | DDC 344.7303/219669208—dc23/eng/20250505
LC record available at https://lccn.loc.gov/2025021767
LC ebook record available at https://lccn.loc.gov/2025021768

This book is printed on acid-free paper, and its binding materials are chosen for strength and durability. We strive to use environmentally responsible suppliers and materials to the greatest extent possible in publishing our books.

The manufacturer's authorized representative in the EU for product safety is Mare Nostrum Group B.V., Mauritskade 21D, 1091 GC Amsterdam, The Netherlands. Email: gpsr@mare-nostrum.co.uk.

Manufactured in the United States of America

10 9 8 7 6 5 4 3 2 1

Also available as an ebook

To my family—thank you for all the love, support, and laughs.

CONTENTS

Introduction 1

1. A Range of Regulatory Options 15
2. The Development of Traditional and Advanced Assisted Reproductive Technologies 28
3. The Evolving Law of Assisted Reproduction 48
4. Life, Embryos, and Abortion: Religious and Moral Influences on the Federal Regulation of Traditional ART in the United States 64
5. The Genetic Revolution: Past and Present 84
6. Self-Regulation, Techno-Anxiety, and the Growing Role of the Federal Government in the Regulation of Genetic Innovation and Embryonic Research 98
7. "Lost" FDA Files, Morality, and the Abortion Debate: The Influence of Politics on Regulation 121
8. Reproductive Genetic Innovation, Subterranean Regulation, and Ways to Reduce Political Influence on Reproduction 146

Conclusion 160

Acknowledgments 165

Appendix A: Letter to Sponsors / Researchers 167

Appendix B: Letter About Human Cloning 171

Notes 173

Index 235

About the Author 249

Introduction

From 1978 to 2010, in vitro fertilization (IVF) led to the birth of more than 4 million children worldwide.[1] By 2019, an estimated 6 million children had been born worldwide as a result of in vitro fertilization.[2] As of 2024, estimates indicate that IVF has led to more than 8 million children worldwide.[3] In the United States alone, over 1 million babies have been born using IVF or other forms of assisted reproduction involving the handling of embryos or eggs in a lab; this number excludes the use of artificial insemination.[4] Celebrity stories of fertility treatments have also increased the public's awareness of these techniques. Readers of Michelle Obama's *Becoming*, for example, received some insight into the former first lady's and former president's fertility journey, which included Michelle Obama self-administering daily injections to stimulate viable eggs to be retrieved by medical professionals, and fertilized using in vitro fertilization, with the resultant embryos to be implanted into her.[5] Michelle Obama's fertility journey resulted in the birth of her two children. Many other women, including Kim Kardashian, Céline Dion, Amy Schumer, Kandi Burruss-Tucker, and Brooke Shields, have joyful stories of how IVF (sometimes combined with surrogacy) has led to the expansion of their families.[6] Earlier usage of IVF tended to focus on aiding married, opposite-sex couples; today partnered individuals, single people, and queer families can all use assisted reproductive technology (ART) to have children. Celebrities, including Andy Cohen and Anderson Cooper, have shared their experiences with IVF and surrogacy.[7] In many instances the public has celebrated these fertility successes. In 2018, approximately one-third of American adults reported that they have undergone fertility treatment or that someone they know personally has.[8]

Regulating Conception: Science, Politics, and Reproductive Genetic Innovation frames the story of IVF and the unfolding story of reproductive genetic innovation around socio-legal responses to innovation in reproduction. It focuses on social events and trends (and societal and legal responses to those trends)—like the birth of children through IVF, the increasingly common usage of assisted reproduction, and the increasing salience of genetic knowledge—to see how the law has responded (or not) to these phenomena, and the significance of those regulatory positions. It also examines the motivations for regulation and how those regulatory decisions connect to the larger social context in the United States and globally. Part of that examination includes inquiries into institutional and legal design: more specifically, what level of regulation is used, what level of regulation is best, and what can each level of regulation achieve? Moreover, *Regulating Conception* considers whether the current regulatory position should remain as it is.

As childbearing decisions are made later in life and the nuclear family declines in popularity, often leading to increasing medical intervention to achieve pregnancy, it is worth reconsidering the current tendency to place regulatory authority in the federal government or any other entity that has subjugated minorities or women.[9] After considering the implications of third-party involvement in reproduction, the book advocates for a hands-off approach to the regulation of reproduction to reduce the domination of conservative social and political views in regulation.

Definitions of assisted reproduction vary. Some entities, such as the United Kingdom's National Health Service, include artificial insemination as a form of assisted reproduction; other groups, like the Centers for Disease Control and Prevention, do not.[10] This book focuses on modern forms of ART such as in vitro fertilization and gamete (egg or sperm) freezing. People have been creating families by using assisted reproduction, though, since at least the late 1940s, and we might trace the timeline back to biblical times, given the story of Abram (later named Abraham), who impregnated his servant Hagar because his wife Sarai was barren.[11]

The recent openness about IVF and surrogacy starkly contrasts with previous historical treatment of assisted reproduction. In the early years of ART, court cases and legislation had to address whether artificial insemination was adultery as well as clearly determine the legal parentage of the children conceived using ART.[12] Further, because of the stigma that accompanied ART and the shaming of individuals with fertility difficulties, patients had limited options, and it was easier for physicians to conceal medical wrongdoing.[13] The advent of popular genetic databases has played a significant role in exposing physicians who used their own semen in artificial insemination without their patients' knowledge, making themselves the genetic parents of their patients' children.[14] Genetic databases have also changed the meaning of "anonymity" in a field that has historically referred to the often-commercialized system of "anonymous donation" where purportedly "anonymous donors" receive money and "donees" pay for gametes based on advertised characteristics that may or may not be true.[15]

This is a book about regulation and societal change. Even just the past five years have been marked by significant changes in society, medicine, and assisted reproduction. In 2020, for example, the public saw, in the legal and societal responses to the COVID-19 pandemic, the influence of politics on the practice of medicine and on decision-making in the area of public health, which many would have expected to be, instead, objective and scientific.

Political preferences can influence legislative actions, like statutes, funding decisions, and even informal interactions between legislators and the public. Political preferences and beliefs also influence the actions of individuals, whether in their personal capacities, including beliefs and voting preferences, or in their capacities as public servants or private employees. Over time, litigation, public statements, and academic scrutiny have revealed how political preferences can impact the regulatory decisions of legislators and bureaucrats involved with the day-to-day implementation of vague laws, which is significant in light of the increasing number of reproductive decisions that require interactions with physicians or the government.[16]

The Laws of Medicine and Assisted Reproduction

In general, two levels of regulation are relevant to medicine and assisted reproduction—state regulation and federal regulation. This book will detail the operation of these types of law as necessary. At the state and federal levels, generally, the legal literature often refers to the "practice–products" divide in medicine, which indicates a demarcation of state authority over the practice of medicine and federal authority over the products used in that practice.[17] Thus, states regulate the practice of medicine through the enactment of statutes governing and defining the practice of medicine, the licensing of health care providers (and prosecution of the unauthorized practice of medicine), and the operation of tort law systems—namely, medical malpractice regimes and also products liability regimes.[18] Many individuals are already familiar with the operation of state law, as state law tends to touch on many important areas of life, including marriage, inheritance, medical licensing, vehicle registration and titling, organ donation, and medical malpractice. Some may be less familiar with the broader role of the state in "family law," which at the state level covers a broad swath of issues including marriage, divorce, cohabitation, and parentage. So, even though one might not notice the particulars of it, state law is particularly relevant to one's life.

The federal government regulates the products used in the practice of medicine, like drugs and biologics, which are covered under patent law from the perspective of innovation and federal food and drug law in a system that sites marketing approval with the US Food and Drug Administration (FDA).[19] Chapter 1 will detail the disputes that surround the practice–products divide as well as the debates that have accompanied both state and federal approaches to the regulation of assisted reproduction. It will also discuss the advantages and disadvantages of regulating at each level, including issues of uniformity, efficiency, and resource availability.

The law discussed in this book involves a broad range of sources, including state and federal statutory law, appropriations decisions (with an emphasis on federal law and state responses when Congress refuses to fund certain types of research), case law or common law (mostly at the state level, but with some aspects of federal law), presidential executive orders, and, at the federal level, an extensive amount of administrative law and federal agency–issued documents that, while not necessarily "law," in the "hard" law or conventional sense of the word, operate with the effect of law.[20] The use of agency-issued documents that fall short of enforcement action or "official" agency regulations is particularly pronounced in the story of what I call the "subterranean regulation" of forms of assisted reproductive technology involving genetic innovation.

Reproductive Genetic Innovation

IVF did not (and still does not) address everyone's infertility issues, and scientists continue to research potential solutions. In the 1990s physicians in the United States, including Dr. Jacques Cohen at the St. Barnabas Medical Center, used a technique called "cytoplasmic transfer" that combined in vitro fertilization with small amounts of genetic substitution in order to improve fertility outcomes. Ultimately, at least 23 children were born using the technique.[21] When the FDA learned of these births, it effectively prohibited the use of the technique in humans in the United States; this regulatory story will be detailed in Chapter 7. The FDA's assertions of jurisdiction deterred physician-researchers in the area of cytoplasmic transfer, but they did not preclude later scientists from conducting research on mitochondrial transfer, a similar technique involving slightly less modification. Mitochondrial transfer, like cytoplasmic transfer, could be used to improve fertility outcomes, but also to preclude the transmission of harmful genetic disease.[22] Yet, as will be detailed, mitochondrial transfer has been targeted by the FDA similarly to cytoplasmic transfer and remains unavailable in the United States.[23]

Cytoplasmic transfer, mitochondrial transfer, and germline gene editing (a technique that would involve far more modification than cytoplasmic and mitochondrial transfer) are all subject to an FDA advisory that states that these techniques require the submission of an investigational new drug application, which is what pharmaceutical companies submit on the path to marketing approval.[24] I argue that this characterization is incorrect, although as of June 2025, no one has challenged this FDA statement in court. In this book I refer to techniques like cytoplasmic transfer, mitochondrial transfer, and germline gene editing as *reproductive genetic innovation*—a term I use to refer to forms of assisted reproductive technology that combine in vitro fertilization with genetic modification or substitution.[25]

In this book I make several normative claims and observations. First, there is a trend, especially in American law, that the law has to "catch up" to science and society. For example, as will be emphasized in the narrative regarding state regulation of assisted reproduction, many individuals have used assisted reproduction techniques to facilitate family creation, which in turn has led to litigation of these novel issues. In assisted reproduction, this litigation has largely unfolded in state court, as discussed in Chapter 3. The existence of so many decisions in state court is notable because it connects to the prevailing scholarly argument that assisted reproduction is the "Wild Wild West," meaning unregulated, a perspective with which I disagree for several reasons, as outlined in Chapters 3 and 7. First, assisted reproduction is actually highly regulated at the state level, insofar as states have passed statutes addressing the consequences of assisted reproduction through the enactment of statutes modeled on the Uniform Parentage Act, for example. Moreover, reproduction is highly regulated in the United States through mechanisms that are not clearly applicable legislation. Similarly, setting aside the issue of reproductive genetic innovation, in more recent developments in the realm of ART there is increasing litigation in various states that essentially establishes that fertility clinics owe certain duties to their customers and by breaching those duties, such as by allowing embryos and eggs to thaw, significant liability can be imposed.[26] Moving to the issue of reproductive genetic innovation, several chapters of the book are focused on the FDA's gradual regulation of techniques of reproductive genetic innovation through administrative law tools that have the impact of law but that are not law per se and are difficult to access. The effect of these federal agency actions, combined with recent, past, and likely recurring congressional funding decisions is to create an extensive and effective method of obstructing the use of reproductive genetic innovation in the United States.

Politics and Ethics

One could divide the story of reproductive genetic innovation by topic areas: (1) legislation, (2) politics, and (3) regulation. Politics are a large part of the story related to reproductive genetic innovation. Political decisions accompany a number of aspects related to reproductive genetic innovation, such as (1) research funding (including a lack of governmental funding), (2) levels of regulation (with ART being highly unregulated at the state level and highly regulated at the federal level when genetic modification or substitution is involved), and (3) decisions about whether the techniques should be covered under federal and private health insurance.

There are many negative reactions to assisted reproduction that often parallel the bioethical criticisms that have accompanied assisted reproduction since its inception, including concerns about exploitation, the appropriate role of persons in directing the fates of others, and the impact of such techniques on women and future generations. However, as will be detailed in Chapter 2, the more modern version of Hagar's biblical surrogacy—artificial insemination by known sperm donor into a woman who is not married to the sperm donor and who carries the child to term (traditional surrogacy)—is highly disfavored due to the well-known *Baby M* case, which involved multiple court dates, controversy, and the transport of a minor child across state lines. Similarly, less celebratory and controversial stories include the furor generated by Nadya Suleman's use of IVF to conceive octuplets while she was receiving public assistance;[27] Sofia Vergara's lengthy litigation with her ex-fiancé, who wished to use their frozen embryos against her will;[28] stories of fertility clinic "mix-ups";[29] fraudulent donor profiles;[30] and freezer failures that resulted in the loss of cryopreserved eggs and embryos.[31]

Beyond that, a number of other political debates and decisions, such as those related to stem cell research, implicate ART, because IVF has been the source of many of the embryos used in stem cell research; this leads directly into debates about abortion, as many inquire into the origins of life and when life begins. Many of these issues were highlighted during George W. Bush's presidency, during which President Bush's decision on the funding of stem cell research by the National Institutes of Health (NIH) and his support for the Snowflakes Frozen Embryo Adoption Program were particularly newsworthy.[32] Today, issues related to "personhood"—including personhood legislation, related abortion legislation, and fetal tissue research—remain salient for the ART field.[33] Further, these political concerns inevitably connect to a number of bioethical debates, including those related to human hubris (the idea that scientists and physicians are "playing God"); disparities based on race, economics, and health; and concerns about access, disability, the consent of future generations, and parental autonomy.[34]

Fertility treatment is expensive in the United States. The cost of fertility treatment is partly due to regulatory choices, including whether fertility treatments should be the subject of health insurance mandates at all, assuming the treatments are not banned or hindered by government actors. As techniques become more commonplace, insurance coverage increases whether as a result of state statutes or employer health insurance decisions.[35] For example, Michelle Obama benefited from employer-provided health insurance coverage of fertility treatments.[36]

Health insurance or employer-provided coverage is significant, as estimates of average costs of IVF in the United States range from approximately $12,000 to $17,000 per cycle (excluding fertility drugs like hormone injections to stimulate egg production).[37] With fertility drugs, the costs can average approximately $25,000 per cycle, a factor that motivates some women to try to source those medications, and even fertility services themselves, from suppliers abroad.[38] Moreover, many women must undergo multiple cycles of IVF in order to become pregnant or must spend money on multiple IVF cycles, even though they do not result in a pregnancy. All of this can easily add up to extensive costs in the pursuit of a genetically related baby, although some clinics have "shared risk" programs that minimize these costs, and some private organizations offer grants.[39] Cost estimates of ART focus on the price charged for services and omit costs such as travel costs (including flights and hotel stays), travel time, and time off from work.[40] Today, the fertility industry is valued at $8 billion.[41]

For noncelebrities, egg freezing is also increasing in popularity. Today, in addition to free meals, stock options, and remote work, Google, Facebook, and Apple offer "egg freezing" to their employees as a "perk."[42] In 2019, news stories covered women traveling to Spain for both vacation and egg freezing; the women's reasons included saving money, at a time when in Spain egg freezing cost $3,500 to $4,000 (excluding travel costs), instead of the $15,000 to $25,000 it cost in the United States.[43] By 2020, early COVID-19 pandemic news stories recounted the experiences of American and British women who stored their eggs in European Union member states in order to minimize the cost of egg freezing but later found that they could not access those eggs in Spain due to pandemic-related travel restrictions (although international shipping was an available option).[44] In spite of the costs of ART services, fertility clinics reported an uptick in women using their egg-freezing services during the COVID-19 pandemic.[45] This uptick corresponded with an increasing knowledge that after age 35, pregnancy becomes far more dangerous for the fetus and mother as well as unlikely.[46] In other words, "each month that she tries, a healthy, fertile 30-year-old woman has a 20% chance of getting pregnant. That means that for every 100 fertile 30-year-old women trying to get pregnant in 1 cycle, 20 will be successful. By age 40, a woman's chance is less than 5% per cycle."[47] ART can, in certain instances, "turn back time" and offer better fertility outcomes than would occur naturally.

Administrative Law and Subterranean Regulation

Colloquial discussions of politics and governments are full of references to "red tape," "bureaucracy," "bureaucrats," and "gridlock." Most of these references are about the federal government, more specifically, federal administrative agencies. There are over 400 administrative agencies in the federal government.[48] Generally, federal administrative agencies are housed within the executive branch of the government, although some administrative agencies are more "independent" of the president than others.[49] In general, federal agencies derive their authority from enabling statutes that have been passed by the US Congress.[50] The US Department of Health and Human Services is a federal agency whose operating divisions include the Centers for Disease Control and Prevention, Food and Drug Administration, Health Resources and Services Administration, and National Institutes of Health.[51]

While many expect these administrative agencies to be "objective" scientific decision-making agencies, they are still political entities, not only in organization, as they are housed within the executive branch of the federal government, but also in action, as evidenced by politically biased decision-making. I argue that there are a number of hidden ethical and moral views that have led to such a hidden, hostile regulatory regime; and even though it is not clear from FDA-issued documents how those views impact regulation, examining the views of politicians and agency employees in other areas reveals what motivates the current regulatory status of reproductive genetic innovation. The regulatory regime is especially hostile to reproductive genetic innovation, saddling it with extensive regulatory barriers, which is contrary to the prevailing scholarly view that assisted reproductive technology is minimally regulated or unregulated. Ultimately, in this book I address three broader questions: (1) What moral, social, or political views impact regulation? (2) Should Americans create a regulatory state that aims to reduce the influence of political, social, or moral views on the regulation of reproduction? (3) How can individuals reduce the influence of politics on the regulation of reproduction?

Chapter Summaries

The following chapters analyze and critique the role of regulators and legislators in relation to law, innovation, and societal views. I argue that an awareness of path dependence—combined with increasing political and religious controversy related to abortion, cloning, embryonic stem cells, and assisted reproduction in general—has led to a regulatory regime that exists outside of conventional legislation and may never be overturned. I also highlight the initial actors in the story of America's subterranean regulation of reproductive genetic modification, including physicians, scientists, administrative agency officials, legislators at the federal, state, and local levels, individuals in need of fertility treatments, current and future parents, and society overall.

The beginning of this book focuses on legal, scientific, and medical background. Chapter 1 discusses regulatory options. Chapters 2–4 focus on societal and legal reactions to traditional assisted reproductive technology, meaning ART without genetic modification or substitution. Chapter 2 will discuss the medical and scientific developments in traditional ART. Chapter 3 will then cover state regulation of ART. Chapter 4 moves into the moral, political, and social issues that might underlie those decisions in depth. Chapters 5 and 6 focus on genetic innovation beginning with the advances in recombinant DNA technology in the 1970s, as well as the regulatory and societal reactions to these advances. The latter part of the book discusses the largely federal regulatory reaction to reproductive genetic innovation, including an expansion of jurisdiction, and argues for a regime that would treat reproductive genetic innovation in a hands-off manner, in order to preserve reproductive rights and increase transparency. Chapters 7 and 8 focus on the influence of politics on regulation including the subterranean regulation of reproductive genetic innovation as well as the regulation of reproduction more broadly, including contraception and abortifacients.

Chapter 1, which covers the regulatory sphere and is intended for both specialists and nonspecialists, provides an overview of potential regulatory options, so that the reader understands and considers these options as they read later chapters related to scientific advances and societal and legal responses to those advances. Along with an overview of relevant federal and state law, this chapter discusses the many ways of regulating, which include economic policy, innovation policy, criminal prohibitions, and bureaucratic hurdles or facilitative options. It also emphasizes the roles of both extensive regulation and hands-off approaches to regulation and provides relevant background on federal agency authority. The chapter provides a broad overview of the scope of congressional authority as well as how Congress has used its power to legislate in the areas of scientific and medical innovation. Also included are an overview of the scope of individual states' jurisdiction, how they have exercised that jurisdiction so far in the areas of scientific and medical innovations, as well as the practice of medicine in general. The chapter also emphasizes federal actions outside of creating substantive legislation, such as appropriations legislation, licensing and gatekeeping functions, and funding restrictions.

Chapter 2 provides a brief scientific overview of contemporary forms of assisted reproductive technology (ART), including in vitro fertilization and artificial insemination as well as add-ons such as preimplantation genetic testing, which allows parents to select embryos with certain traits. The chapter's historical narrative begins with the development of ART in England, the site of the world's first baby born as a result of in vitro fertilization and includes scientific advances, societal responses, and the regulatory environment that developed in the United Kingdom, in order to show the different regulatory options available to respond to ART. The latter half of the chapter briefly discusses the development of "advanced assisted reproductive technology"—a term I use to refer to ART involving genetic modification or substitution.

Chapter 3 covers historical reactions to ART in the United States and the trend of science outpacing the law at both federal and state levels. Because the law often reflects or highlights moral views, such as the early characterizations of artificial insemination as being akin to adultery, the chapter discusses historical reactions and debates to show why the law surrounding traditional assisted reproductive technology is scant. The chapter also discusses the prevailing scholarly view that assisted reproductive technology is "minimally regulated" or "unregulated," a view that will be substantially rebutted in Chapters 7 and 8.

Chapter 4 discusses the debate over the technologies detailed in Chapter 2 and centers the opposition to ART within the larger American political and bioethical debates, particularly how religion greatly influences American perspectives on issues related to reproduction and assisted reproduction, including abortion. Chapter 4 also provides an overview of congressional hearings related to ART and how these connect to larger debates in the United States related to abortion and religious views. These debates provide useful comments from legislators, revealing the underlying political views that affect their legislative and regulatory decision-making, including the use of budget riders that prevent the funding of certain activities and restrict the use of funds on certain activities by federal agencies. The chapter also discusses how ethical views or concerns, which are often a proxy for religious views, impact regulatory decision-making not only for traditional ART but also for scientific innovation more broadly.

Chapter 5 is a general historical overview of the genetic "revolution." It begins with a discussion of significant genetic innovations and technologies: (1) The 1980 Nobel Prize in Chemistry, described by the Nobel Committee as awarding "[half of the prize to] Paul Berg 'for his fundamental studies of the biochemistry of nucleic acids, with particular regard to recombinant-DNA' and the other half jointly to Walter Gilbert and Frederick Sanger 'for their contributions concerning the determination of base sequences in nucleic acids,'" (2) human and animal cloning, (3) embryonic stem cell research, and (4) the 2020 Nobel Prize in Chemistry "for the development of a method for genome editing." The chapter also discusses the bioethical concerns that accompanied various genetic innovations before transitioning into the FDA's regulation of reproductive genetic innovation through an extremely preclusive regime. The FDA has treated reproductive genetic innovation, such as mitochondrial transfer and cytoplasmic transfer, with significant regulatory hostility—as evidenced by subterranean regulation, which has effectively made those technologies unavailable in the United States.

Chapter 6 begins with the scientific self-regulation that has accompanied recombinant DNA technology, which occurred at the 1973 and 1975 Asilomar conferences. It discusses various legal issues and regulatory choices that accompany genetic innovation, including patent law and federal funding restrictions. The chapter also briefly discusses the popular and scientific furor that accompanied the announcement by Dr. He Jiankui, at the International Human Gene Editing Summit in 2018, that he used CRISPR-Cas9 technology to gene-edit two embryos before their implantation into a woman who gave birth to two girls, purportedly named Lulu and Nana.[52]

Chapter 7 shows how the political debates and societal discourse related to traditional ART influence regulation not only in Congress but also at the level of administrative agency decision-making. It also details the impact of politics and morality on regulation, not only in laws passed by legislators but also in regulations and actions of federal agency employees. The chapter critically examines the regulatory history in which the FDA slowly increased its power over techniques combining ART and genetic modification, even though legislative history indicates that Congress never considered the FDA as an agency to regulate ART.

In addition to this widely accessible, publicly available history of congressional hearings, Chapter 7 analyzes a hidden regulatory regime, what I call subterranean regulation. Subterranean regulation of ART is evidenced by documents obtained through Freedom of Information Act (FOIA) requests and the FDA's issuance of untitled letters and warning letters, which the agency sometimes makes publicly available on its website (in contrast to other agencies that have more robust systems for retaining documents). For example, the FDA posted on its website an untitled letter that had the effect of causing physician-researchers to stop providing cytoplasmic transfer, an ART technique involving reproductive genetic modification; however, in response to an FOIA request for the list of addressees, the FDA reported that it "could not find the admin file," which is shocking in light of the nature of administrative agency operation.[53]

Chapter 7 also discusses the FDA's subterranean actions in the targeting of OvaScience, a defunct company (as of 2018) that stopped providing AUGMENT, its fertility treatment, after receiving an untitled letter from the FDA. In its case, the FDA's untitled letter stated that the AUGMENT treatment would require an investigational new drug application (IND) for marketing in the United States because, contrary to the company's assessment, the treatment did not fall within the regulatory exemption for "minimally manipulated" products that do not require an FDA license.[54] After receiving the letter, the company only provided the technique abroad. Moreover, the company had to expend legal resources on a shareholder suit; after shareholders were informed of the FDA's letter, a shareholder sued the company, alleging that the company defrauded investors when it previously stated that the treatment would not need FDA approval. While that lawsuit was eventually dismissed, it illustrates the significance of the FDA's determination. The case studies in Chapter 7 support this book's argument that subterranean regulation can result in significant legal and practical barriers, including the halting of innovation, lawsuits, and even potential criminal action.

Chapter 8 discusses the failures of state bureaucracy in safeguarding reproductive rights. I also argue here, though, that the current method of state-based regulation of the practice of medicine enables the private market to operate more freely and hinder regulatory interference with what should be personal decisions. While it may seem that the choice is between the federal government (and the status quo) and the states (which have arguably engaged in more encouragement of reproductive medical innovation than the federal government), the states offer the least intrusive mechanism of reproductive regulation due to their general hands-off stance. A state-based approach quickens the pace of innovation, which is often seen as a normative good even though that good comes with trade-offs.

As a matter of legal scholarship, Chapter 8 argues for the wholesale "minimal regulation" of all forms of assisted reproductive technology, especially forms of assisted reproductive technology involving genetic modification or substitution. To relax federal regulation would achieve the standard that many scholars believe is currently the status of ART.

More importantly, for this book's argument, in light of the partisan nature of federal decision-making related to health care and public health matters, it is necessary to increase transparency in the realm of reproductive rights. Based on the less than complementary involvement of the federal government (and state governments) in the regulation of reproduction, the book concludes its argument for the "hands-off" regulation of ART and ART involving genetic modification. The Conclusion also includes a "nod to the future" of assisted reproductive technology involving genetic modification, including in vitro gametogenesis, along with international and comparative perspectives on access to reproductive genetic innovation including mitochondrial transfer and germline gene editing of embryos.

1

A Range of Regulatory Options

This book responds to many questions, including: (1) Why is reproduction regulated the way it is in the United States? (2) Do assisted reproduction and reproductive genetic innovation have to be regulated the way they currently are? and (3) Are there better ways to regulate reproduction—namely, advanced assisted reproductive technologies and germline gene editing? To provide a legal foundation for these broader questions, this chapter provides an overview of the many options that exist when decision-makers are deciding (1) whether to regulate an area at all, and (2) how to regulate that area.

Federalism: Who Should Regulate—States, the Federal Government, or Both?

Federalism, the general concept of splitting power into various spheres—state and federal—will be referred to throughout this book, as will the separation of powers, although the term "separation of powers" will not be invoked as much.[1] Federalism is a concept that has spawned a significant literature, which focuses on many concepts related to whether primary regulatory power over an area is held by individual states or the federal government.[2] While not delving into the debates within the federalism literature, this chapter and this book are ultimately focused on federalism-related issues of regulatory choice.

One of the federalism-induced debates discussed in this book centers on whether the better regulator of reproductive genetic innovation is the federal government or the states. Both the federal government and state government offer advantages and disadvantages. State and local governments were well-known for their role in creating separate facilities and countless other mistreatments of minorities.[3] At the same time, the federal government has engaged in the same.[4] Moreover, while this book tends to focus on the decision between state government and federal government, it is worth acknowledging that municipalities have a growing role in politics as they create plans for the exercise of prosecutorial discretion (where prosecutors refuse to enforce certain laws, such as laws criminalizing abortion) and the refusal to cooperate with federal immigration enforcement actions, sometimes through the creation of "sanctuary cities."[5] At the same time, municipal law is increasing in significance in the area of reproductive rights, often in reaction to the US Supreme Court's decision in *Dobbs v. Jackson Women's Health Organization*.[6]

Beyond funding, states have a significant role in many aspects of family law and parentage, as Chapter 3 will explain. States have licensing roles for many types of employment that involve public health and safety, like positions in cosmetology, dentistry, and medicine.[7] States' regimes also deal with issues related to the scope of medical practice, which can connect to politically salient issues—for instance, by creating scope of practice laws that relate to medical procedures, such as those that say that only physicians, but not physician assistants or other health care providers, can perform abortions.[8] Similarly, much attention has been paid to the potential role of midwives and doulas in reducing maternal mortality, but some state laws have made it difficult for these individuals to be licensed in the state.[9]

In addition to federal statutes that apply to issues of national concern, often with a connection to interstate commerce, federal law sometimes relies on state law. Assisted reproduction leads to assorted unexpected issues. With the development of cryopreservation, gametes can be frozen and thawed long after their originator dies. The application of the federal Social Security Act connects with state law as the Social Security Administration provides benefits to posthumously conceived children, a term that refers to children born after their gamete provider has died, based on parentage determinations. These parentage determinations mean that the law of an individual state as to the parentage of posthumously conceived children directly affects the provision of federal benefits.[10] As a result, while some states provide parentage recognition to posthumously conceived children, others do not or provide temporal and practical limitations on when a deceased individual can be named the parent of a child born after their death.

Another concern is the level of government that is the siting of the majority of regulatory decisions in an area, as state governments and federal governments often cooperate in regulation.[11] No area is perfect. In many ways, decisions related to reproduction involve decisions about what is the lesser of regulatory evils. Historically, reproduction has been treated in a way in which individuals make decisions related to reproduction, and the law (and sometimes society) catch up afterward. Later chapters show a way in which the federal government has preemptively precluded decisions related to reproduction, without a clear pathway to remove those regulatory barriers.

Federal Legislation and Regulation

The source of Congress's extensive power in many areas stems from the Commerce Clause. Article I, Section 8, Clause 3 of the US Constitution permits the US Congress "To regulate Commerce with foreign Nations, and among the several States, and with the Indian Tribes." The Commerce Clause is the basis for a number of well-known statutes, including the Sherman Antitrust Act, the Securities Act of 1933, and other statutes regulating securities and financial exchanges, and the Lanham Act, which provides trademark protection in commerce.[12] Congress's commerce power is the basis for legislation related to the existence and jurisdiction of the US Food and Drug Administration (FDA), including the Federal Food Drug and Cosmetic Act (and subsequent amendments).[13]

Congress first enacted the Federal Food, Drug, and Cosmetic Act (FDCA) in 1938 and has subsequently amended it several times.[14] The 1938 Act established the current system, in which manufacturers must obtain premarketing clearance from the FDA before legally marketing their drugs in the United States.[15] As part of the 1962 Amendments to the FDCA, Congress added the often-mentioned safety and effectiveness standard, which drugs need to meet in order to obtain and maintain marketing approval.[16] In general, a drug is considered effective "if there is general recognition among experts, founded on substantial evidence, that the drug in fact produces the results claimed for it under prescribed conditions."[17] Safety similarly has a specific meaning within the realm of the FDA. As noted by the US Supreme Court in *U.S. v. Rutherford*, "few if any drugs are completely safe in the sense that they may be taken by all persons in all circumstances without risk."[18] As a result, the FDA "generally considers a drug safe when the expected therapeutic gain justifies the risk entailed by its use."[19]

ADMINISTRATIVE AGENCIES

The most relevant federal administrative agencies in the realm of assisted reproduction are the US Department of Health and Human Services and the Federal Trade Commission. The US Food and Drug Administration, the National Institutes of Health (historically a significant source of funding for medical research in the United States), and the Centers for Disease Control and Prevention (which has many responsibilities, including collecting data on fertility clinic success rates) are operating divisions within the US Department of Health and Human Services.[20] Genetic innovation also implicates the US Patent and Trademark Office, as CRISPR-Cas9 has been the subject of a patent battle that has stretched on for years, and some innovators, like OvaScience, entered into contracts to license patents after they were granted by the US Patent and Trademark Office.[21] The Federal Trade Commission also routinely investigates companies, including biomedical innovators, for fraudulent claims.[22]

Administrative agencies have been described as a "veritable fourth branch of the Government."[23] After Congress passes a law, administrative agencies are the bodies that individual entities interact with for the actual application of those laws.[24] Administrative agencies issue regulations, approve applications so that products can be introduced into interstate commerce, conduct inspections of workplaces, and generally serve as gatekeepers to industries.[25] Many agencies are organized around licensing actions and enforcement actions.[26] Enforcement actions, which involve enforcing laws and regulations, can range from letters that identify wrongdoing to criminal penalties such as fines or even imprisonment.[27]

Administrative agencies often cooperate, including on jointly signed warning letters notifying individuals of purported violations of federal statutes. These letters can implicate the agencies' licensing and enforcement actions. For example, officials from the FDA and FTC both signed an FDA-issued letterhead to Dr. Norbert Gleicher, a fertility doctor who was the subject of a *Washington Post* article discussing the lack of efficacy of his drugs.[28] In the letter, the two agencies explained that the products were "drugs" that were not FDA-approved for marketing and were thus "misbranded."[29] The letter also alleged violations of the Federal Trade Commission Act for advertising drugs without a "reasonable basis consisting of competent and reliable scientific evidence, including, when appropriate, well-controlled human clinical studies, substantiating that the claims are true at the time they are made."[30] Further discussion of these agencies, analysis of their jurisdictional scope, and their impact on people's lives will occur in Chapters 4 through 7.[31]

FEDERAL RESEARCH FUNDING

Congress and administrative agencies can foster certain innovations by subsidizing or encouraging them through research grants. Government funding of a technique often leads to de facto regulation because grantees must comply with agency regulations such as regulations protecting human subjects and approval of projects by institutional review boards.[32] Similarly, the government can subsidize fields through grants that minimize student loans for promising researchers and provide graduate school stipends for lab members.[33] Federal funding is a significant source of innovation funding.[34] Funding estimates are often divided into defense and nondefense spending, although defense spending can lead to innovations that are relevant to the general public, such as components of smartphones and techniques like germline gene editing.[35] In fiscal year 2022, the federal government spent $910 billion on nondefense spending, compared to $751 billion used for defense,[36] and the National Institutes of Health (NIH) spent $33.3 billion of its $45.2 billion appropriation on grant awards.[37] In fiscal year 2023, the NIH spent $34.9 billion of the agency's $47.7 billion appropriation on competing and noncompeting grant awards.[38] The NIH website notes that "NIH is the largest public funder of biomedical research in the world," despite the recent actions and turmoil related to the allocation and distribution of federal funding during the second Trump administration.[39]

FEDERAL FUNDING RESTRICTIONS

Reproduction, contraception, abortion, assisted reproduction, and stem cell research are controversial topics that have been the target of appropriations legislation as well as executive action. Due to these logistical challenges of enacting legislation, Gillian Metzger writes that Congress members are "more likely . . . to seek to attach substantive measures to appropriations bills to take advantage of appropriations' must-pass status and the greater ease of getting appropriations measures to the [congressional] floor."[40] For example, the Hyde Amendment, which is a recurring appropriations rider that hinders federal spending on abortion procedures, states:

> (a) In General.—No funds authorized or appropriated by Federal law, and none of the funds in any trust fund to which funds are authorized or appropriated by Federal law, shall be expended for any abortion.
> (b) Health Benefits Coverage.—No funds authorized or appropriated by Federal law, and none of the funds in any trust fund to which funds are authorized or appropriated by Federal law, shall be expended for health benefits coverage that includes coverage of abortion.[41]

The success of the Hyde Amendment, in being passed (and confirmed each subsequent year) and in withstanding constitutional challenges, inspired politicians to add what Marlene Gerber Fried calls "Hyde-type" language to "other appropriations bills, including a Department of Defense bill, a District of Columbia bill, and a Treasury–Postal Service bill."[42]

FEDERAL EXECUTIVE BRANCH INFLUENCE

Federal funding is directed not only by Congress, which provides the funding, but also by the executive branch. Executive action, agency policy, the president, federal agencies, and Congress all have important roles in the funding of medical and scientific research.

The president of the US also shapes the direction of administrative agency action, as indicated by the varied history of the Mexico City Policy (also known as the Global Gag Rule) and the interpretations of the Dickey-Wicker Amendment.[43] The Dickey-Wicker Amendment, another appropriations rider, was added to part of the congressional budget for fiscal year 1996 and has been passed every year since.[44] Its implementation has also been the subject of litigation as different Presidents have managed to contract and expand the scope of the amendment's impact on federally funded research.

The Dickey-Wicker Amendment, which arises in the context of debates related to human embryos and stem cell research, notes:

> (a) None of the funds made available in this Act may be used for—(1) the creation of a human embryo or embryos for research purposes; or (2) research in which a human embryo or embryos are destroyed, discarded, or knowingly subjected to risk of injury or death greater than that allowed for research on fetuses in utero under 45 CFR 46.204(b) and section 498(b) of the Public Health Service Act (42 U.S.C. 289g(b)).[45]

State Legislation and Regulation

State parentage law in many ways arose out of necessity. Family matters are generally sited within states, as states provide laws related to marriage and parentage.[46] Some family-related matters are governed by federal statutes or involve an interplay between state and federal jurisdiction, and Congress can act on issues of national concern although it has largely failed to do so in the realm of ART.[47] Two examples of federal statutes related to child custody include the Indian Child Welfare Act and the Parental Kidnapping Prevention Act. Due to several concerns, including "that an alarmingly high percentage of Indian families are broken up by the removal, often unwarranted, of their children from them by nontribal public and private agencies and that an alarmingly high percentage of such children are placed in non-Indian foster and adoptive homes and institutions," Congress enacted the Indian Child Welfare Act, which has led to several US Supreme Court cases.[48] Notably, these adoptions and child removals would occur under state law, which led to congressional findings that "the States, exercising their recognized jurisdiction over Indian child custody proceedings through administrative and judicial bodies, have often failed to recognize the essential tribal relations of Indian people and the cultural and social standards prevailing in Indian communities and families."[49] The Parental Kidnapping Prevention Act responded to parents who would attempt to flee to other states with their children without the required parental or judicial permission.[50]

States and private organizations also supplement federal funds.[51] Human embryonic stem cell research has been controversial in the United States for many reasons. Responses to federal restrictions have varied over time, including California creating the California Institute for Regenerative Medicine.[52] Similarly, even when there is federal law on a matter, states also pass legislation. For example, between 1999 and

2008, "after President George W. Bush's administration limited federally funding for ESC research in 2001," over 450 bills were introduced in state legislatures related to human embryonic stem cell research.[53] Of those bills, 14 percent—67 in total—were enacted into law.[54]

States also create medical malpractice regimes, which compensate patients for harms incurred during their medical treatment.[55] The estimated amount of time from an injury to a malpractice settlement is two to three years.[56] Trial makes the timeline even lengthier.[57] Physician licensure regimes have often been criticized for their failures to curb serious harms to patients and their delay in revoking the licenses of particularly egregious physicians.[58] Medical malpractice regimes also operate in an industry that is also full of malpractice insurance, which renders financial penalties for physicians and health care providers less onerous.[59] Like the federal government, individual states also have legislation related to fraud. Just as the federal government can interpret the Commerce Clause in an especially expansive way, some states also do the same with their constitutional and legislative provisions.[60] Similarly, states have products liability regimes, which, subject to certain exceptions, generally provide causes of action for those who are injured by defective products like pharmaceuticals and even defectively constructed vehicles and tools.[61] Chapter 3 focuses on state regulation of assisted reproductive technology and parentage as the early regulation of ART and family law were state-centric.

This chapter and this book significantly emphasize state law, but state law is not without its downsides. Early state laws prohibited interracial adoptions; and many court battles ensued over the parentage of children conceived as a result of traditional surrogacy, artificial insemination, gestational surrogacy, and in vitro fertilization.[62] Yet the nature of family law in the United States is particularly state-centric and there are very few federal laws that relate to the family.[63] This state-centric focus has been emphasized in the few Supreme Court cases that have dealt with issues related to the family, such as *Troxel v. Granville* (grandparent visitation) and *Obergefell v. Hodges*.[64]

Self-Regulation

Doing nothing is a regulatory option. Nothing, of course, is a misnomer. If the US Congress or other legislative body fails to pass legislation, then self-regulation by an industry—such as that which occurred with scientists in relation to research and use of recombinant DNA and fertility specialists as it related to the use of IVF in the United States—likely fills in the vacuum. Professional norms and self-regulation are a form of regulation, even though they do not have the direct backing (and enforcement) of the law.[65]

Self-regulation is an important tool for many professions and often supplements statutory regimes. It is important to the legal profession as well as many aspects of the scientific and medical professions.[66] Recombinant DNA, discussed in Chapters 5 and 6, was the subject of the Asilomar conference of 1975.[67] At this conference, scientists agreed to adhere to "stringent guidelines" for recombinant DNA research, based on safety concerns and risk assessment.[68] The fertility industry also is self-regulating. Two important groups related to self-regulation in the fertility industry are the American Society for Reproductive Medicine (ASRM) and the Society for Assisted Reproductive Technologies (SART).[69]

There are downsides to self-regulation. Institutional review boards (IRBs), for instance, review the research proposals for human subjects research that has been or will be supported by federal funding. Some note that IRBs tend to "rubber stamp" the proposals presented by individuals from home institutions, thus reducing or negating the significance of IRB review.[70] Similarly, self-regulation does not come with enforcement mechanisms.[71] Thus, while the scientific collaboration related to recombinant DNA was effective, the self-regulation of physicians in the realm of ART is not always effective. For example, in spite of SART/ASRM norms that individuals should not implant more than one to three embryos, Dr. Michael Kamrava implanted 12 embryos into Nadya Suleman, who is often referred to as "Octomom," leading to the birth of eight children.[72] Self-regulation will receive more detailed treatment in Chapters 5 and 8.

Health Insurance Coverage and Regulation

Health insurance companies and markets are regulated by law.[73] Insurance companies exhibit a de facto regulatory role by facilitating or limiting the availability of funds for certain procedures. One of the first steps of a patient's visit to a physician's office is the patient providing their insurance card or some other guarantee of payment for services.[74] Front desk staff often can give a patient an initial estimate of how much the physician's visit will cost the patient.[75] Health insurance coverage of a technique also encompasses restrictions such as limitations on the numbers of embryos transferred, the number of rounds of IVF, and limitations on who can access assisted reproduction based on age and sexual orientation.[76] As noted by Dr. James Grifo, a fertility specialist and innovator, "insurance companies dictate what kind of care you can provide, and what you can do. They dictate protocols for clinical practice, and patients aren't protocols."[77] Similarly, the National Society of Genetic Counselors explains that not having insurance coverage can cause some individuals to forgo genetic testing or genetic counseling.[78] For those patients whose fertility treatments are not covered by insurance, out of pocket costs are significantly higher.

Health insurance in the United States is largely connected to employment status or marriage, despite the innovations of the Patient Protection and Affordable Care Act.[79] Health insurance often does not cover fertility treatment in the United States, and scholars often categorize ART as a "highly unregulated" technique, a characterization that will be addressed from different angles in the subsequent chapters.

Even with the expansion of health insurance coverage in the United States as a result of the Patient Protection and Affordable Care Act, there is no federal mandate to cover ART services as "minimum essential health benefits" or otherwise. In fact, due to the success of conservative opposition in politics and litigation, "minimum essential health benefits" only covers contraception in a limited fashion in certain instances.[80]

Insurance coverage of fertility treatment has been slowly expanding. Seventeen states mandated insurance coverage of fertility treatment, as of 2025, although the extent of that treatment varies significantly. The applicability of such mandates also varies, due to limitations like the complicated relationship between the federal Employment Retirement Income Security Act of 1974 and state laws related to health insurance coverage.[81] Similarly, the list of private employers providing coverage for reproductive services through health insurance or other methods of providing employee benefits continues to expand.[82] In the United States, even in states without health insurance mandates, some employers provide fertility treatment to employees as an employee benefit. In her book

Becoming, Michelle Obama wrote that she and former President Obama were "inordinately lucky that [her] university health insurance would cover most of the bill" for their use of in vitro fertilization to conceive their children.[83] Employer-sponsored access to ART is not the focus of this chapter, but it is worth noting that as ART usage increases, so do subsidies of it and state mandates related to ART.[84] For example, in 2021, 36 percent of large employers provided coverage for IVF, and 15 percent covered egg freezing.[85] As of 2024, 47 percent of large employers provided coverage for IVF, and 21 percent covered elective egg freezing.[86]

The federal government directly provides health care to certain groups, such as enrolled members of Native American tribes, military service members, and certain veterans; it also provides health insurance coverage for specific groups, including federal civilian employees.[87] Insurance can be a tool for legislators, as evidenced by congressional action permitting coverage of assisted reproduction for individuals whose service-related injuries led to infertility, especially in the aftermath of the Iraq and Afghanistan wars.[88] While some individuals who are covered by TRICARE, the health insurance plan for active duty and retired military members and their dependents, can access in vitro fertilization and other fertility services, TRICARE provided more expansive coverage to current service members as opposed to those who accessed ART services through the Department of Veterans Affairs. Additionally, some service members who are not injured are sometimes able to access subsidized ART through certain military medical centers' reproductive endocrinology and infertility programs at obstetrics/gynecology graduate medical education locations.[89] Beginning in 2017, the Department of Veterans Affairs began covering certain assisted reproduction services, like infertility and genetic counseling, blood testing, sperm testing, ultrasounds, reversals of vasectomies or tubal ligations, and other medications and treatments, as part of the VA medical benefits package covering ART for eligible veterans.[90] In March 2024, the Department of Defense (DoD) and Department of Veterans Affairs (VA) announced expanded access to IVF for more groups, including eligible unmarried veterans, eligible veterans in same-sex marriages, certain veterans using donated sperm or eggs, seriously or severely ill/injured (category II or III) active duty service members regardless of marital status, and seriously or severely ill/injured (category II or III) active duty service

Table 1.1: Assorted Regulatory Options

Regulatory Option	State Examples	Federal Examples
Direct provision of services	• State National Guard units when deployed by state governors	• U.S. military branches • National Guard units when deployed by the president
"Direct" substantive legislation, (specific identification of an area for regulation as well as specific regulation about that area)	• Statutory tort law regimes for medical malpractice and products liability	• Internal Revenue Code
Administrative agency action	• Operations of state medical boards • Gatekeeping functions: licensing of medical professionals	• Internal Revenue Service administering and enforcing the Internal Revenue Code • FDA issuance of pre-marketing approval • U.S. Patent & Trademark Office issuing of patents
Administrative agency inaction	Exercise of enforcement discretion, including safe harbors	Exercise of enforcement discretion (example FDA announcement of enforcement discretion for certain health care institutions and other entities that provide specific fecal transplants to treat clostridium difficile infection under specified conditions)
Law enforcement action	Criminal prosecutions by local prosecutors of state law	Criminal prosecutions by U.S. Attorney's offices, investigations by the FBI including the issuance of target letters
Law enforcement inaction	Sanctuary cities	Prosecutorial discretion, such as failure to prosecute or deferred prosecution agreements
Executive action	Presidential executive orders	Gubernatorial executive orders
Funding restrictions	Congressional appropriations rider banning the use of FDA funding for the consideration of applications involving heritable genetic modification (essentially banning the activity)	State restrictions on the use of state Medicaid funds on abortions
Funding approvals	Awarding federal research grants, such as competitive grants through the National Institutes of Health	Awarding state research grants through bodies like the California Institute for Regenerative Medicine
Health insurance: Contracts for partial, full, or no coverage of certain medical procedures*	Federally provided health insurance plans include Federal Employees Health Benefit Plans, TRICARE	State Medicaid plans and state health insurance coverage mandates for fertility procedures and products
Criminalization/bans (temporary and permanent)	State criminal law	Federal criminal law

* For a discussion of the intersection of state and federal law in the realm of health insurance coverage of fertility treatment, *see* Myrisha S. Lewis, *Reproductive Innovation and Reproductive Exceptionalism: How Private Health Insurance Coverage of Fertility Treatment Complements Hostile Governmental Action and Expands Access to Assisted Reproduction in the United States*, in Health Law as Private Law (I. Glenn Cohen, Wendy Netter Epstein, Christopher Robertson, Carmel Shachar, & Susannah Baruch eds.) (Cambridge University Press) (2025).

members, regardless of marital status, using donor gametes.[91] The DoD and VA issued these policies in response to a lawsuit by various veterans and service members due to various alleged legal violations, including to the potential constitutional deficiencies of the DoD and VA policies.[92]

Table 1.1 (see facing page) provides a brief depiction of regulatory options at the state and federal levels.[93]

Conclusion

This is a book about law and regulation. Regulation comes in various forms and at varying intensities. There are many regulatory options. The current system of regulation is not the only option for regulating traditional assisted reproduction like in vitro fertilization or reproductive genetic innovation. Similarly, although this book does not center on comparative law, a comparative analysis is inevitable, given that the first known use of IVF to give birth to a child was in England. One issue that has accompanied IVF and reproductive genetic innovation since its inception is, Who will pay for the development and use of these technologies? Chapter 2 covers the early history of the development of in vitro fertilization and artificial insemination.

2

The Development of Traditional and Advanced Assisted Reproductive Technologies

In 2023 actress Kerry Washington revealed that her world was turned "upside down" when she learned that her father was not her biological father.[1] In 2018 Washington had planned to appear on Henry Louis Gates Jr.'s PBS show *Finding Your Roots*, a show that uses genealogy and DNA testing to find out celebrities' backgrounds. When Kerry mentioned the genetic testing aspect of the show to her parents, they realized they would have to reveal to her that her father, Earl Washington, was not her genetic father. Her parents approached the team at *Finding Your Roots*, who told them that it would be best to discuss this with their daughter off camera. They did so, and Kerry Washington decided not to participate in the PBS show. Her memoir indicates that her (legal/genetic/biological) mother and (legal but not biological) father were never going to tell her about her sperm donor genetic father. Moreover, under most states' regimes, Kerry would never have a right to the identity of her donor or an affirmative declaration that she was a donor-conceived child.[2]

Assisted reproductive technology (ART) is becoming increasingly commonplace in the United States. Estimates indicate that as of 2022 there were 457 fertility clinics in the United States.[3] Moreover, 1 in 6 individuals suffer from infertility. Fertility often declines with age for women, and because many individuals now are marrying or reproducing later in life, the fact that female fertility declines after age 35 causes many individuals to turn to assisted reproduction. "Elective" egg freezing—women choosing to freeze their eggs due to age-related decline in fertility or as a preventative measure, instead of due to a medical condition—is increasing around the world.[4] Many of these eggs will be used in in vitro fertilization procedures. Ideally, eggs are frozen earlier in a woman's reproductive life. Women who freeze their eggs later in life are likely to require more rounds of fertilization to achieve pregnancy.[5]

It has been estimated that as of 2022 there were approximately 1.5 million frozen embryos in the United States, and that number that has been steadily increasing.[6] The Kaiser Family Foundation (KFF) analyzed survey data from 2015 to 2017 and found that "10% of women ages 18–49 say they or their partner have ever talked to a doctor about ways to help them become pregnant."[7] A Pew Research poll concluded approximately the same from data from 2017 to 2019, and noted that the share has "remained relatively stable since the early 2000s."[8] The KFF analysis also noted, "Data and research often assume cisgender identities and may not systematically account for people who are transgender and non-binary. . . . [T]he data we are citing uses gender labels that we cannot change without misrepresenting the data."[9] Data reported to the CDC indicates that approximately 2 percent of US infants are conceived using in vitro fertilization services each year.[10] The CDC does not track the use of fertility drugs or artificial insemination, but a Pew Research poll found that "between 2017 and 2019, 10% of American women ages 15 to 44 said they had received some form of fertility service." In that poll, the term "fertility service" included fertility advice and fertility testing.[11] Many of these individuals pay out of pocket for fertility services, although private employer decisions to include fertility services in employee health plans, as well as state health insurance mandates and coverage for certain current and former service members, can subsidize costs.[12] Data submitted by fertility clinics to the CDC in 2021 suggest that the use of ART (which for the CDC does not include artificial insemination) led to 94,039 live births (deliveries of one or more living infants) and 98,289 live born infants.[13]

This chapter has three larger goals: (1) to discuss the scientific development and regulatory responses to traditional ART—namely, in vitro fertilization—but also briefly discuss artificial or intrauterine insemination; (2) to briefly discuss advanced assisted reproductive technologies (AARTs), which are innovations in the realm of assisted reproduction that combine traditional ART like in vitro fertilization with genetic modification or substitution; and (3) to introduce the ethical issues that accompany these reproductive technologies.

Traditional Assisted Reproductive Technology: Artificial Insemination and In Vitro Fertilization

This book is focused on ART. Which specific procedures are included as elements of ART depends on the source. For example, the drafters of the Uniform Parentage Act of 2017 and the Eunice Kennedy Shriver National Institute of Child Health and Development include artificial insemination within the category of ART. Others consider ART to be more expansive; the Centers for Disease Control and Prevention (CDC), for instance, defines ART as "all fertility treatments in which either eggs or embryos are handled outside a woman's body."[14] The CDC's definition stems from the 1992 Fertility Clinic Success Rate Act, which requires the CDC to collect information from fertility treatment providers in the United States.[15]

Artificial Insemination

Various forms of artificial insemination are used to improve fertility outcomes. People used artificial insemination successfully in animals for hundreds of years before physicians and researchers adapted it for use in humans.[16] Generally, artificial insemination involves the placement of sperm directly into a person's uterus (intrauterine insemination) or directly into the cervix, which can be done outside of a physician's office as various sensationalized court cases remind us.[17] The development of modern artificial insemination implicates a number of historical figures, including Antonie van Leeuwenhoek (the individual who discovered sperm), J. Marion Sims (the so-called father of gynecology, who is also known for his torturous experimentation on enslaved peoples), and later William Pancoast, a Philadelphia physician.[18] Developing a successful method of artificial insemination then facilitated the use of banked donor semen, which led to ethical controversy for assorted reasons that will be discussed in Chapter 3.[19] Nonetheless, artificial insemination became prevalent in the United States in the 1940s and is still used today, especially with cryopreservation.[20] The use of donor insemination declined between 1995 and 2013; from 2015 to 2017 the increase in its use was "precipitous."[21] Intrauterine insemination in a medical setting costs between $300 and $1,000, excluding insurance coverage; in 2023 the FDA approved the first at-home kit for intravaginal insemination.[22] Chapter 3 will discuss how state law regulates artificial insemination by known and unknown donors in the United States as well as later-revealed controversial aspects surrounding the first reported artificial insemination in the United States.

The Early History of In Vitro Fertilization in the United States and United Kingdom

For some, artificial insemination was sufficient to address their reproduction concerns, but for many it was not. Individuals in various countries worked to develop in vitro fertilization into a successful technique. In vitro fertilization is a technique in which a female egg is fertilized by male sperm outside of the body.[23] The resulting embryo is implanted into the intended mother or another woman who is serving as a gestational surrogate.[24] The first IVF baby, Louise Joy Brown, was born in England in 1978; the second, Candice Reed, was born in Australia in 1980; the third, Elizabeth Jordan Carr, was born in Norfolk, Virginia, on December 28, 1981.[25] Media coverage of the first children conceived as a result of IVF often referred to them as "test tube babies," even though the embryos that led to their birth were created in a petri dish, not a test tube.[26]

SOCIETAL AND LEGAL REACTIONS TO THE USE OF HUMAN IVF IN THE UNITED KINGDOM

This book discusses the regulatory regime of the United Kingdom because the UK was the site of the first child born as a result of IVF and the UK took a very different approach to the regulation of assisted reproduction (and later mitochondrial transfer), which is a helpful starting point when one considers the various regulatory options available regarding assisted reproduction in the United States. Robert G. Edwards, an English physiologist, began his research on fertilization during the 1950s.[27] He collaborated with Patrick Steptoe and Jean Purdy to further the development of human IVF in England.[28] Their work culminated in the birth of Louise Brown on July 25, 1978, in England.[29]

In July 1982, the UK established a committee to investigate ethical issues related to in vitro fertilization and to consider the potential legal regulation of IVF in the UK.[30] The Committee of Inquiry into Human Fertilisation and Embryology is often referred to as the Warnock Committee, in reference to the committee's chair, Dame Mary Warnock.[31] In addition to the perspectives of the committee members, the committee considered evidence submitted by various groups. The ultimate report of the Warnock Committee included 64 recommendations.[32] The committee recommended, among other things, the formation of a licensing body, the funding of fertility treatment, limitations on embryonic research, various legal guidelines related to the establishment of parentage for children conceived using assisted reproduction, the unenforceability of surrogacy contracts, and temporal limitations on the storage of gametes.[33]

The political economy of the UK is very different from that of the United States. In the United Kingdom, ART is highly regulated. To operate legally in the UK, a fertility clinic must have a license from the Human Fertilisation and Embryology Authority (HFEA), the UK's independent regulator of fertility treatment and research involving human embryos. As of March 31, 2024, there are 135 fertility clinics licensed by the HFEA in the UK.[34]

The UK's National Health Service (NHS) provides health care directly to individuals in the United Kingdom; by contrast, few Americans directly access their health care through the federal government. The National Health Service in the UK is actually composed of separate NHS systems for each individual country: Scotland, Wales, Northern Ireland, and England.[35] NHS Northern Ireland funds one round of IVF.[36] The Belfast Trust (NHS in Northern Ireland) will cover the storage of sperm or embryos for two years, after which time individuals have to pay for the storage.[37] A number of other requirements must be met in order to be referred for ART services in Northern Ireland; for example, individuals cannot have had three or more IVF cycles previously (whether publicly or privately funded), must have met "HFEA requirements on the welfare of any child," and must meet body mass index requirements (referred to as "healthy weight").[38] In Wales, "the policy on who can have NHS-funded IVF in Wales is governed by the advice of the Welsh Health Specialised Services Committee (WHSSC)."[39] Moreover, some clinics do not provide IVF for patients with communicable viral infections; these clinics can be identified at the HFEA website.[40] Moreover, as with all health care, there can be delays in accessing the treatment, which is significant because delays in accessing assisted reproduction can greatly curtail the success of those treatments, as female fertility declines with age.[41]

The availability of assisted reproduction varies according to not only the individual UK country but also local criteria. For example, NHS Lothian, a region of NHS Scotland, requires that neither partner use alcohol prior to or during the treatment.[42] Despite having a national regulator, the NHS admits that "the provision of IVF treatment varies across the country, and often depends on local [Integrated Care Board (ICB)] policies."[43] Integrated Care Boards can impose additional criteria for accessing NHS-provided IVF, including being childless, at a healthy weight, under the age of 35, and a nonsmoker.[44] Critics of the NHS's system for determining access to fertility treatment in England have noted that "unlike the devolved nations, decisions on provision of fertility treatment in England are made locally . . . difficulties conceiving are distressing enough without finding that your postcode precludes you from accessing treatment."[45] Even though IVF was first developed in England, NHS England has lagged behind other UK nations in the funding of fertility treatment.[46] Just as medical care is largely concentrated in urban areas in the United States, most fertility clinics in the UK are located in London.[47] In short, even with publicly regulated ART and a system with increased access to health care, there are many hurdles to accessing assisted reproduction in the UK, even though public funding is available to some.[48]

DIFFERING REGULATORY REACTIONS: THE UNITED STATES

Elizabeth Jordan Carr, born on December 28, 1981, at Norfolk General Hospital in Virginia, was the first child born via IVF in the United States. Howard and Georgeanna Jones established the first in vitro fertilization clinic in the United States at Eastern Virginia Medical School (EVMS) in Norfolk, Virginia.[49] Previously Georgeanna Jones, MD, was the director of "the first division of reproductive medicine in any medical school in the United States" at Johns Hopkins University. Howard Jones, MD, also worked at Johns Hopkins as "director of the university's international program on fertility control"; the couple moved to EVMS after reaching the mandatory retirement age at Johns Hopkins University.[50] The Jones Institute for Reproductive Medicine at EVMS opened in 1983.[51]

In the United States, Howard W. Jones Jr., one of the physicians who used IVF to create the embryo that would become Elizabeth Jordan Carr, expressed surprise at the subsequent controversy, which had surfaced not only in societal discussions and newspaper articles but also in regulatory hearings related to the opening of the Jones Institute for Reproductive Medicine at EVMS.[52] Due to hospital licensing requirements in the state of Virginia, like many other states, the center needed to obtain a Certificate of Need in order to operate. At this time, many individuals in the community voiced their opposition to assisted reproduction. On June 30, 2021, the Jones Institute moved from EVMS and became part of Shady Grove Fertility.[53]

Efficacy, Innovation, and Contemporary Trends in Traditional ART in the United States

There have been significant changes in ART usage since the first baby was born via IVF. In the United States, about 2.3 percent of all infants are born as a result of ART.[54] This means that, on average, approximately 86,000 children per year are born as a result of ART, using the CDC's definition of ART, which does not include intrauterine insemination.[55]

Egg freezing and embryo freezing are relatively recent innovations, with embryo freezing advancing ahead of egg freezing.[56] In 1997 many news outlets reported the birth of a child from a woman's frozen eggs, which were thawed, fertilized, and implanted, resulting in the birth of healthy twins.[57] NBC News anchor Brian Williams noted while introducing the segment on that birth:

> The procedure, the first ever in the US, has big implications, since eggs have always been too fragile to freeze and use. It's important news for the estimated 5 million couples in this country who experience infertility every year, and it could change the lives of women everywhere, giving them choices they've never had before.[58]

Before cryopreservation, physicians routinely implanted all of the embryos created through IVF back into the intended mother because otherwise they would be destroyed.[59] Cryopreservation changed physician practices and continues to increase in use in the United States.[60] Health care providers previously suggested cryopreservation only for individuals who would undergo medical treatments that could lead to infertility, but individuals without identified health conditions increasingly use cryopreservation, although insurance coverage tends to be more inclusive for individuals facing medically induced infertility.[61] Moreover, cryopreservation enables physicians to save embryos for later transfers and can reduce multiple gestation pregnancies.[62] Due to the availability of fertility treatments, currently there are more than 1.5 million embryos in storage in the United States.[63] Moreover, cryopreservation is available at many fertility clinics and is even covered by health insurance or employee benefits for many individuals in the United States.[64]

Cryopreservation is used with most IVF cycles, especially as individuals await the results of preimplantation genetic testing.[65] Although egg freezing is increasing in popularity, as a practical matter, one physician notes that "it's easy to freeze eggs, but it's harder to thaw these eggs, add sperm, make embryos and get someone pregnant."[66] IVF success can also vary widely: for women under 35, the likelihood of a successful live birth is just over 20 percent;[67] for women 35 to 37 years old it drops to 17 percent;[68] for women 38 to 40 it drops to 11.1 percent;[69] and for women over 41 the rates of ART success are in the single digits.[70]

Moreover, in recent years debate has intensified over whether fertility treatments may lead to increased cancer risk.[71] Without government funding, many of these debates related to efficacy may remain unresolved, because a largely market-based industry has less incentive to research such issues when demand remains high regardless of skepticism. Beyond those statistical and practical difficulties, there is also the issue of negligence, as evidenced by well-publicized lawsuits against fertility clinics whose freezers have failed, resulting in the loss of frozen eggs and embryos.[72] These legal cases are briefly discussed in Chapter 3.

Pregnancies with multiple babies are riskier and more expensive.[73] Giving birth to multiple babies ("multiples") after a single pregnancy is also common with IVF. This is often due to the implantation of multiple embryos, either to produce multiples or to increase the likelihood that at least one of the embryos will become a baby.[74] Multiples from

ART procedures are more common in the United States, where the insertion of multiple embryos is allowed, as opposed to abroad, where government-mandated coverage of ART often requires that only a single embryo be implanted, although industry groups in the United States have increasingly advocated for single embryo transfers in fertility treatment.[75] In the United States, state-mandated insurance coverage also tends to require single embryo transfers.[76]

Ethical Issues That Accompany the Use of Traditional Assisted Reproduction and Preimplantation Genetic Testing

The phrase "First do no harm" is often quoted in the context of physicians' duties to their patients, in association with the Hippocratic oath.[77] It is generally believed that the medical profession is guided by certain ethical principles, including beneficence, non-maleficence, truth telling, and respect for patient autonomy. Similar ethical principles govern scientific research as well, although science and medicine are full of ethical breaches.

Ethical issues regarding assisted reproduction received attention after the actual births of children via IVF. That these children were—and sometimes still are—referred to as "test tube babies" implied that they were different from other babies in a way that merited mention.[78] Some feared the use of IVF for reasons that ranged from techno-anxiety to religious opposition. Others were excited by the promise of the new technology. In 2010 the Nobel Committee awarded the Nobel Prize in Physiology or Medicine to Robert G. Edwards for the development of human IVF.[79] The Nobel Committee noted that IVF is a "safe and effective therapy . . . regulated by strict ethical guidelines . . . [and that] IVF children are as healthy as other children."[80] In the announcement of the Nobel Prize, Professor Christer Höög noted that many children born because of IVF conceive their own children without the aid of IVF.[81] Professor Höög also noted that Edwards "had to overcome strong opposition from the establishment that tried to stop his research."[82] In response to media questioning on ethical issues related to IVF, a Nobel Committee representative noted that all medical treatments come with ethical issues, but the Nobel Committee provides the award for the discovery itself.[83]

As indicated by the Noble Prize press conference in 2010, the ethical issues that have accompanied ART since its inception still exist. Moreover, many of the concerns that accompany ART also accompany AARTs. Ethical issues regarding both assisted reproduction and germline gene editing, as well as social, political, and ethical matters can influence regulation in the areas of ART and germline genetic modification.[84] Volumes could be written about all of these ethical concerns, and they could be separated in different ways. The following is a brief overview.

Ethical issues regarding in vitro fertilization tend to focus on extramarital reproduction, the sanctity or dignity of marriage, and humans "playing God."[85] As noted by Mary Warnock, in relation to her committee's deliberation on matters of assisted reproduction, issues related to the family and to research using embryos were overlapping but distinguishable questions.[86]

Preimplantation genetic testing is often combined with assisted reproduction, and decisions made as a result of this knowledge often lead to ethical debates. Preimplantation genetic testing (PGT) encompasses both preimplantation genetic diagnosis (PGD) and preimplantation genetic screening (PGS).[87] PGT can be used to ascertain some abnormalities in embryos, which allows patients and physicians to determine whether those embryos should be implanted into a woman with the aim of a pregnancy and subsequent birth. PGT cannot, however, ascertain all abnormalities in an embryo or mitochondrial defects.[88] Even when abnormalities have been identified, some individuals still implant the embryos, for various reasons, including (but not limited to) the uncertainty of medical testing, especially when aiming to have a genetically related child, an indifference to potential abnormalities, or the aim to have children with specific genetic conditions like deafness. Decisions to discard or use embryos with genetic conditions, or to edit in favor or against genetic conditions, arise in bioethical debates, especially in relation to the disability community. Many are concerned about the implications of specifically discarding embryos or fetuses that are affected with certain genetic conditions. Debates also exist about parental decisions to deliberately select for embryos that have conditions that many regard as disabilities, like deafness or dwarfism.[89]

Disparities are another issue for ART. The demographics of ART use have changed over time. For example, a study published in 1988 found that, of the people using ART, "90% percent of the men are married, 95 percent are white and 99 percent are heterosexual."[90] Today trends have changed, although it appears that there are wealth-related disparities in the use of ART. Many studies also find disparities in access to ART related to race and sexual orientation.[91] Some of these disparities are caused by bias against or hatred of various groups, especially in relation to individuals in the LGBTQ+ community.[92]

Some ART techniques involve the creation and destruction of embryos. Thus, there are ethical issues with ART related to the moral status of embryos. Are embryos people? tissue? or something in-between? These debates will arise in Chapters 3 and 4. Chapter 4 focuses on societal responses to IVF in the United States, as examined through the lens of Congressional hearings related to funding of IVF research and access in the United States, stem cell research, and fears related to human cloning. Notably, unlike in the United Kingdom, where there was a Warnock Committee, there has generally been a lack of societal discussion of IVF and ART more broadly in the United States.

Reproductive Genetic Innovation: AARTs

In spite of some religious and political opposition, ART is relatively "mainstream" in the United States.[93] Several recent innovations in the realm of assisted reproduction are not available in the United States, despite American researchers having innovated in some of the areas. Many individuals in the United States would like to avail themselves of innovative techniques like mitochondrial transfer and cytoplasmic transfer but cannot due to federal restrictions that will be discussed in depth in Chapter 7. Advanced assisted reproductive technologies include cytoplasmic transfer and mitochondrial transfer, both of which involve the genetic modification of non-nuclear DNA. Both germline gene editing (a controversial version of genetic modification that has reportedly been carried out in China) and AARTs fall within this book's category of "reproductive genetic innovation."

Some believe that selecting embryos for various traits is better than engineering or altering embryos to have certain traits.[94] On the other hand, as a practical matter, physician-researchers like George Q. Daley have noted that genetic engineering could possibly save some embryos by editing out genetic abnormalities that would render them unsuitable for implantation.[95] Many individuals are also concerned that ART could be used for eugenic purposes, especially when combined with genetic alteration.

Similarly, there are various perspectives on genetic engineering. Some, like Julian Savulescu, argue that parents have an obligation to "make their children better." Others disagree with engineering or "designing" children, suggesting that it can create a genetic "arms race." The fear is that once some parents start using these technologies to "design" their offspring, others will feel obligated to do the same. Nowadays, news accounts refer to children born via IVF as "designer babies"—children who are created to fit their parents' specifications, including eye color and hair color.[96] Many traits, such as intellect and height, cannot actually be engineered, but the possibility of engineering for such traits is the basis of various fears related to children conceived via ART or ART using genetic modification or substitution.

Moreover, some are concerned that once a genetic technology is used, even for the treatment of medical disorders, this eventually will pave the way for using such technologies for "enhancement," an issue that arises in a heightened fashion in connection with techniques involving genetic modification or substitution, like mitochondrial transfer or germline gene editing. These concerns about a move from treatment to enhancement are often categorized as "slippery slope" concerns. There are concerns that wealthier individuals will have the ability to access these technologies and engineer "better" children but that lower-income individuals will not have access to these techniques because they will not be able to afford them.

Julian Savulescu would support his arguments in favor of genetic engineering by noting that parents, exercising their own autonomy, already undertake many actions that undermine children's autonomy. The US Supreme Court has recognized parental autonomy, and it is part of the care and custody of a child, as will be discussed in Chapter 3. Reproductive autonomy, broadly described as the right to bear or beget a child, will also arise. Many of those who object to genetic engineering argue that it reduces a child's autonomy and right to self-determination.

Autonomy concerns also connect to issues of consent. Such issues do not receive much attention because ART results in children with the same genetic makeup as their parents. The concern for the future child's consent becomes magnified in the context of AART and germline gene editing, as individuals object to parents determining the genetic makeup of the child. Moreover, in the context of ART and AARTs the standard "informed consent" issue of medical ethics arises. Informed consent, a legally recognized concept in the United States after the landmark case of *Canterbury v. Spense*, generally requires that a physician disclose all material information related to a procedure. Consent will arise especially in the context of the first artificial insemination as well as a recent use of germline gene editing, discussed in Chapters 3 and 6.

Cytoplasmic Transfer

Before delving into the development of AARTs, I present a brief discussion of the cell that explains the names and operations of the AART techniques cytoplasmic and mitochondrial transfer. In simple terms, a cell is bordered by a membrane that contains the cytoplasm of the cell, which in turn contains the nucleus of the cell.[97] The cytoplasm and nucleus both contain various cell parts, but for this discussion the relevant organelles are the cytoplasm and the mitochondria. The nucleus, located in the middle of the cell, contains nuclear DNA; a little more than 99.9% of the DNA in the cell is nuclear DNA.[98] The nucleus is surrounded by the cytoplasm, which contains, among other organelles, mitochondria.[99] Scientific and popular media conversations routinely refer to mitochondria as "the powerhouse of the cell."[100] Mitochondria provide energy to the cell and are especially relevant to parts of the body that require a significant amount of energy, like the brain and nervous system, and they are the subject of studies related to aging and attempts to reverse or slow the aging process.[101] Cytoplasmic transfer and mitochondrial transfer are ART processes that involve the replacement of the cytoplasm (sometimes referred to as ooplasm) and mitochondria of an egg cell or embryo with donor material.[102]

Jacques Cohen and others developed cytoplasmic transfer in the United States at the Saint Barnabas Medical Center in New Jersey. CBS News reporter Jacqueline Adams described it as a "groundbreaking fertility treatment."[103] The technique was national news, as evidenced by a CBS News segment titled "Baby Emma Conceived in Laboratory

Through Cytoplasmic Treatment."[104] The CBS News segment as well as other media publications focused on Maureen Ott, a woman who had been told she would likely never have children but who later gave birth to a child as a result of cytoplasmic transfer.[105] Adams described it by saying, "It's a new high-tech treatment for infertility. . . . Doctors removed a small amount of the cytoplasm from the healthy egg of another woman, a donor. They inserted it into Maureen's egg, along with her husband Michael's sperm. Then the embryo began to develop. Despite the involvement of another woman, genetically Emma is purely Michael and Maureen's."[106] The characterization of the child as "purely Michael and Maureen's" is slightly inaccurate because Emma would contain some genetic material from the donor, but it does highlight the fact that over 99.9 percent of the child's DNA comes from her intended parents. Moreover, cytoplasmic transfer was significant because at that time women with egg quality similar to Maureen Ott's would traditionally have had to use egg donation, and a child conceived in that way would have had a genetic relationship only with the father.[107] *The Lancet*, a peer-reviewed medical journal, published the results of cytoplasmic transfer, and print and television media covered the technique's success.[108] At the time of the CBS News report, physicians were not sure why cytoplasmic transfer improved fertility outcomes, and the CBS News report ended by noting that the technique had been performed on six women, resulting in two pregnancies, one of which was Maureen Ott's.[109]

Although Emma Ott has been described as "something of a scientific miracle," she is far less well-known than Elizabeth Carr or Louise Brown.[110] When Emma Ott's birth was first reported, *The Virginian-Pilot*, a local Hampton Roads, Virginia, newspaper noted that the technique was built "in part" on work at the Jones Institute for Reproductive Medicine.[111] The article noted, "The Jones Institute is doing work similar to that done by the doctors in New Jersey, Hodgen [Dr. Gary D. Hodgen, president of the Jones Institute] said, although he wouldn't elaborate."[112] In the regulatory story in Chapter 7, it will become clear that the Jones Institute was one of the known providers of cytoplasmic transfer in the United States, due to its public response after receiving an untitled letter from the FDA on July 6, 2001. In the UK, the HFEA reported that it had "serious concerns" about the safety of cytoplasmic transfer and that it probably would not grant a license for the use of the technique.[113]

Cytoplasmic transfer was miraculous for some, but like many medical interventions, it was not miraculous for everyone. For at least two pregnancies via the technique, the fetuses had Turner syndrome.[114] An FDA employee mentioned these occurrences at an advisory committee meeting held after the FDA sent letters to physician-researchers who provided cytoplasmic transfer in the United States, informing them that they would need to participate in the FDA's onerous drug-approval process if they wished to continue providing cytoplasmic transfer in the United States. Parents whose healthy children resulted from cytoplasmic transfer had particularly positive views of the technique, and at least one mother who birthed a child via cytoplasmic transfer was disappointed to learn, when she sought to use it for a second child, that the technique was no longer available in the United States.[115] Cytoplasmic transfer was not legalized in the UK, although some UK-based individuals did access the technique and use it to bear children. By the early 2000s, US-based providers stopped providing the technique after receiving warning letters from the FDA.[116]

Mitochondrial Transfer

Researchers in various countries pioneered mitochondrial transfer, a technique that is similar to cytoplasmic transfer but involves less genetic modification or substitution. In the United States, mitochondrial transfer has been treated similarly to cytoplasmic transfer by the regulatory regime and is subject to an FDA Advisory. Nevertheless, American researchers have innovated in the area. Notably, Dr. Shoukhrat Mitalipov of Oregon Health Sciences University has developed mitochondrial transfer techniques and received federal funding for his nonhuman primate research. As of June 2025 his research has not been reported as used in the birth of any children, although Paula Amato, a physician and embryologist, has mentioned plans for clinical trials in Asia.[117] Reportedly, researchers at Columbia University have used mitochondrial transfer to create embryos that "would be ready for transfer if a legal path could be found," but they will not impregnate anyone with such embryos until they obtain FDA approval.[118]

In 2015, Dr. John Zhang, a doctor based in New York City, used a form of mitochondrial transfer to help a couple conceive a child. The child, born in 2016, was reportedly the world's first birth of a child conceived via mitochondrial transfer. The parents at the time had two children born with Leigh syndrome. The aim of mitochondrial transfer in this instance was to maintain the genetic connection between the child and the genetic mother and father but to avoid passing on Leigh syndrome to the child; this was made possible by using genetic material from a female donor's mitochondria.[119] The couple's first two children had died from Leigh syndrome, one at eight months old and the other at six years old.[120] Some of the mother's siblings had also died of Leigh syndrome, as had the children of her surviving sibling.[121] The patient was offered the option of selecting between the two methods of performing mitochondrial transfer: maternal spindle transfer or pronuclear transfer. She "[chose] spindle transfer over pronuclear transfer for religious reasons (to avoid disrupting a zygote)."[122] The embryos were created in a New York City clinic, but the embryo that was selected after testing was shipped to the New Hope Fertility Clinic site in Mexico for transfer into the patient.[123] While the patients and Dr. Zhang were US-based, Mexico was the site of the embryo transfer because, according to Dr. Zhang, in Mexico "there are no rules [against the procedure]."[124] The baby, a boy, was born at 37 weeks.[125] Dr. Zhang and his collaborators reported that the child's "male gender . . . eliminates the risk of transferring the disease to his offspring."[126] While the complexities of mitochondrial DNA have not been completely resolved, the general view is that the mitochondrial DNA used in the procedure should come from a woman, not a man.

Another complexity of mitochondrial DNA transfer is also relevant here: It is often difficult to predict exactly how mitochondrial DNA will be passed on to a child. As evidenced by the story of the family affected by Leigh syndrome, the inheritance of mitochondrial DNA is often unpredictable. Moreover, it is generally expected that defective mitochondria, which can lead to health conditions, are passed on matrilineally, although some researchers have found otherwise.[127] Dr. Zhang noted, "It is inevitable that a certain amount of cytoplasm will be carried over into the enucleated donor oocyte . . . leading to heteroplasmy in the reconstituted oocyte. The mutated [mitochondrial DNA] load observed here, however, is low, and we expect the offspring to remain asymptomatic."[128]

At the time of Dr. Zhang's initial publication, the child was seven months old.[129] In that publication he noted that many follow-up studies were planned, including following the child every three months in his first year of life, every six months in the child's second year of age, and annually every year after until age 18.[130] Clinic health care providers and researchers plan to assess the child's fertility function when he reached age 18.[131] Yet, it can be difficult to conduct follow-up studies. Many parents choose to opt out of them once it is apparent that their child is healthy. Dr. Zhang noted in the initial publication that "the family does not wish the baby to undergo retesting for mutant mitochondrial DNA load after the initial test, unless there is a clinical benefit."[132]

A now-defunct company, OvaScience, advertised mitochondrial transfer to patients in the United States and several other countries, including Canada and Jordan, through a technique called AUGMENT. The Delaware-incorporated company operated out of its main offices in Cambridge, Massachusetts.[133] OvaScience explained the steps of its procedure in a Securities and Exchange Commission filing:

(1) Obtain ovarian tissue
(2) Identify and isolate EggPC cells: After the company "receive[s] the ovarian tissue and perform[s] all AUGMENT related proprietary procedures needed to isolate the EggPC cells."
(3) Prepare mitochondria from EggPC cells: "[OvaScience] perform[s] all AUGMENT related proprietary procedures needed to isolate the mitochondria from EggPC cells."
(4) Inject EggPC cell mitochondria into egg: An embryologist at a partner clinic, trained by OvaScience, receives the preparation of mitochondria and injects it into the egg, in a single injection alongside the sperm, during the ICSI (intracytoplasmic injection) step of the IVF process.[134]

In a regulatory story that will be told in Chapter 7, after leaders of the company told shareholders that the technique would not require FDA approval, the FDA sent an untitled letter to the company explaining that it did. I obtained the letter, reproduced in Appendix A, through a Freedom of Information Act request. After receiving the untitled Letter from the FDA, the company stopped advertising the technique to patients in the United States but continued to provide it abroad.[135] It seems that a few pregnancies resulted from the use of AUGMENT in

Canada and Turkey, and at least one child was born in Canada, according to various media stories.[136] Eventually the technique was only available through an exclusive license to a clinic in Japan.[137] The story of AUGMENT, which, according to a Spanish study, provided "no benefit in terms of pregnancy or live birth rate," also implicates themes related to the funding of studies, the funding and efficacy of IVF research, and the ways in which profit incentives can potentially harm patients.[138] In 2018, through a merger, Millendo Therapeutics acquired OvaScience.[139] The OvaScience company name was no longer used after the merger, and in 2021 Tempest Therapeutics acquired Millendo Therapeutics.[140] The impacts of the regulatory system on OvaScience, as well as a lawsuit filed against the company by its own shareholders, as well as the settling of fraud charges brought against the former CEO of OvaScience will be discussed in Chapter 7.[141]

As of April 20, 2023, mitochondrial transfer had reportedly led to the birth of "fewer than five" children in the United Kingdom.[142] After an extensive public consultation in the UK, Parliament amended the law to permit the use of mitochondrial transfer in the UK under specific conditions.[143] Only one fertility clinic in the United Kingdom has received a license to provide the technique to families.[144] Each case of mitochondrial transfer has to be approved by the HFEA, and at least 30 cases have been approved.[145] Very little information has been provided about the children who reportedly were born as a result of mitochondrial transfer in the United Kingdom. More information may be forthcoming in the next several years. According to "a spokesperson for Newcastle Hospitals NHS Foundation Trust and Newcastle University . . . 'Academic publications have been submitted and are going through the process of scientific peer review. This means we are unable to comment further at this time in order to avoid prejudicing the process.'"[146]

Mitochondrial transfer has been provided to women at the Institute of Life Clinic in Athens, Greece. According to the clinic, at least six babies have been born using maternal spindle transfer, a form of mitochondrial transfer.[147] The baby born in Greece in 2019 was reportedly "the first successful birth in a clinical trial [of mitochondrial transfer]."[148] The clinic's list of available services does not include mitochondrial transfer, and the babies born using maternal spindle transfer were born as part of a clinical trial.[149] In addition to Mexico and Greece, mitochondrial transfer has resulted in the birth of babies in Ukraine.[150] The regulatory treatment of mitochondrial transfer will be discussed further in Chapters 7 and 8.

The ethical issues that accompany traditional ART also accompany mitochondrial transfer. Additionally, mitochondrial transfer involves some genetic substitution, which leads many to object solely because they oppose all genetic modification of embryos.[151] Due to these genetic changes, many are concerned that the genetic modification at issue in mitochondrial transfer would be irreversible and could be inherited by future generations.[152] This book treats mitochondrial transfer separately from germline gene editing. There is some debate as to whether "heritable" gene editing includes mitochondrial transfer, an issue that will be discussed in Chapter 7 in the context of the recurring congressional budget rider barring the use of the FDA's budget on techniques involving "heritable genetic modification." Other ethical issues, including issues related to sex selection in the context of mitochondrial transfer, will arise in Chapters 5 and 8.

Conclusion

One larger matter at issue in this book is the growing regulatory gulf that exists between the United States and early innovators in IVF—notably England and Australia—in the world of reproductive genetic innovation. The world's second child born as a result of IVF was born in Australia, and Australia recently enacted Maeve's law to legalize mitochondrial transfer. Meanwhile, the United States lags behind the UK and Australia in the realm of reproductive genetic innovation, even though many innovators live in the United States. Several authors have written about whether it would be advantageous to impose a more UK-centric regime in the United States, although in this book I argue against a federal-centric regime for several reasons that are outlined in Chapter 8.[153]

Religion has long influenced regulation in the United States. For instance, divorce is now no-fault; but in the past, divorce was fault-based and required proof of certain infractions, such as adultery. Even though artificial insemination does not lead to as much opposition as in vitro fertilization or gamete donation, the strong moral, ethical, social, and (initial) legal reactions to its use are part of a broader history of opposition to assisted reproduction. Chapter 3 will briefly discuss how artificial insemination was seen by many as adultery. Assisted reproduction met with significant opposition, especially from the Catholic Church, due to its role in permitting reproduction outside of the marital relationship. There were also other religious and bioethical objections. Moreover, as will be explored in Chapter 4, these ethical objections have arguably led to subterranean regulation of AARTs and germline gene editing.

3

The Evolving Law of Assisted Reproduction

Assisted reproduction continues to spawn new legal issues. Moreover, those legal issues tend to be the subject of court cases after the technology has been used, as opposed to beforehand, which differs from the general regulatory approach. In 2024, the entertainment outlet TMZ reported that "[a] popular IVF clinic frequented by the likes of Kim Kardashian, Paris Hilton and Chrissy Teigen is about to face some legal woes . . . we've learned former patients are gearing up to sue the practice" over 16 embryos that were allegedly wrongfully discarded.[1] This lawsuit would not be the first such lawsuit in the United States. Notably, significant political and legal capital focused on the Alabama Supreme Court decision in *LePage*, where the Court ruled that a fertility clinic could be liable for wrongful death after a patient wandered into an embryo storage area, removed a vial containing embryos, and then dropped the vial onto the floor, rendering the embryos unavailable for implantation.[2]

Embryo disposition cases are routine when couples divorce or separate. Actress Sofía Vergara was embroiled in a multiyear, multistate pattern of litigation against her ex-fiancé Nick Loeb. In happier times the two underwent in vitro fertilization (IVF), leading to the existence of frozen embryos that Loeb wanted to use, against Vergara's will, after their breakup. Loeb wrote an Opinion piece about it in *The New York Times*.[3] Although he had no connection to Louisiana, Loeb even initiated a lawsuit in Louisiana, where embryos are "juridical persons," in hopes that a ruling there would eventually lead to the thawing and implantation of the embryos against Vergara's will, even though the embryos were frozen in California.[4] Loeb named the two embryos Emma and Isabella and advocated for them in the news as well as through attorneys in various lawsuits, but a judge eventually granted a permanent injunction precluding Loeb from using the embryos without Vergara's consent.[5]

The United States never commissioned a national body like the UK's Warnock Committee on matters related to assisted reproduction.

Instead, a state-by-state "patchwork" of regulations emerged. This chapter has four main goals: (1) to show how the law has historically lagged behind innovations in assisted reproduction; (2) to show the relevance of state law to family formation and the legal recognition of the family; (3) to engage with the scholarly literature; and (4) to show that, contrary to many scholars' assertions, assisted reproductive technology (ART) is actually highly regulated because it is, at the very least, as regulated as medical innovations at the state level, where such innovations are subject to medical malpractice regimes. Traditional assisted reproductive technologies such as intrauterine insemination and in vitro fertilization are part of the practice of medicine, and the state-based legal regime reflects that position.

The Legal Recognition of Parentage

The legal system has historically exhibited a delayed response in recognizing intended parents. In other words, the legal system has historically reacted to parentage disputes as opposed to creating a proactive scheme for regulation. While there is now a comprehensive scheme for ascertaining parentage, it has evolved over the centuries, and largely over the past few decades as it relates to ART (and by default, AARTs like cytoplasmic transfer). A person who gives birth to a child has historically been presumed to be the child's parent.[6] Similarly, the marital presumption operates such that the law presumes that children born into a marriage are children of the two spouses.[7]

In the past, children born "out of wedlock" were stigmatized and often had no legally recognized father.[8] Because laws regarding reproduction focused on marital sex (as well as husband-wife marriages), parentage schemes were particularly gendered and children could only have two parents: specifically, a mother and a father.[9] Moreover, because women could only give birth to their own genetic children, motherhood status was clear.[10] Over time, marriage rates started to (and have continued to) decline in the United States.[11] Even though there was still a stigma attached to out-of-wedlock birth early in that period of decline, women who became pregnant through nonmarital sex could list fathers on birth certificates and obtain child support, with minimum awards established by statute.[12] States established registries for putative fathers.[13] The advent of DNA testing has rendered the establishment of parentage even more accurate, the emphasis, historically, being on ascertaining paternity.[14]

The law used to treat marital and nonmarital children differently. In 1973, the Uniform Law Commission promulgated the first Uniform Parentage Act (UPA), responding to Supreme Court decisions that held state actions to treat marital and nonmarital children differently unconstitutional.[15] The UPA of 1973 provided a model statute that state legislatures could adopt. The 1973 version contained provisions that addressed children born to unmarried parents. Subsequent modifications addressed innovations in assisted reproduction as well as same-sex marriage.[16] There have been subsequent amendments that respond to other societal and technological changes.[17] The 2002 version of the Uniform Parentage Act has been adopted in some form by nine states, and the 2017 version has been adopted by eight states, with Colorado enacting a "substantially similar" statute.[18] While not significant to the discussion in this chapter, it is worth noting that parentage law has evolved in many other ways over the years, including through the recognition of doctrines of "functional parentage" or "holding out," which can also be used to ascertain legal parentage, especially when more than two putative parents might exist.[19]

Artificial Insemination

Artificial insemination, which occurred long before in vitro fertilization, added some complications to determining parentage. After individuals began to use artificial insemination to conceive children, courts, legislatures, and society began to consider how this practice would affect the parentage of children, the criminality of their parents' actions, and the appropriate role of physicians.

In the late 1800s the infamous J. Marion Sims performed several artificial inseminations, none of which resulted in the birth of a child.[20] The first successful artificial insemination took place in 1884, although it was not public knowledge until 1909.[21] A married couple had been experiencing infertility, likely due to the husband's having been infected with gonorrhea in his youth. The husband's semen contained no sperm, and subsequent medical treatments did not cure his infertility.[22] Upon finding that two months of treatment did not resolve the issue, one of the treating physician's students joked that "the only solution of this problem is to call in the hired man."[23] The "hired man" in this case was a medical student. The treating physician, Dr. William Pancoast, secretly artificially inseminated the wife when she was unconscious.[24] While the wife was unconscious, Dr. Pancoast selected the "best-looking member of the class" to be the semen donor.[25] The physician swore the six medical students present at the time of insemination to secrecy. Years later, after first contacting the then 25-year-old adult who had been conceived via the artificial insemination, one of those six medical students wrote a letter to *Medical World*.[26] Reportedly, after the insemination and long before the letter to *Medical World*, the physician told the husband what he had done, and the husband was "delighted with the idea, and conspired with the Professor in keeping from the [wife] the actual way by which her impregnation was brought about."[27] The *Medical World* letter provides no indication that the physician ever explained to the wife that she was artificially inseminated with a medical student's sperm without prior consent.[28]

A legal regime developed for the use of artificial insemination after some courts ruled in the 1950s that artificial insemination was adultery.[29] This legal regime was an amendment to state parentage rules. While the first artificial insemination was shrouded in secrecy, an industry slowly developed. Written consent was crucial to this industry and its accompanying regime for parentage as well as divorce.[30] In general, physicians artificially inseminated women after both the husband and wife consented in writing to the use of the technique. That the artificial insemination was performed by a physician meant that under statutory law the donor of the semen was not the father of the child who would result.[31] Instead, the father was the husband of the wife, as a husband was generally the default parent of a child born into a marriage, even if the wife used artificial insemination to conceive the child.[32] Exceptions to this rule existed in the context of divorce and, later, in the context of unmarried individuals using artificial insemination. Today, state legal regimes generally distinguish between known and unknown or anonymous sperm donors.[33]

Intrauterine insemination has declined in prevalence as a fertility treatment because in vitro fertilization is more effective, yet stories abound of individuals who use artificial insemination outside of the medical context. These stories often focus on "turkey basters" and instances where individuals use the semen of individuals they know to impregnate themselves or their partners.[34] These "turkey baster" inseminations often lead to parentage disputes and, in certain instances, the same legal treatment that children who are conceived through natural reproduction would have due to proof issues.[35] Thus, the role of physicians or intermediaries in artificial insemination is often to create a situation in which a special legal framework applies, as opposed to the default legal rule when genetic parentage is established: legal parentage.[36]

Commercialization of Gamete Donation

In 1989, it was estimated that couples spent "$1 billion per year on infertility treatments with $30 million to $40 million spent specifically on IVF procedures."[37] Today, billions are spent on ART (as of 2023 it was at least a $10 billion industry).[38] In addition to the fees paid to physicians and other health care providers for their services, there are hefty costs for the many other participants in the process. Cryobanks freeze the gametes of individuals who plan to use their own genetic material in future assisted reproduction cycles. Cryobanks and fertility treatment providers enlist individuals to "donate" their eggs or sperm to their cryobanks. The cryobanks store the genetic material and screen it for sexually transmitted infections.[39] After being cleared, the material is available for individuals who are willing to pay for those products. Cryobanks market many of these human products on websites to individuals who are searching for donors with particular educational or racial backgrounds.[40]

With regard to egg and sperm donors, the terms "known," "unknown," and "anonymous" are legal fictions. For example, the law distinguishes between "known" and "unknown" donors, even though there is a way to ascertain who all of the donors are. Use of the term "donor" to refer to gamete providers is misleading because many of these individuals receive various forms of compensation. For instance, they are paid for their time and effort at rates that reflect market demand. *The New York Times* reports that sperm donors who donate twice a week for a month may receive $1,500 per month, although $100 per donation seems more likely, based on coverage from other news outlets as well as sperm banks themselves.[41] Sperm donors with more desirable traits are in higher market demand. Sperm donation is far less intrusive and dangerous than egg donation, so egg donors receive higher payment. Over the years there have been many media reports of Ivy Leaguers and models receiving large payments for their eggs; back in 2009 rates were reportedly up to $150,000 for models and up to $50,000 for Ivy Leaguers, far more than the "standard" rate for egg donation.[42] Professor Diane Tober, an anthropologist who focuses on egg donation, wrote in 2019 that the highest payment she had heard of was $250,000, reported to her by "the founder of a US egg donation agency that specializes in 'elite' Asian donors. The egg recipient was a wealthy woman from China, who wanted the egg donor to meet a specific set of criteria, such as small hands and a degree from Massachusetts Institute of Technology."[43] In earlier days such offers were posted in newspaper ads and flyers on college campuses. Today Facebook ads target potential egg donors as well as female gestational surrogates, all of whom are compensated, with a 2020 news article discussing an ad offering $200,000 to the egg donor and $50,000 to the charity of the egg donor's choice or for the donor's own egg freezing.[44] Compensation to the egg donor is couched as payment for the donor's time and effort as opposed to the gametes themselves.[45] Similarly, surrogates are compensated for their time and effort and are often able to contract for various services, such as specific diets, and for damages in case they become infertile as a result of their surrogacy roles; but they are not compensated in terms of the value of the child itself.[46] Instead, as will be detailed, surrogacy payments after the birth of a child are said to be for the "relinquishing" of parental rights, as opposed to for the child itself, as baby-selling is illegal.[47]

The commercialization of assisted reproduction has met with various lawsuits. Notably, society uses the word "donation" in the context of assisted reproduction even though parties receive compensation, and the genetic products have monetary value. Parents have sued sperm banks for failing to reveal genetic traits that are carried by the sperm donor or are in the donor's family history—especially when those traits lead to undesirable health conditions in the child born via donor's sperm.[48]

Moreover, in a reminder of the market-based nature of gamete donation, vials of donor semen can sell for far more than $1,000. Some sperm banks, such as California Cryobank, allow semen purchasers to pay $70,000 to ensure that the entirety of the cryobank's vials from a donor will be used only by the purchaser.[49] Lower payments can purchase partial exclusivity.[50]

States often impose restrictions on the commercial cryobanks that collect and freeze gametes, although market actors are not the only individuals who can provide ART services. Over time, assisted reproduction has increased in its "do it yourself" nature. During the COVID-19 pandemic, for example, many commercial cryobanks and medical providers closed. Those who wanted to conceive children during that time had to find work-arounds. Sacrificing the potential security provided by the legal regulations governing commercial cryobanks, many individuals turned to Facebook and other internet sources.[51] Facebook sperm donors shipped their sperm directly to their customers. Back in 2011 the FDA targeted Trent Arsenault for providing his sperm to individuals across state lines, but from time immemorial people have reproduced without intermediaries.[52] Since the COVID-19 pandemic, individuals have continued turning to Facebook groups and other informal methods to obtain sperm, in spite of the legal difficulties for the donors.[53] Moreover, some donors, like Kyle Gordy, a participant in the show *90-Day Fiancé: Love in Paradise*, have arranged sex with putative mothers instead of providing samples.[54]

Distinctions regarding known and unknown gamete providers tend to focus on protections for intended (and eventually legal) parents or donors (who are not the recognized "parents" of children conceived using their genetic material) as opposed to the children conceived.

While not the subject of this volume, there are calls for changing the statutes related to gamete donation, especially in relation to children's "rights," which are largely nonexistent in this area. Reasons for these calls include concerns regarding incest (that adults who were conceived via gametes from the same donor, but unaware of this fact, might reproduce) and failure to provide information about negative health conditions that might be inherited from the donor. Arguably, genetic testing can resolve some of these issues and has indeed been a way for many children to uncover their "donor siblings" or to ascertain information on their genetic background. Yet genetic databases come with their own disadvantages, including the commercialization of genetic information, privacy issues, and the possibility that they might be used by law enforcement. In the UK, children conceived through ART have the right to identifying information related to their donors, but that is not the case in the United States. A movement to require that donor-conceived children receive more information about the donor is slowly developing in the United States.[55] This movement is reflected in current and prospective legislation as well as state court decisions.[56]

Baby M and the End of Traditional Surrogacy

Traditional surrogacy, where a potential carrier (and biological/genetic mother) was inseminated by a donor, is rarely (if ever) used today. The well-publicized *Baby M* case from 1988 serves as both a social and legal story of traditional surrogacy and its demise. The story also invokes many of the ethical issues that still accompany ART today. William and Elizabeth Stern were a married couple who wanted to have a child, but Elizabeth Stern suffered from multiple sclerosis and was anxious about the potential health risks of pregnancy.[57] William Stern entered into a contract with Mary Beth Whitehead and her husband, which provided that Mary Beth Whitehead would be artificially inseminated with William Stern's sperm with the aim of conceiving a child who would be genetically related to William. According to the contract, after the child was born, William Stern would pay $10,000 to Mary Beth Whitehead upon delivery of the child.[58] Notably, Elizabeth Stern was not party to the surrogacy contract, "presumably . . . to avoid the application of the [New Jersey] baby-selling statute to this arrangement."[59] Professor Carol Sanger and others have written about the many interesting (and unenforceable) terms of those contracts.[60] Although she was not a contract signatory, Elizabeth Stern was mentioned in the contract, as the surrogacy agreement provided that sole custody of the child would go to Elizabeth in the event of William's death.[61] Mrs. Whitehead became pregnant after several artificial insemination attempts, and Baby M was born on March 27, 1986.[62] News broadcasts documented the entire story at the time, but for the purposes of this book, Mrs. Whitehead felt "bonded" with the unborn fetus during her pregnancy.[63] Things went especially awry in the arrangement shortly after the birth of Baby M (later identified as Melissa), who, according to Mrs. Whitehead, looked like Mrs. Whitehead's other daughter.[64] Mrs. Whitehead eventually relinquished the child to the Sterns, but it was later revealed that initially she felt that she could not live without the child and "that she must have her, even if only for one week, that thereafter she would surrender her [biological and genetic] child."[65] Mrs. Whitehead did not surrender the child after a week. Mr. Stern went to court to obtain enforcement of the contract, and in the process of having the contract enforced, "Mr. Whitehead fled with the child, who had been handed to him through a window while those [law enforcement officials] who came to enforce the order [in favor of Mr. Stern] were thrown off balance by a dispute over the child's current name."[66]

The Whiteheads then fled to Florida.[67] In Florida, they stayed with Mrs. Whitehead's parents and then at "roughly twenty different hotels, motels, and homes in order to avoid apprehension."[68] A trial court "held that the surrogacy contract was valid; ordered that Mrs. Whitehead's parental rights be terminated and that sole custody of the child be granted to Mr. Stern; and, after hearing brief testimony from Mrs. Stern, immediately entered an order allowing the adoption of Melissa by Mrs. Stern, all in accordance with the surrogacy contract."[69] Mrs. Whitehead appealed the decision and the Supreme Court of New Jersey granted direct certification.[70] The Supreme Court of New Jersey concluded that the surrogacy contract was unenforceable for several reasons, including conflicts with at least three New Jersey statutory provisions and public policy considerations.[71] In its conclusion, the New Jersey Supreme Court began, "This case affords some insight into a new reproductive arrangement: the artificial insemination of a surrogate mother. The unfortunate events that have unfolded illustrate that its unregulated use can bring suffering to all involved."[72]

Legal Lessons, Societal Realities, and Ethical Illustrations from the *Baby M* Case

Opponents of ART often suggest adoption as a "substitute" for assisted reproductive technology, but adoption is a complex and expensive process.[73] The Sterns considered adoption but were "discouraged" by the length of the process and "by the potential problem they saw arising from their age and their differing religious backgrounds."[74] While not mentioned as a reason for the Sterns' preferring traditional surrogacy, adoption also comes with many legal rules. Not only do states have methods for recognizing the parentage of children who are adopted (as well as terminating parental rights), many states have "waiting periods" during which time a mother (and potentially a father) can decide whether to go through with terminating their parental rights after birth.[75] For example, New Jersey provides three separate methods for terminating parental rights.[76] Additionally, consent to a private-placement adoption can be "revocable."[77] This was one of the many reasons the contract in *Baby M* was ultimately unenforceable.

In an article briefly summarized in Chapter 2, I outlined the ethical issues that accompany ART and AARTs.[78] The *Baby M* story implicated some of those ethical issues, such as exploitation, commodification, and consent. Socioeconomic disparities between the surrogate and the commissioning couple arose. While there is a literature on individuals who act as surrogates out of altruism, often to help someone they are related to as family, more often surrogacy involves an exchange of funds from a wealthier, more privileged individual to a lower-income individual. William and Elizabeth Stern met at the University of Michigan, where they were both PhD students.[79] Elizabeth Stern also obtained an MD.[80] Commodification of a woman's reproductive capacity was another ethical issue that arose as a result of the arrangement in *Baby M*. Others found concerning the brokerage role the Infertility Center of New York played in the arrangement. Not only should there have been far more screening of the surrogate mother, it was argued, but the fee of $7,500 paid to the Infertility Center of New York for its "services" could be viewed as high as compared to Mrs. Whitehead's $10,000.[81] In its decision, the New Jersey Supreme Court observed, "There are, in a civilized society, some things that money cannot buy."[82]

Due to the many issues that arose in the *Baby M* case, traditional surrogacy is almost never used anymore.[83] Instead, health care providers implant gestational surrogates with embryos that are not genetically related to the surrogates.[84] Even gestational surrogacy is not without controversy. Generally, surrogacy contracts are unenforceable in Arizona, Indiana, Michigan, and Nebraska.[85] Some states—Arkansas, California, Connecticut, Delaware, Florida, Illinois, Louisiana, Nevada, New Hampshire, New Jersey, New York, North Dakota, Oklahoma, Texas, Utah, Virginia, Washington, and West Virginia—have statutory regimes permitting gestational surrogacy. Some allow it only under specific conditions, such as when the parents are married; other states' regimes rely on judicial decisions that indicate that gestational surrogacy is permissible.[86]

Cryopreservation and Frozen Embryo Disputes

Cryopreservation has led to assorted legal disputes and more parenting possibilities. Just as the US Supreme Court decided in 1973 that a fetus was not a person, courts have had to make similar decisions as to whether embryos are people (in the wake of *Dobbs*, the directions of these decisions may change).[87] For example, in the 1992 case *Davis v. Davis*, the Tennessee Supreme Court "conclude[d] that preembryos are not, strictly speaking, either 'persons' or 'property,' but occupy an interim category that entitles them to special respect because of their potential for human life."[88] Ultimately, in a dispute between a previously married couple over the disposition of the embryos created during their marriage, the court sided with the party who wanted to avoid procreation.[89] Court cases in other states have decided similarly, sometimes on different grounds.[90] In short, regardless of the legal reasoning employed by the court, courts generally favor procreative autonomy and decide against forcing an individual to procreate against their will, with one recent notable exception in Illinois involving an unmarried couple.[91] For example, individuals have the following options for their leftover IVF embryos: (1) use them, (2) donate them to other individuals, (3) donate them to research, or (4) discard them; although discarding embryos and donating them to research are not mutually exclusive categories.[92]

In addition to these family law disputes, commercial disputes have also arisen in connection with cryopreserved gametes and embryos. Other disputes related to frozen embryos have resulted, including cases in which fertility clinics have lost gametes or embryos and where clinics' freezers have failed, causing embryos or gametes to thaw before they could be fertilized or implanted.[93] These instances of fertility clinic failures have led to multimillion-dollar legal judgments.[94] There have also been cases involving fertility specialists mistakenly implanting the wrong embryos into prospective parents.[95]

(Scarce) Federal Law Regulating ART in the United States

So far this chapter has focused on the development of state law. This lack of discussion of federal law is significant. There is one substantive federal law that specifically addresses assisted reproductive technology:

Fertility Clinic Success Rate Act of 1992.[96] The existence of only one statute that addresses assisted reproduction, and in such a nonsignificant way—requiring reporting of fertility clinic outcomes but providing no enforcement mechanism for the CDC to ensure compliance—has been the basis for various scholars' characterization of ART in the United States as "minimally regulated" or "highly unregulated."[97]

The Fertility Clinic Success Rate Act of 1992 requires clinics to report the success of their procedures to the Centers for Disease Control and Prevention (CDC); the Act does not contain an enforcement provision. The Act is often criticized for its lack of an enforcement mechanism, but it has led to relatively high rates of voluntary compliance. For example, 91.6 percent of fertility clinics performing ART in the United States in 2019 provided data to the CDC.[98] In 2019 ART, excluding artificial insemination, led to the conception of approximately 2.1 percent of all infants in the United States.[99] And in 2019, of all births of multiples, such as twins and triplets, 10.6 percent were via ART.[100] Fertility treatments have led to higher rates of multiple births, which has led to efforts over time to reduce those rates.[101] From 2013 to 2022, the rate of multiples in ART pregnancies steadily declined, at least partially as a result of a reduction in the number of embryos transferred in an IVF cycle.[102] California, an early leader in the use of ART—as evidenced by not only the proliferation of clinics specializing in ART but also state case law related to ART—is also the state with the largest number of fertility clinics providing data to the CDC.[103] New York and Texas contain the second and third largest numbers of fertility clinics in the United States.[104] The CDC maintains statistics on a number of other related subjects, including percentages of preterm births among women who conceive using ART, and ART success rates. Its IVF Success Estimator allows individuals seeking to become pregnant to insert personal data, such as age, height, weight, pregnancy history, and other factors influencing fertility, to find their "cumulative chance of live birth" after, for example, one to three egg retrievals (or using donor eggs).[105] Laboratory safety, with an emphasis on communicable disease prevention, is the subject of state and federal regulations as discussed in Chapter 7.[106]

After the births of Louise Brown and Elizabeth Carr in 1978 and 1981, Congress held many hearings related to in vitro fertilization technology, some of which are discussed here and others of which are the focus of Chapter 4. By 1989, Congress members were concerned about fraudulent advertisements and the lack of regulation of the fertility industry, particularly individuals who seemed to fraudulently advertise themselves as fertility specialists. A March 1989 hearing featured JoBeth Williams, an actress and director, as a witness. By the time of the hearing, Williams had starred in classic movies like *Poltergeist* and *Poltergeist II: The Other Side.*[107] She also starred in the ABC miniseries, *Baby M.*[108] Her portrayal of Mary Beth Whitehead in the miniseries earned her an Emmy nomination for outstanding lead actress in a miniseries or special in 1988.[109] Williams was also the honorary chair of the National Infertility Awareness Week and shared her story of her experiences with unsuccessful fertility treatment.[110] She ultimately adopted a child after many unsuccessful years of trying to conceive.[111] In her testimony, she noted that she acknowledged the "horror stories" of other individuals who had unscrupulous doctors and noted that "the doctors that I dealt with were all honest and kind men, but I felt that they should have been more open about their limitations and referred me to others who really could help me. The years were slipping away and the age factor is a vital one in infertility."[112] Her written testimony similarly noted that she had difficulty finding the appropriate physician because "all gynecologists, including my own, claimed to handle infertility," which meant that she had to rely on friends' recommendations.[113] Nowadays people seeking fertility help are aware of the importance of specialists like reproductive endocrinologists, but the role of these specialists was not clear in the 1980s.[114] The House subcommittee later published data they had gathered from a survey of clinics that practiced IVF and gamete intrafallopian transfer. This data was not comprehensive; some clinics did not respond, and some misinterpreted one of the questions on the survey.

Today, the FTC, often in conjunction with the FDA, routinely targets entities and medical professionals who advertise unproven technologies. For example, in 2021 both the FDA and the FTC sent a warning letter to an infertility specialist who made many unsubstantiated claims about one of his products, including that his fertility supplements were the "best fertility supplements to boost your chance of pregnancy or improve your IVF success rate."[115]

Regulation of Medical Practice and Medical Research

A large part of any health law course focuses on a specific section of tort law—medical malpractice liability. More specifically, physician liability is a significant issue in any health law course and in the medical field more broadly. The most-cited journal in medicine, *The New England Journal of Medicine*, routinely publishes articles related to medical malpractice litigation. Surgery is especially known for introducing innovations through clinical use without preapproval.[116] Similarly, physicians introduced ART into practice without federal or state regulatory preclearance. When medical treatment harms patients, medical malpractice lawsuits focus on proving harm and causation—namely, that the patient's harm resulted from the physician's actions, which violated the "standard of care"—the generally recognized minimum medical care provided in a specialty.[117]

Moreover, for physicians with an interest in innovating beyond the status quo or standard of care, research regulation is often at issue. Individuals at institutions receiving federal grants, for example, have to comply with federal research regulations, which include protections for human subjects in research, the submission of research protocols to institutional review boards, and other obligations such as those related to confidentiality and compliance with ethical principles. Individuals who plan to issue FDA-regulated products, like small-molecule drugs and biologics, must obtain premarket approval. Practitioners of ART are often criticized for using procedures without proof of clinical effectiveness, yet the field of ART is not alone in this. Many other common medical practices, such as the use of stents, statins, and certain breast cancer treatments, were later revealed to be less (and sometimes extremely less) effective than originally thought.[118] Those products and treatments have not been banned from the market, although physicians no longer consider them to be the standard of care.

Conclusion

As noted in Chapter 2, after the birth of Louise Brown the Warnock Committee in the UK considered the ethical, social, and potential legal implications of ART. Such a comprehensive and documented national conversation did not occur in the United States. Even in the three years between the birth of Louise Brown and that of Elizabeth Carr, American society (and the law) largely did not react until after the birth of the child. The same occurred in the realm of artificial insemination, which this chapter discusses to provide historical context. Instead of a national response analogous to that in the UK, the states resolved the issues on their own. The few attempts made to achieve uniformity included drafting various iterations of the Uniform Parentage Act, which various state legislatures ultimately adopted in part, and passage of the federal 1992 Fertility Clinic Success Rate Act, which was far less sweeping than the significant regulatory structure created in the United Kingdom.[119]

This chapter has discussed three general methods of becoming a (legal) parent: sex or natural reproduction (inside or outside of marriage), artificial insemination (inside or outside of marriage although historically, generally inside of marriage), and in vitro fertilization (an umbrella term that includes specific methods like intracytoplasmic sperm injection). In vitro fertilization accompanies many parental options, including the use of a donor egg, donor sperm, or both in the creation of an embryo that will later be implanted into the intended legal mother or a gestational surrogate. Adoption of an already existing child (or a child conceived using IVF and a gestational surrogate in a state where gestational surrogacy is legal), is also an option.

This chapter has provided an overview of the role of state law in family arrangement, with an emphasis on family law as opposed to medical malpractice regimes, which are also relevant to ART procedures. In this book I focus on egg freezing, in vitro fertilization, and AARTs, but artificial insemination, which became mainstream in the United States in the 1940s, "was the first successful technique of assisted conception."[120] The conception of a child via artificial insemination in 1884 did not become public knowledge until 1909. In 1964, Georgia was the first state to enact a statute related to donor insemination.[121] Law professor Walter Wadlington testified in Congress that "now" in 1978 was the time to start the process of creating model legislation related to assisted reproduction, "long before the process becomes widely or even moderately used by those seeking to avoid infertility."[122] Congress did not pass substantial legislation related to assisted reproduction, but the states did.

The historical hearings related to ART often invoked the status of state law. Expert witnesses like law professors Alexander Capron and Lori Andrews referenced state law related to artificial insemination and assisted reproduction in the United States.[123] This included Professor Capron's note that the law had, at least in some states, contributed to early confusion by characterizing artificial insemination as adultery.[124] Assisted reproduction in its early days largely focused on married, opposite-sex couples, although that focus has changed over time, in spite of the preferences of many politically conservative individuals in the United States (and sometimes abroad, like in Italy).[125]

As indicated by congressional hearings in the 1980s and 1990s, the success of fertility clinics, as well as the efficacy of the treatments they offered to the public, concerned legislators and members of the public more broadly. A study of congressional transcripts surrounding failed legislation shows just how much religion greatly influences American perspectives on issues related to reproduction and assisted reproduction. Even before the litigation related to the Affordable Care Act's contraceptive mandate, the controversy over abortion played a large part in destroying legislation aimed at increasing funding for women's health and infertility services; it also hindered funding for ART and stem cell research.[126]

Unscrupulous actors are generally inevitable. The Netflix series *Our Father* told stories of a physician who used his own semen to inseminate patients.[127] A similar documentary, *Baby God*, aired on HBO.[128] With the rise in genetic testing, many more such situations continue to arise as previously unnoticed misrepresentations come to light. Unscrupulous actors persist throughout medicine as well as other areas of life. Usually, the existence of unscrupulous actors does not lead to the banning of a medical technology altogether. Chapters 5 and 7 will show how heavily the federal government regulates ART involving genetic innovation and will reconsider the role of federal consumer protection law in the regulation of ART advertisements involving interstate commerce. The next chapter will cover matters related to the funding of assisted reproduction that have been controversial due to ethical, moral, social, and political controversies.

4

Life, Embryos, and Abortion

Religious and Moral Influences on the Federal Regulation of Traditional ART in the United States

Moral and social views have greatly influenced debates, jurisprudence, and legislation related to the origins of life, especially in the realms of reproduction and scientific research. Legislative conversations about assisted reproduction rarely occur without discussions of (and associations with) abortion and morality. My focus is largely on federal action, but similar disputes related to abortion and IVF occur at the state level.[1] A study of congressional transcripts accompanying legislative debates on health insurance, fetal personhood, abortion, IVF, stem cells, and human cloning shows just how much religion influences American perspectives on issues related to reproduction and assisted reproduction by emphasizing beliefs related to the potentiality and personhood of embryos as well as views that oppose reproduction outside of marriage. This chapter will show how the lack of federal funding for ART stemmed from religious views and political choices related to the many bioethical objections that accompany ART, many of which were outlined in Chapter 2. Given the lack of federal funding, the private sector took over the development of IVF procedures. This exacerbated some of the access issues for ART; it is still not routinely covered by health insurance, and innovation in the area tends to stem from private research funds as opposed to public funding. Moreover, bioethical objections to stem cell research often overlap bioethical objections to ART. Stem cell research, like ART, involves the creation, and often the destruction, of embryos, and implicates the issues related to personhood, abortion, and contraception that continually derailed research funding through both legislative policy and executive branch spending policies.

Path Dependence and In Vitro Fertilization

To take no action will avoid controversy.[2]
—Multiple Memoranda circulated within the National Institutes of Health regarding the funding of IVF research

Path dependence is a theory that is difficult to test but worth considering. In his book *Reinventing American Healthcare*, Professor Ezekiel Emmanuel summarized path dependence as a social science concept

> that helps explain how decisions made in previous circumstances that may no longer be relevant today nonetheless shape and limit how current decisions are made. In other words, path dependence means that the institutions and arrangements created before—often created haphazardly or as an expedient—now constrain and shape the changes that are possible today. So the history of health care can help us understand why certain aspects of the health care system exist today, and this in turn helps us understand the constraints imposed on any health reform proposal.[3]

In 1974, after the public became aware of the harms done in the Tuskegee syphilis experiment, Congress passed the National Research Act.[4] One way this Act changed the federal research landscape was by establishing the National Commission for the Protection of Human Subjects of Biomedical and Behavioral Research.[5] The commission considered many issues, including research on humans and in vitro fertilization. Its findings influenced the Department of Health, Education, and Welfare's subsequent regulations, including a 1975 regulation that members of the scientific and medical communities characterized as a moratorium: "No application or proposal involving human in vitro fertilization may be funded by the Department or any component thereof, until the application or proposal has been reviewed by the Ethical Advisory Board and the Board has rendered advice as to its acceptability from an ethical standpoint."[6]

In 1977, a Vanderbilt researcher submitted a proposal for human in vitro fertilization research, which was then subject to peer review by the NIH.[7] In February 1978, members were appointed to an Ethics

Advisory Board (EAB) to review the research, but in July, Louise Brown was born. Her birth led the secretary of the Department of Health and Human Services (HHS) to broaden the committee's inquiry, which led to 11 public hearings.[8] Ultimately, the EAB in 1979 published a document, "Support of Research Involving Human In Vitro Fertilization and Embryo Transfer" in the *Federal Register*.[9] The short-lived Ethics Advisory Board purposefully avoided "the question of the level of funding, if any, which such research on IVF without embryo transfer because the EAB considered the question . . . troublesome for the Board in view of the uncertain risks, the dangers of abuse, and because funding the procedure was seen as morally objectionable by many."[10] Even so, after the *Federal Register* published the document, the HHS "received comments from approximately 13,000 members of the public and 80 Members of Congress. The overwhelming majority expressed opposition to Federal funding of the procedure, particularly if the procedure were to involve the intentional destruction of human embryos or increase the risk of embryos being otherwise harmed."[11] While many recommended reconstituting the Ethics Advisory Board, the federal government never reconstituted it, and the Ethics Advisory Board was unavailable after 1980.[12] Additionally, research projects that had previously been received for review were held in abeyance as they awaited EAB review.[13] An NIH employee reported that since 1975, the NIH had approved only three projects dealing with human IVF and that it "withdrew or withheld support of direct attempts to fertilize human ova in some of these" because they were approved after the August 1975 requirement that the EAB approve such projects.[14] Two of the three grants were to fund Luciano Zamboni's work, which involved animal and human research; the third project, which was also mentioned in congressional hearings, was the work of Pierre Soupart titled "Cryogenetics of Human Preimplantation Embryos."[15]

Louise Brown, the first child born via IVF, was born on July 25, 1978, in England.[16] Reactions to her birth ranged from fear to amazement to joy.[17] On December 28, 1981, Elizabeth Carr, the first baby born in the United States as a result of in vitro fertilization was born at Norfolk General Hospital in Virginia.[18] Like Louise Brown's birth, Elizabeth Carr's birth elicited a variety of reactions. A little over six years after the birth of Louise Brown and three years after the birth of Elizabeth Jordan Carr, a congressional subcommittee held a hearing on human embryo transfer.[19] Albert Gore Jr., then a representative from Tennessee, led the questioning for the August 1984 subcommittee hearing.

Early congressional hearings on IVF focused on the lack of consensus on IVF and the lack of regulation of the technique. While the August 1984 hearings aimed to "look at how a consensus on these issues might be developed," arguably no such consensus occurred.[20] There was significant discussion of physician self-regulation by representatives of organizations such as the American Fertility Society and American College of Obstetricians and Gynecologists (ACOG) as well as the lack of consensus on the status of the embryo.[21] While many have criticized physician self-regulation, Representative Gore commended the American Fertility Society and ACOG "for going into this field and trying to establish some guidelines where none exist."[22] At the same time, the default result of a lack of consensus is that these matters were left to "the smaller units of society—the family, the married couple, the individual."[23] Thus, IVF regulation—meaning, decisions about parentage and physician malpractice, if any—fell within the ambit of state jurisdiction like other matters regarding family and regulation of physicians.

Lack of consensus is not automatically negative. The lack of consensus on IVF corresponded with a lack of federal regulation, which allowed IVF to flourish. This lack of federal regulation led to model statutes like the Uniform Parentage Act and state-based "gap filling." No choice is without disadvantage. One law professor, Alexander Capron, noted that he thought the law had "contributed to confusion" because of early cases that categorized artificial insemination as being akin to adultery.[24] These characterizations led physicians to not keep records of the identity of sperm donors so that those donors could not be identified.[25] Similar regulatory uncertainty chilled physician action in other states, like Illinois, in the early days of IVF.[26]

Many opponents of IVF note that adoption is a substitute for in vitro fertilization or other forms of ART and renders ART unnecessary. Yet, congressional hearings in the 1980s provided insights into the expense of adoption as well as the restrictions that prevented adoption for a "large portion of the infertile population."[27] Many individuals who pursued IVF did not meet adoption agency requirements that "both partners be under the age of 40, of the same race and religion [as the child they would adopt], and that one of the partners stay at home until the child goes to school."[28]

A 1988 hearing that focused on the difficulties of receiving covered fertility treatments from the Department of Veterans Affairs also highlighted the bias that physically disabled individuals faced in adoption and child custody determinations.[29] The hearing also highlighted the difficulties of international and private adoptions.[30] Moreover, those who pursue ART or AARTs do not see adoption as a substitute.[31]

Even though the US House of Representatives August subcommittee hearings in 1984 often referred to the Warnock inquiry, including its declarations related to the status of the embryo, lack of support for surrogacy, and the suggested creation of a licensing board, the United States never had a similar inquiry. The findings of the Warnock inquiry and its report were unenforceable, but the UK later moved to make its recommendations law, as indicated by the creation of the Human Fertilisation and Embryology Authority.[32] On the second day of the 1984 hearings Representative Gore noted that the members of the subcommittee were not proposing a national regulatory agency that would require licensing, although they were in agreement with the creation of a national commission "to stimulate dialog on the biological implications of these issues."[33] The kind of open, purposeful, public discussion and inquiry regarding the ethical and regulatory issues posed by IVF that occurred in the United Kingdom did not occur in the United States.

Embryo destruction is an inevitable aspect of innovation related to IVF or genetic alteration. At a hearing after the birth of Louise Brown, Representative Gore noted that her birth "was preceded by 200 embryos that were discarded for various reasons."[34] Thus, the issue of leftover embryos has existed since the early use of IVF in the United States.

Members of Congress and experts debated the issue of what to do with the leftover embryos, even before egg or embryo freezing was as widespread as it is today. In August 2001, President George W. Bush addressed the nation from his ranch in Crawford, Texas.[35] He thanked the public for their time in permitting him to discuss research involving stem cells derived from human embryos, an issue the president called "one of the most profound of our time."[36] President Bush noted that research on human embryos "at its core . . . forces us to confront fundamental questions about the beginnings of life and the ends of science. It lies at a difficult moral intersection, juxtaposing the need to protect life in all its phases with the prospect of saving and improving life in all its stages."[37] President Bush also advocated for the Snowflakes Frozen Embryo Adoption program, in which couples who have leftover embryos from IVF can donate those embryos to others who are interested in expanding their families.[38] Today, HHS still funds programs meant to increase education related to embryo adoption options.[39] Thus, efforts to preserve human embryos receive support from administrative agencies but embryo destruction is often the reason for general opposition to, and refusal to fund, ART and human embryonic stem cell research. Subsequent chapters will show how administrative agencies, which are a part of the executive branch of government, implement these personhood-based conservative policies in the context of reproductive genetic innovation, which is significantly stymied by agency policies and threats that do not have clear origins or clear explanations.

Human Stem Cells

Cloning technology often arises in discussions related to stem cell research. Cloning technology can be used to create embryonic stem cells. This is often controversial because it involves the creation of human embryos for the sole purpose of using them for research, which requires their eventual destruction. This also leads to "slippery slope" concerns that instead of being used to harvest stem cells, the cloned embryos will be implanted into a human for gestation and eventual birth. When scientists at Advanced Cell Technology in Massachusetts succeeded at creating a cloned human embryo, the company's vice president explained, "Our intention is not to create cloned human beings, but rather make lifesaving therapies for a wide range of conditions, including diabetes, stroke, cancer, AIDS, and neurodegenerative disorders such as Parkinson's and Alzheimer's disease."[40] Researchers value embryonic stem cells because they are "pluripotent," meaning that they can become any human cell and could be customized for specific patients.[41] Adult stem cells are valuable but generally less valuable than embryonic stem cells because they cannot divide into any kind of cell. Even though embryonic stem cells are different from adult stem cells, discussions related to stem cell research and regenerative medicine have historically been curtailed by controversy over the moral status of embryos. Volumes have been written about the morality of stem cell research as well as the practical limitations of that research, including the merits of choosing stem cells derived from human embryos as opposed to adult stem cells.[42] Two things worth noting are that "the most potent cell-based therapies of the future are likely to require complex genetic engineering to maximize the efficacy and safety of the therapeutic cells and tissues," and that it is expected that it will be "much easier—and potentially safer—to perform the necessary engineering steps with pluripotent stem cells."[43]

Funding Restrictions and Reproductive Rights

The government is an important source of funding for innovation, as well as an innovator itself. Politicians use funding restrictions or refusals to fund research as ways to target techniques that are abhorrent to politicians. Limiting federal funding to certain kinds of research cuts off a significant source of funding for that research and can effectively prohibit access to techniques without private demand, which may not exist for early-stage innovations. Moreover, funding restrictions can prohibit administrative agencies from using their budgets on approval of techniques that some find offensive, as has occurred with mitochondrial transfer, which also effectively bans those techniques in the United States.

Federal funding restrictions are often connected with reproduction. For example, the Dickey-Wicker Amendment prohibits the use of federal funds for

> (1) the creation of a human embryo or embryos for research purposes; or (2) research in which a human embryo or embryos are destroyed, discarded, or knowingly subjected to risk of injury or death greater than that allowed for research on fetuses in utero under 45 C.F.R. 46.204(b) and [42 U.S.C. 289g(b)].[44]

In the United States, today's funding discussions of abortion and genetic alteration tend to focus on the Hyde Amendment (which restricts federal funding of abortions in the Medicaid program), restrictions on American foreign aid being used for abortion services, and the NIH's policy of not funding proposals involving germline genetic alteration.[45] IVF also faced a significant research funding restriction: the NIH refused to fund proposals related to human IVF, a factor that may have contributed to the lack of regulation of the technique.[46] This refusal resulted from a 1975 ruling by the secretary of the Department of Health, Education, and Welfare (today's US Department of Health and Human Services).[47]

Even before the litigation related to the Affordable Care Act's contraceptive mandate, abortion played a large part in defeating legislation aimed at increasing funding for women's health and infertility services, as well as in hindering funding for assisted reproductive technology research and clinical use and human embryonic stem cell research. This treatment of reproduction in an exceptional manner has spread from Congress to the executive branch, and vice versa, as indicated by the many ways matters related to reproduction have been the subject of creative legal and policy barriers that do not accompany other medical treatments.

The fact that human IVF research faced significant barriers in federal funding received extended media coverage when Dr. Gary D. Hodgen, a physician who had spent 15 years at the NIH, moved to the lab of Howard and Georgeanna Jones, the physicians responsible for the birth of Elizabeth Carr in Norfolk, Virginia. When in front of a congressional subcommittee, Dr. Hodgen noted, "It is my clear opinion that the American people are not adequately treated by a policy that hinders their receipt of optimal reproductive and developmental health."[48] In live congressional testimony, Dr. Hodgen highlighted the fact that his departure was due to the NIH's policy; so did his submitted congressional testimony, which included the 1984 *Science* magazine article related to his departure, "Scientist Quits NIH over Fetal Rules."[49]

Congressional testimony by IVF practitioners in the 1980s included many references to the "restrictive policies of the National Institutes of Health toward funding research" regarding the area of IVF.[50] These policies limited the use of federally funded research to monkeys, and precluded research related to human IVF and embryo transfer as well as general funding for human IVF research.[51] Many bioethical analyses of assisted reproduction today focus on disparities in access to these technologies, with an emphasis on economic and racial disparities.[52] One possible explanation for these disparities is the lack of federal funding, which physicians cited as "damaging" because only those who could afford it could access the technology, and further, the incentives to reduce costs meant that "precious little money is left over to support research itself."[53] Similarly, Dr. Hodgen noted that the "debate of relevant scientific, ethical, and legal issues" could have taken place during the NIH grant review process, yet that was not possible with the NIH policy on the funding of human IVF research.[54]

More specifically, many witnesses noted that the expiration of the Ethics Advisory Board meant that one would need to submit a grant application to the NIH in order to obtain NIH funding, making it impossible to obtain funding for IVF research.[55] The NIH's Ethics Advisory Board expired in 1980, and as noted by Gary B. Ellis of the Office of Technology Assessment, "this moratorium on human in vitro fertilization research has created a chilling effect in the research community. The researchers know there is no channel for their research proposals to get review, so they do not submit them."[56]

In 1988, a congressional subcommittee held a hearing on whether IVF research should be federally funded. While not a member of that subcommittee, Representative Henry Hyde, the namesake of the Hyde Amendment, provided a prepared statement claiming that that "as currently practiced IVF poses several threats to the sanctity of human life."[57] Representative Hyde's statement also identified a number of his other concerns about IVF, including accidental embryo loss, "deliberate discarding and destruction of the [embryo]," and experimentation on human embryos.[58]

In 1989, Gary Ellis testified before a congressional subcommittee again and noted, on the topic of the Ethics Advisory Board, that the failure of the HHS to "deliver on its pledge to publish a final charter and revive the Ethics Advisory Board" had "essentially halted" research on human IVF, even though "such a Board is required by Federal regulation to advise the Department of Health and Human Services."[59] Ellis then re-emphasized the significance of this "de facto" ban on federally funded human IVF research. Ellis noted that this failure "robbed infertile couples seeking IVF of the ultimate consumer protection . . . research."[60]

These concerns continued to surface in debates about human cloning as experts like Dr. Bryan Cowan, who testified on behalf of the American Society for Reproductive Medicine at a meeting of the US House of Representatives, noted: "The decision to deny Federal funds for research involving human IVF has harmed the millions of Americans suffering from infertility."[61] Funding restrictions including refusals to include IVF and other forms of ART in health insurance coverage also harm individuals suffering from infertility by rendering IVF more difficult to access. Moreover, Chapters 7 and 8 will explore the tension in the government's decision to treat IVF and other ART techniques, which involve the practice of medicine, like pharmaceuticals, which require millions of dollars in research funding (which is recouped through high pharmaceutical prices, which are in turn covered by insurance in the United States) and approval by the FDA, an especially political agency when reproduction of any kind is involved—traditional or assisted.

Bioethics, Religion, Life, and Personhood

Volumes have been written about religion and its influence on politics and its role in the law. Relevant portions of the First Amendment, for the purposes of this book, include "Congress shall make no law respecting an establishment of religion or prohibiting the free exercise thereof."[62] These two clauses are referred to as the establishment clause and the free exercise clause. The free exercise clause, in particular, is relevant to this book because it has led Congress to enact laws that purport to foster the free exercise of religion.

Recently, the protections ascribed to the free exercise clause tend to focus on theistic religions, with an emphasis on various forms of Christianity, as opposed to secularism.[63] With regard to reproduction, decisions have favored religious views, promoting embryo adoption programs, abstinence-only education, and crisis pregnancy centers (which present an appearance of offering abortions but in fact do not).[64]

The influence of religion on the law and regulatory decisions is apparent in all chapters of this book. As detailed in Chapter 2, many of the bioethical concerns regarding assisted reproduction reflect religious and secular views about reproduction in general. Even though individuals in legal, scientific, and medical fields tend to refer to "bioethical" views, such views may also be synonymous with "moral," "religious," "ethical," or "political" views. Below is a brief listing of the bioethical concerns that accompany assisted reproduction, some of which have already been discussed in this chapter and in previous chapters. The terms used in bioethical discourse did not tend to appear in congressional testimony but evidence of their influence was clear. The bioethical terms and concerns that shaped testimony included, often for politically conservative individuals, concerns about hubris, "playing God," the appropriate role of humans in decision-making about potential lives, "dignity," and appropriate limits on parental action. Other bioethical concerns at issue, especially for politically liberal individuals, include reproductive autonomy, parental autonomy, patient autonomy, and eugenics, especially regarding the rights of those with disabilities. Such "bioethical concerns" underlie the testimony of legislators and expert witnesses. Disability concerns and eugenics are included in Chapter 5's discussion of background information related to the mechanics of genetic alteration as well as concerns that the information provided by ART and genetic testing can lead to decisions that remove certain traits from the population or that indicate that certain traits are more desirable than others.

The 1987 congressional hearing before the Select Committee on Children, Youth, and Families, titled "Alternative Reproductive Technologies: Implications For Children and Families," included testimony from professors Lori Andrews, George Annas, and John A. Robertson, as well as Dr. Gary D. Hodgen (all of whom appeared before the 1984 House subcommittee).[65] At the hearing, experts referred to babies conceived via IVF as "test tube babies" and babies conceived via gestational surrogacy as "host-uterus babies."[66] This hearing focused on the implications of alternative reproductive technologies, as well as the reasons for using those technologies, which included references to infertility and delayed childbirth.[67] Much of the terminology focused on "married couples" and their rights to access these technologies, even though marriage was not a prerequisite for access to assisted reproduction.[68] More specifically, the hearing participants were particularly concerned with the "profound questions and difficult choices for women."[69]

In spite of the often-evoked separation of church and state, religious views often influence legislators and judges and the individuals who carry out their directives. Legislators often express their religious views in various media outlets and legislative hearings. Judges should rule impartially, but there is a robust literature on how their personal views can influence legal proceedings and decisions. Congressional hearings and articles have devoted substantial time to how Supreme Court Justices' backgrounds (age, parental status, race, religion, etc.) might influence their decisions.[70] There is sometimes less information on local judges, but in a well-written judicial opinion the judges' views would at least be identified. It is much more difficult to know the views of the many civil service employees who may eventually interpret regulations, or to know how their views shaped their interpretations or enforcements of regulations or their responses to the public.

Religious and bioethical views connect to legislation in various ways. Certain political groups are guided by their moral views, as illustrated by the decades-long debate related to the legality of abortion. Religious activist organizations can impact federal funding allocations. Groups motivated by reproductive autonomy tend to support legislation that strengthens access to and protection for abortion rights as well as funding for ART. Conservative religious groups tend to oppose abortion and ART. Catholic religious views were steadily well-represented at congressional hearings related to in vitro fertilization, stem cell research, and abortion. Catholicism does not represent the views of all Christians, and evangelical Christians tend to be Protestant. Protestant Christian are known to be more open to the use of IVF than Catholics are.[71] And there is a broad range of Protestant denominations.[72] The Southern Baptist Convention has been described as "the nation's largest and most politically powerful Protestant denomination."[73] It has 50,000 churches and 14 million adherents to its increasing anti-abortion activism.[74] Some of those denominations, however, are just as concerned as Catholics about the creation of "designer babies," or gamete donation, even if those views (and opposing views) are not represented before the US Congress.[75] Nonetheless, evangelical Christians also tend to be opposed to abortion rights.[76] Recently, in a concurring opinion in *LePage v. Center for Reproductive Medicine*, Alabama Supreme Court Chief Justice Tom Parker wrote the following in support of recognizing destroyed human embryos as destroyed human lives:

> Human life cannot be wrongfully destroyed without incurring the wrath of a holy God, who views the destruction of His image as an affront to Himself. . . . Even before birth, all human beings bear the image of God, and their lives cannot be destroyed without effacing his glory.[77]

In 2024, the Southern Baptist Convention also voted to "to reaffirm the unconditional value and right to life of every human being, including those in an embryonic stage, and to only utilize reproductive technologies consistent with that affirmation, especially in the number of embryos generated in the I.V.F. process."[78]

Individuals on all sides of the political spectrum (for instance, liberal, in-between/moderate, and conservative) can ascribe to various religious (and secular) views, but conservative religious views tend to have significant political impact, especially lately, as evidenced by successful conservative legislation and policies that are inimical to autonomy. The media often refer to the "religious right," and religious views often correspond with "pro-life" or conservative views. Opposition to abortion, contraception, and stem cell research tends to reflect "pro-life" views. In 1973, the Supreme Court decision in *Roe* noted:

> We need not resolve the difficult question of when life begins. When those trained in the respective disciplines of medicine, philosophy, and theology are unable to arrive at any consensus, the judiciary, at this point in the development of man's knowledge, is not in a position to speculate as to the answer.[79]

The *Roe* court subsequently discussed the views of various religious traditions, including Judaism, Roman Catholicism, and Protestantism, on when life began.[80]

Abortion: Moral Controversy and State Regulation

Value judgments—judgments about the morality of certain actions or their value to society—often motivate regulatory choices. There is a sizable literature on the regulation of abortion, for example, which legislatures in various states had criminalized before the Supreme Court's decision in *Roe v. Wade* (1973), which recognized a federal constitutional right to an abortion, using a trimester framework that was later modified in subsequent cases.[81] For example, in the lead-up to the overturning of *Roe v. Wade* in *Dobbs v. Jackson Women's Health Organization*, significant commentary focused on TRAP laws, the term given to laws that were "targeted regulation of abortion providers."[82] These laws, passed by state legislatures, aimed to render pre-viability access to abortion more difficult in the absence of a ban on abortion.[83] Common TRAP laws have included requirements related to room size and corridor width as well as requirements that abortion providers have admitting privileges at local hospitals, that ambulatory surgical centers providing abortions meet different requirements than those of centers offering riskier medical procedures than abortion, in spite of the lack of health benefit for these requirements.[84] Legislators based some of these laws on model legislation created and provided by advocacy groups.[85] Often, once one state passes a law, other interested legislatures pass similar laws.[86]

In the lead-up to *Dobbs*, Jackson Women's Health Organization filed suit to prevent the enforcement of Mississippi's Gestational Age Act.[87] The Supreme Court's decision overturning the federal constitutional right to an abortion focused on a provision of Mississippi's Gestational Age Act:

> Except in a medical emergency or in the case of a severe fetal abnormality, a person shall not intentionally or knowingly perform . . . or induce an abortion of an unborn human being if the probable gestational age of the unborn human being has been determined to be greater than fifteen (15) weeks.[88]

Penalties for violations of Mississippi's Gestational Age Act include the revocation or suspension of one's medical license for intentionally or knowingly performing or inducing an abortion on a fetus that has gestated for more than 15 weeks.[89] The lengthy *Dobbs* opinion, which was substantially similar to the version that was leaked to the press in April 2022, concluded by noting:

> We end this opinion where we began. Abortion presents a profound moral question. The Constitution does not prohibit the citizens of each State from regulating or prohibiting abortion. *Roe* and *Casey* abrogated that authority. We now overrule those decisions and return that authority to the people and their elected representatives.[90]

While the *Dobbs* opinion (as well as the well-publicized prior leaked version) noted that it was "not based on any view about if and when prenatal life is entitled to any of the rights enjoyed after birth," it very clearly is.[91] Not only did the majority opinion continually invoke these specific issues related to the point at which life begins, Justice Kavanaugh's concurring opinion did as well. Thus, as the dissenting opinion in *Dobbs* indicated in 2022, physicians who provide ART services as well as genetic testing services were (and are) rightly concerned about the implications of *Dobbs* on other matters related to reproduction. In fact, in 2024 the Alabama Supreme Court ruled that IVF embryos are children, a decision that led clinics to cease providing IVF in Alabama until the legislature clarified the matter.[92]

The *Dobbs* majority opinion referenced several topics including moral and ethical debates as to what point "life" exists and the moral status of the embryo. These same concerns from the *Dobbs* opinion have accompanied assisted reproduction since its inception.

Personhood, or more specifically, when an entity becomes a person, has significant political and legal ramifications.[93] The US Supreme Court concluded in *Roe* "that the word 'person,' as used in the Fourteenth Amendment, does not include the unborn."[94] Nevertheless, debates about fetal personhood were rife (and still are). Fetal personhood debates often correspond with religious views about when "life" begins, with conservative Christian beliefs corresponding to particularly restrictive regulatory decisions. Debates about when life begins are implicated in arguments about in vitro fertilization, especially in relation to embryo disposition and stem cell research. Thus, those who place "life" at conception are generally opposed to treatments involving the destruction of embryos.

Estimates indicate the following makeup of religions in the United States: White mainline (non-evangelical) Protestant (13.9 percent); White evangelical Protestant (13.6 percent); White Catholic (12.6 percent); Hispanic Catholic (8.6 percent); Black Protestant (7.7 percent); Hispanic Protestant (3.5 percent); other nonwhite Protestant (2.5 percent); other nonwhite Catholic (1.9 percent); Jewish (1.9 percent); New Age religions (1.6 percent); Mormon (1.5 percent); Jehovah's Witness (1.1 percent); Buddhist (0.7 percent); Hindu (0.7 percent); Muslim (0.6 percent); Unitarian/Universalist (0.5 percent); Orthodox Christian (0.5 percent); and Unaffiliated (meaning nonreligious) (26.8 percent).[95] Even given these estimates, the United States is a religious country as compared to Western European countries.[96] When individuals who hold these conservative views on when life begins are politicians or represent a particularly conservative political party (or sect) or constituents, these beliefs often influence their policies.

While it can be difficult to define "public discourse," congressional hearings are certainly part of that discourse. The various positions of religious groups tend to dominate these conversations because religions tend to have varied positions on when life beings, whereas secular or scientific positions are inclined to classify embryos as "tissue" or in intermediate categories demanding respect. Representatives of the National Conference of Catholic Bishops have often testified before Congress, as have abortion opponents, abortion supporters, and representatives of physician groups (which tend to support access to abortion and contraception).

The Republican Party is not a monolith, and "conservatives" do not all hold the same beliefs. Moreover, sometimes individuals vote strategically. Nonetheless, a Pew poll about the electorate in the 2016 election, in which President Trump prevailed, noted that "White evangelical Protestants, who constituted one out of every five voters, consistently have been among the strongest supporters of Republican candidates and supported Trump by a 77% to 16% margin."[97] The Pew analysis also found that voters who identified as Catholic "were more evenly divided" than Protestant voters; 52 percent of Catholic voters reported voting for President Trump and 44 percent said they voted for Hillary Clinton.[98] Additionally, the Pew Research Center study found that "Protestants constituted about half of the electorate and reported voting for Trump over Clinton by a 56% to 39% margin."[99] An analysis of the religious affiliations of Trump 2020 voters found that 43 percent were evangelical, 21 percent were Catholic, 16 percent were non-evangelical Protestant, 16 percent were unaffiliated, and 4 percent were classified as other.[100]

Other religions besides Catholicism and Evangelicalism have views on assisted reproduction but tend to be indifferent to or supportive of it, and those views rarely are expressed in congressional hearings. For example, religions with views generally receptive to ART include Judaism, Islam, Buddhism, and Hinduism.[101] Judaism, in particular, is known for its particularly pro-natalist views that "gladly accommodate assisted reproductive technologies."[102] For example, the prepared testimony of Lois C. Waldman, acting director for the Commission on Law and Social Action of the American Jewish Congress, noted: "The fetus is not a 'person' in the Jewish tradition until the moment of birth. . . . Whatever has not come forth into the lift of the world (i.e., the mother's birth canal) is not a human life. In no circumstances is abortion a capital offense."[103] Views on genetic modification of humans, which will be the topic of Chapter 5, also often correlate with religious views.

Congressional Debates Related to Insurance Coverage and Fertility Treatment Coverage

IVF has been treated similarly to some other medical innovations insofar as the innovations had to occur in the private sector as opposed to with public funding. Thus, for decades insurance companies and some physicians characterized IVF as "experimental," which generally prevented it from being covered by insurance.[104] Even when physicians considered IVF "a standard and accepted medical practice," a classification that occurred as early as 1988 by some, NIH funding remained unavailable.[105] Congress has held hearings on whether infertility treatment should be a part of federal employee insurance coverage. Federal employees' neighbors in states like Maryland can benefit from private insurance coverage of infertility treatment but federal employees remain largely uncovered for treatments like IVF, although some plans cover other fertility-related services, such as artificial insemination.[106] Some found this lack of coverage ironic, given that many federal health insurance plans cover costs associated with procedures to produce deliberate infertility, like vasectomies and tubal ligation, or the diagnosis of infertility, but not the treatment of infertility.[107]

Recent stories have focused on insurance coverage of fertility treatment for employees of companies like Amazon and Starbucks, but individuals have been pursuing health insurance coverage for IVF for years.[108] Materials submitted by the Alan Guttmacher Institute in a 1986 hearing noted:

> Unlike many private health insurance plans written by other employers for their employees, [Federal Employees Health Benefit] plans essentially do not cover medically necessary abortion services. Since 1983, insurance plans offered to federal employees and their dependents have been prohibited—as a result of a congressionally imposed ban—from covering abortion except if the life of the woman would be endangered if the pregnancy were carried term.[109]

In 1988 a federal employee whose wife left the federal service in search of better insurance coverage for fertility treatment noted that Maryland required fertility benefits and that "of the 15 women who testified in favor of [Maryland's health insurance policy], 14 have since had children."[110] Even in 1988, some legislators were disappointed to hear that individuals left federal service for private employers who provided greater insurance benefits for fertility treatment.[111]

In the earlier days of IVF, when physicians considered IVF experimental, expert witnesses from areas with military personnel, like Norfolk, Virginia, noted that it was heartbreaking to tell service members that their incomes were too low to afford IVF at places like the Jones Institute at Eastern Virginia Medical School (named for Howard and Georgeanna Jones, the physicians responsible for the birth of Elizabeth Carr) and also that their insurance did not cover IVF.[112]

The lack of insurance coverage did not mean that "enterprising" physicians were not able to bill insurance companies for infertility-related charges, but an expert witness from the Office of Technology Assessment viewed this as a "disingenuous" action.[113] Nevertheless, methods of physician billing to include fertility services in the absence of clear insurance company coverage continued to surface in congressional hearings, as did stories about those who could not obtain insurance coverage for their fertility treatments.[114]

Today some private and federal employee insurance programs cover some fertility drugs and treatments. Stories continue to circulate about individuals who select specific employers in order to obtain fertility benefits.[115] Private companies are leaders in the provision and subsidization of fertility treatment to their employees through private health insurance plans and fertility benefits companies.[116] The actions of the federal government as it relates to covered procedures have significant consequences because the federal government is associated with multiple insurance programs, including federal employee health benefits, Medicare, Medicaid, Indian Health Service, CHAMPVA (available through the Department of Veterans Affairs), and TRICARE, previously CHAMPUS (available through the Department of Defense).[117] Moreover, since the 1980s, the military health system has made some changes for service members whose combat injuries necessitate the use of fertility services.[118] TRICARE, the health insurance provider for active duty military service members and their dependents, for some time did not cover IVF or intrauterine insemination, although it did cover some services like cryopreservation and storage of embryos, IVF, artificial insemination, and sperm and egg retrieval for certain service members who lost their reproductive abilities due to a "serious illness or injury" sustained while on active duty.[119] Similarly, the Department of Veterans Affairs has amended its regulations to provide IVF to certain service members who suffered severe service-related injuries that resulted in their infertility.[120] In 2024, the Department of Defense announced expanded coverage of ART for service members and veterans in response to lawsuits asserting that the preexisting policies violated the Patient Protection and Affordable Care Act and the Fifth Amendment of the US Constitution, and the Administrative Procedure Act.[121] In spite of the slow expansion of health insurance coverage to include fertility treatment, even though IVF is no longer considered experimental, insurance plans often exclude IVF from routine health insurance coverage due to lack of mandate or statutory exceptions.[122]

Conclusion

The development of ART in the United States continues to be accompanied by ethical controversy. Early in the use of ART, that controversy stymied access to federal funding, which led to the development of ART in the private sector, where funding is provided by patients/consumers. The ethical controversy arguably led to a very slow rollout of insurance coverage for ART. In the United States, coverage for ART has largely been driven by private employers.

While the literature tends to treat abortion, assisted reproduction, and stem cell research separately, ART often appears in conversations about other controversial topics. Animal cloning led to anticipatory, yet ultimately unnecessary, conversations at both the federal and state legislative levels related to human reproductive cloning. Similarly, individuals who oppose abortion or ART rarely separate assisted reproduction from abortion because of their focus on defining when life begins. The chronological starting point for this chapter was 1978, with the birth of Louise Brown in England, which was after the Supreme Court's 1973 decision in *Roe v. Wade* (1973). Because the hearings discussed in this chapter were after *Roe* but before *Dobbs*, many experts specifically referred to the constitutional right to an abortion or alluded to it in a manner that indicated that the existence of *Roe* appeared to affect their analysis.[123] Without *Roe*, how will their arguments and the impacts of those arguments change? State responses to *Dobbs* continue to unfold, but at the very least the impact of these arguments seem to be that (1) in certain states, legislatures have curtailed access to abortion even when a pregnant person's health is at stake, and (2) the legislatures and or judiciaries of states like Alabama have identified assisted reproduction as the next target for potential legal barriers. In the lead-up to President Trump's election in 2024, in vitro fertilization and abortion were significant portions of the societal and political discourse and of candidate and campaign statements.[124] During their 2024 campaigns, candidates Harris and Trump both mentioned issues related to assisted reproduction and ultimately, both expressed support for IVF, a notable decision in light of the prior opposition of many Republican candidates to assisted reproduction. Moreover, the Alabama Supreme Court decision in *LePage v. Center for Reproductive Medicine* holding that embryos are "extrauterine children" and "unborn children" led to vocal support for assisted reproduction among many already supportive Democratic politicians and supporters but also individuals who had not previously voiced support for ART, like Alabama's Republican governor Kay Ivey, President Trump, and the many politicians in the Alabama Assembly who passed legislation providing civil and criminal immunity to individuals providing or receiving IVF services, a necessary measure for the continuation of IVF services after the *LePage* decision.[125]

This chapter has focused largely on Christianity and its influence on politics, regulation, and legislation. This focus is due, not to a bias for or against Christianity, but to an acknowledgment of the impacts of conservative religious views on politics and legislation, especially in the area of reproductive rights. Chapter 5 will begin by considering genetic alteration on its own, before moving into the potential combination of assisted reproduction and genetic alteration.

5

The Genetic Revolution

Past and Present

Just as assisted reproduction becomes more commonplace, there is an increasing emphasis on the role of genetics in medicine and society. Genetic databases now help to unite donor-conceived children, conduct genealogy searches, unearth lost relatives (or relegate to another status persons previously classified as blood relatives), and discover criminal perpetrators (such as the Golden State Killer).[1] In a world in which genetics are becoming increasingly salient in medical treatment, the awarding of the 2020 Nobel Prize in Chemistry to the creators of the gene-editing system, CRISPR-Cas9, is also notable.[2] The Nobel Committee awarded this prize after a well-publicized use of CRISPR gene-editing technology to edit human embryos (not by the inventors) that led to the birth of children in China, which the inventors of CRISPR denounced, as did much of the world.[3]

Often the literature atomizes assisted reproduction and genetic alteration, unless techniques involving genetic alteration would also include the modification of gametes or embryos, yet earlier debaters of the appropriate regulatory regime for ART continued to consider the relevance of preceding debates in Congress related to new genetic technologies—namely, recombinant DNA. In 1984, the first witness to testify before a congressional subcommittee on human embryo transfer was Clifford Grobstein, a professor who previously testified in 1982 on the topic of human gene transfer, which at that time caused nonheritable genetic alteration.[4] Grobstein was a professor of biological science and public policy at the University of California San Diego. At the hearing, he noted the connections between IVF, embryo transfer, and human gene transfer before arguing that assisted reproduction and human gene transfer "should be considered by the same oversight mechanism."[5] Grobstein also noted that society would be "better off to try to anticipate" the issues raised by genetic engineering and assisted reproduction instead of using a piecemeal approach that could be "conceivably . . . contradictory."[6] Yet the hands-off, piecemeal approach is exactly what the United States adopted.

At the same hearings, Dr. Howard Jones, who was part of the team whose IVF procedure led to Elizabeth Carr's birth, testified that the method of "handling genetic problems" involved either amniocentesis or selective termination, yet he thought "it would be infinitely better if it were possible to alter the genes so that we did not terminate those pregnancies."[7] In furtherance of that view, he offered the example of Tay-Sachs disease, a well-known debilitating condition, and noted that it would be a "tremendous step forward" if one could "overcome" the gene for Tay-Sachs or a similar genetic condition that leads to selective termination.[8]

Genetic testing has become increasingly important in the world. Individuals can access it not only from health professionals but also via direct-to-consumer genetic testing. The genetic counseling industry has existed since at least the 1956, when the first genetic test was performed in the field of cytogenetics.[9] In a 2022 article, Professor Khiara Bridges noted that the entire premise of the genetic counseling industry rests upon the idea that parents have a "legitimate interest in avoiding the birth of a health-impaired child."[10] Family planning and achieving pregnancy are the most common reasons individuals seek genetic counseling and testing.[11] As a practical matter, exercising this legitimate interest requires exercising the right to an abortion (often referred to as "selective reduction" in the fertility industry or "selective termination") if a fetal abnormality is detected or using preimplantation genetic testing to identify preferred embryos for implantation. Bioethical issues related to parental autonomy also arise in debates over the possibility that parents could genetically engineer their children or select embryos with certain traits.

In this book, I focus on newer techniques of genetic modification or substitution, like cytoplasmic or mitochondrial transfer or germline gene editing. But these techniques did not develop in a vacuum. Gene therapy, the nonheritable analog of germline genetic modification, builds on recombinant DNA technology that was pioneered in the 1970s.[12] This chapter traces the increase in genetic modification and genetic knowledge, from recombinant DNA technology to scientific efforts at (successful) self-regulation, the patent regime, and gene editing, including CRISPR-Cas9 and prime editing. This chapter has two goals: (1) to briefly describe innovations in genetic science and revisit germline gene editing, which involves the modification of nuclear DNA, and AARTs, both of which fall within the category of reproductive genetic innovation; and (2) to briefly introduce some of the regulatory responses to genetic technologies and reproductive genetic innovation in the United States.

Recombinant DNA

Recombinant DNA is the basis for many medical innovations and therapies, including insulin, human growth hormone, and other pharmaceutical products.[13] Vaccine production and development have also been facilitated by recombinant DNA technology.[14] At first, recombinant DNA elicited many fears, and its regulators were largely a combination of scientists' self-regulation and the NIH's Recombinant DNA Advisory Committee.[15] In the realm of self-regulation, scientists met at the Asilomar conferences, where they agreed upon future uses of recombinant DNA technology.[16]

The experience with recombinant DNA, especially the role of self-regulation as well as local regulation, is a useful model that could be implemented for reproductive genetic innovation. Three individuals are particularly noteworthy regarding recombinant DNA innovation: Stanley Cohen, Herbert Boyer, and Paul Berg. Paul Berg, from Stanford, is credited as being "among the first to produce a recombinant DNA molecule in 1972."[17] In 1980, the "Nobel Prize in Chemistry 1980 was divided, one half awarded to Paul Berg 'for his fundamental studies of the biochemistry of nucleic acids, with particular regard to recombinant-DNA', the other half jointly to Walter Gilbert and Frederick Sanger 'for their contributions concerning the determination of base sequences in nucleic acids.'"[18]

Stanley Cohen, at Stanford, and Herbert Boyer, at the University of California at San Francisco (UCSF), submitted a patent application for recombinant DNA technology in 1974.[19] In 1976, Herbert Boyer and Robert Swanson, a venture capitalist, co-founded Genentech, the first biotechnology company.[20] Herbert Boyer continued to work at Genentech while a professor at UCSF.[21] The US Patent and Trademark Office granted a patent based on Cohen and Boyer's application in December 1980, after the Supreme Court's decision in *Diamond v. Chakrabarty* holding that living organisms produced through genetic engineering were eligible for patent protection.[22] While Cohen and Boyer are the inventors on the recombinant DNA patent, for them and many other university or corporate employees, the patent itself is assigned to the institution or institutions involved.[23] A presentation from Stanford's licensing office lists the following patents as "Big Winners" for the institution: "Cohen-Boyer Recombinant DNA ($255M) [;] Google ($343M) [;] Functional Antibodies ($628M)."[24] That same presentation notes that "~81% of research at Stanford is funded by the US government."[25] Genentech used recombinant DNA technology "to develop recombinant human growth hormone and insulin in the early 1980s."[26] As of 2016, more than 20,000 patents covering inventions made by Genentech researchers had been issued.[27] By 1990, Roche, a pharmaceutical company, owned the majority of Genentech, and in 2009 it fully acquired the company for $46.8 billion.[28]

While recombinant DNA is commonplace today, at the time it was an extremely controversial technology. As Stanford Medical School noted in the press release accompanying the university's notice of Paul Berg's death at 96, Berg's work "set off a political and public firestorm. Soon after he first combined DNA from two different organisms, Berg faced public fears that inserting the genes of one organism into the DNA of another would lead to the creation of new plagues, alter how organisms evolve or wreak environmental havoc."[29]

Asilomar, Self-Regulation, and Recombinant DNA

Recombinant DNA is significant to genetic innovation. Paul Berg, recipient of the 1980 Nobel Prize, wrote, "Without the tools of recombinant DNA there would be no human or any other genome sequence."[30] Patented recombinant DNA technology was licensed by 468 companies, and it was the basis for many important medical innovations, including "erythropoeitin for dialysis patients, insulin for the treatment of diabetes, growth hormone for children with growth deficiencies and interferon for cancer patients."[31] Recombinant DNA was also the foundation for other innovations like genetically modified crops and vaccines.[32]

The historical conception of the early promise of recombinant DNA is very similar to that assigned to reproductive genetic innovation. In 1973, scientists who had attended the 1973 Gordon Conference on Nucleic Acids voted to send a letter to the presidents of the National Academy of Sciences and the National Institute of Medicine.[33] A majority of those scientists also "desired to publicize the letter more widely" and the journal *Science* published the letter.[34] The letter's authors, Maxine Singer of the NIH and Dieter Soll of Yale University's Department of Molecular Biophysics and Biochemistry, observed that news techniques could "combine DNA from animal viruses with bacterial DNA, or DNA's of different viral origin."[35] The letter did not mention the term "recombinant DNA," but the technique was the subject of the letter as evidenced by the letter's description of the methods required to execute the technique.[36] Singer and Soll also noted that recombinant DNA experiments "offer exciting and interesting potential both for advancing knowledge of fundamental biological processes and for alleviation of human health problems."[37] Similarly, reproductive genetic innovation offers the potential for advancing knowledge of fundamental biological processes, especially the impacts of certain genes on certain traits and disease formation, as well as the potential to prevent the inheritance of certain diseases. On the other hand, the 1973 Letter writers Singer and Soll also characterized recombinant DNA as a "matter of deep concern"—a characterization that many would also apply to reproductive genetic innovation.[38]

In January 1973, the NIH and the National Science Foundation sponsored a meeting at the Asilomar Conference Center in Pacific Grove, California, convened by Paul Berg and other scientists. This meeting was "prompted by concerns relating to the possible oncogenic potential of [Simian Virus 40] in humans, [so] Berg and other prominent scientists convened a meeting to assess the risks of working with tumor viruses and recombinant DNAs that contain them."[39] The most prominent concern was that the viruses could possibly have some cancer-causing effects in humans.[40]

After this meeting, in 1974, *Proceedings of the National Academies of Sciences* published another letter. This 1974 letter is often referred to as the Report of the Committee on Recombinant DNA Molecules, titled "Potential Biohazards of Recombinant DNA Molecules."[41] The letter began by acknowledging the potential promise of recombinant DNA, but then moved to potential perils, including the "creation of novel types of infectious DNA elements whose biological properties cannot be completely predicted in advance."[42] This meant that there was a "serious concern that some of these artificial recombinant DNA molecules could prove biologically hazardous."[43] These concerns about biological hazards do not apply to AARTs, but they do apply to germline gene editing, even though they have not prevented the use of germline gene editing of plants, which could affect everyone on the planet, unlike germline gene editing of humans.[44]

The 11 members of the committee who signed the 1974 letter included Paul Berg (later winner of the 1980 Nobel Prize for Chemistry), Herbert W. Boyer and Stanley N. Cohen (the inventors, for the purposes of the recombinant DNA patent), David Baltimore (one of three joint awardees of the 1975 Nobel Prize in Physiology or Medicine "for . . . discoveries concerning the interaction between tumour viruses and the genetic material of the cell"), and James Watson (one of three joint awardees of the 1962 Nobel Prize in Physiology or Medicine "for . . . discoveries concerning the molecular structure of nucleic acids and its significance for information transfer in living material").[45] The letter provided several recommendations.[46] The first recommendation was that "until the potential hazards of [certain] recombinant DNA molecules are better evaluated or until adequate methods are developed for preventing their spread," scientists should voluntarily agree to defer certain experiments.[47] The letter also requested that the director of the NIH create an advisory committee to consider certain issues related to recombinant DNA technology and that there be an international convening of scientists within a year of the letter's publication to review scientific progress and "and to further discuss appropriate ways to deal with the potential biohazards of recombinant DNA molecules."[48] The letter's authors made their recommendations even though complying with their "major recommendations [would] entail postponement or possibly abandonment of certain types of scientifically worthwhile experiments."[49] Some referred to this 1974 letter as the "Berg letter," after its lead author, Paul Berg.[50] Later, another meeting at the Asilomar Conference took place in 1975.[51] This second Asilomar Conference on Recombinant DNA is what individuals are generally referring to when they refer to "the Asilomar Conference."[52]

Genetic Screening, Prenatal Testing, and Genome Sequencing

Now that the human genome has been sequenced, potential gene targets can be identified. Yet even with this sequencing, gene editing leads to unexpected effects. Genetic testing has evolved over time to become more specific, accurate, and applicable.[53] Similarly, the terms used to refer to genetic testing in the context of reproductive medicine have changed. Today, pre-implantation genetic testing (PGT) encompasses what in the past was commonly referred to as preimplantation genetic diagnosis (PGD) and preimplantation genetic screening (PGS).[54] Patients and medical professionals often combine genetic testing with IVF in order to identify and select embryos with or without certain traits, such as to select for sex or against implanting embryos with certain genetic traits, like those that might be carriers for Tay-Sachs disease or mosaicism.[55]

Noninvasive prenatal testing can be used during pregnancy to diagnose potential ailments. This can affect the prenatal care provided to a mother and fetus, as well as, potentially, the care of a child who is born as a result of the pregnancy. Prenatal testing can detect conditions like Down syndrome, which in turn can lead to discussions about eugenics and bioethics as various individuals object when the information gleaned as a result of prenatal testing is followed by abortion.[56] Moreover, some disability advocates become concerned by the potential implications of a technology that can be used to screen for what society deems a "disability," whereas some individuals with that genetic condition do not see it as something that should be screened for and eliminated from the population.[57] Other disability rights advocates are supportive of genetic technologies and prenatal screening.[58] There are some limitations to PGT. For instance, it cannot identify certain diseases, and it does not resolve the issue of embryos that are categorized as being of "poor quality" and thus not suitable for implantation.[59] In the future, if practitioners are able to successfully combine germline gene editing with preimplantation genetic diagnosis and ART, they "could rescue otherwise viable embryos that were carrying the abnormal allele and theoretically double the probability of the birth of the healthy baby."[60] Newborns are also subject to common medical screenings, some as a result of state requirements and others as part of standard medical diagnostics and treatment in some areas.[61]

Human Cloning: Reproductive and Therapeutic

Cloning does not fit neatly into discussions of ART, but it is necessary to discuss it due to its influence on regulators and legislators. Fears about cloning shape not only decision-makers' actions but also the lead-up to their decisions, and ART is often included in conversations about cloning even when it should not be.

Cloning can occur naturally or artificially.[62] Examples of naturally occurring cloning include asexual reproduction, which plants and single-celled organisms can do.[63] In 2023, parthenogenesis as a type of asexual reproduction made headlines when an American crocodile in captivity reproduced on her own, leading to headlines announcing the "virgin birth" of a crocodile.[64] Identical twins are also classified as "natural clones."[65]

Three types of cloning tend to be mentioned in discussions. Reproductive cloning and therapeutic cloning use similar techniques. Reproductive cloning creates copies of entire organisms; scientists used the method to clone Dolly the sheep, an incident that led to significant controversy with regulatory and legislative repercussions.[66] Therapeutic cloning results in "embryonic stem cells for experiments aimed at creating tissues to replace injured or diseased tissues."[67] The third type of cloning, gene cloning, "produces copies of genes or segments of DNA."[68]

Somatic vs. Germline Genetic Modification: Gene Therapy and Gene Editing

"Genome editing (also called gene editing) is a group of technologies that give scientists the ability to change an organism's DNA."[69] Gene editing or therapy is often divided into two forms—somatic and germline—based on the types of cells targeted.[70] Scientists and commentators commonly refer to these two forms of gene editing as gene therapy and germline gene or genome editing, respectively.[71]

Gene Therapy

Some decried gene therapy as being "a paradigm case of hyperbole"; it was also heralded as a "miracle cure" in 1980. In a 2002 hearing, one individual argued that gene therapy had been "far worse than a disappointment" due to the death of Jesse Gelsinger.[72] Gelsinger was an 18-year old man who participated in, and died as a result of, a gene therapy trial that tested a treatment for babies with a fatal form of ornithine transcarbamylase (OTC). The trial was run by the University of

Pennsylvania Medical Center in 1999.[73] Gelsinger had a mild form of the disease, and the treatment would not benefit him as it was intended for babies suffering from a fatal form of OTC.[74] Industry analysts hypothesized that Gelsinger's death led to a lot of caution in the industry, especially given that he was not sick with the disease.[75] Yet, in 2017 the FDA approved the first gene-therapy product, Kymriah, for marketing in the United States.[76]

CRISPR-Cas9 genome editing can result in heritable or nonheritable changes. In 2023, the FDA approved Casgevy, "the first FDA-approved therapy utilizing CRISPR/Cas9 . . . genome editing."[77] Casgevy is "a cell-based gene therapy . . . approved for the treatment of sickle cell disease in patients 12 years of age and older with recurrent vaso-occlusive crises."[78] CRISPR-Cas9 gene editing was the subject of a lengthy patent dispute between the Massachusetts Institute of Technology's Broad Institute and the University of California at Berkeley.[79] As other forms of gene editing develop, experts predict even more patent battles.[80]

Germline Gene (or Genome) Editing

Germline gene (or genome) editing merits analysis in this book because the US regulatory system treats it similarly to reproductive genetic innovation. In other words, the FDA and a recurring congressional budget rider have effectively banned human germline gene editing in the United States. Technologies for editing genes or genomes involve adding, removing, or changing genetic material at specific locations in an organism's DNA.[81] Genome editing can be used on plants, animals, microorganisms, and humans.[82] In 2020, Emmanuelle Charpentier and Jennifer Doudna were awarded the Nobel Prize in Chemistry "for the development of a method for genome editing."[83]

Various systems have been developed for genome editing. For instance, CRISPR-Cas9 can be used to edit somatic cells or the germline. As we have seen, the inventors of CRISPR-Cas9 oppose the use of genome-editing technology in humans at this time. CRISPR-Cas9 is developing in a world that is far more interconnected than the worlds in the 1970s and 1980s, when Louise Joy Brown and Elizabeth Jordan Carr were born. CRISPR-Cas9 is not the only method of gene editing currently being developed. For example, Professor David Liu's method of prime editing is the subject of several patents and is being used in some startup companies.[84] In vitro gametogenesis, a potential reproductive technology that health care providers might use clinically years from now, is a form of ART that has been the subject of many patent applications; the Conclusion briefly discusses this technology.[85]

CRISPR-Cas9 and other gene (or genome) editing systems can be used for somatic or germline gene editing. Germline editing results in heritable genetic modification; somatic editing leads to nonheritable modifications. In 2008, Jennifer Doudna received a grant from the US Department of Energy to fund her research on CRISPR RNA strands and the Cas1 protein.[86] She later used the findings from this research and other investigations to describe "the underlying mechanisms of the CRISPR-Cas9 system."[87] Other proteins have been discovered as well. Mammoth Biosciences, a biotech company co-founded by Jennifer Doudna, has discovered "newer and smaller proteins such as CAS14 [that] could help overcome hurdles faced by older ones, including the CAS9 editing tool."[88] As of 2021, investors valued Mammoth Biosciences at over $1 billion.[89]

While gene editing holds extensive promise, especially for its potential to eliminate various ailments or to reduce the severity of their symptoms, there are many drawbacks to gene editing. Older forms of gene therapy affected only one generation as opposed to multiple generations. Scientists and observers are especially concerned about the potential negative impacts of gene editing, especially when the gene editing impacts the human germline, and there is both scientific and regulatory opposition to heritable genetic gene editing. For example, as noted in various sources, including experiments that aimed to remove disease-causing alleles in animal and human embryos, "gene editing has the potential to reduce disease-causing alleles, but inadvertent changes to the human germ line, including rearrangements, long deletions, and loss of heterozygosity . . . could have serious consequences that affect development, predisposition to cancer and fertility."[90] Additional safety concerns include the potential for off-target effects, which can lead to changes to genes other than the intended targets, mosaicism, and unknown long-term effects.[91]

In spite of these potential concerns, scientists continue to try to improve the accuracy, safety, and efficacy of germline gene editing. For example, in 2018, Dr. Shoukhrat Mitalipov and other researchers replicated an experiment to insert into an embryo a "foreign" gene, meaning a gene that did not match a parent's genes.[92] According to Dr. Mitalipov's experiment, using CRISPR to replace a gene for hypertrophic cardiomyopathy with a novel gene did not work in the CRISPR'd embryos, rendering the likelihood of "designer babies" lower.[93] Due to various federal regulatory restrictions, including those on a clinical trial involving the implantation of a genetically altered embryo into a uterus, Dr. Mitalipov expects that "unfortunately, this technology will just be shifted to unregulated countries."[94] Yet, various leaders in the field, some of whom differed on whether CRISPR could be used successfully in human embryos, expected that the technique was "too unpredictable and unreliable for use in fertility clinics any time soon."[95]

Various books have been written about human germline genome editing. It is worth noting that in 2018 at the International Summit on Human Gene Editing, Dr. He Jiankui announced that he had used the CRISPR-Cas9 gene-editing system to edit embryos.[96] Dr. He had used CRISPR-Cas9 to edit the genes of two embryos before the children, Lulu and Nana, were born. Dr. He later noted that another child had been born via a gene-edited embryo, although that child was not given a name in the press.[97] Dr. He reported that he targeted the CCR5 gene in order to protect the children from HIV infection, a decision that many scientists and members of the public found deplorable.[98] Allegedly, the children, Lulu and Nana, who have not been seen by the public, are doing well, although Dr. He failed to edit the CCR5 gene as he intended.[99] There were other objectionable aspects of his "experiment," including issues related to consent.[100]

Genetically Altered Food and Animals

Animals merit a mention because they matter to scientific innovation. The lead-up to human clinical trials often involves primates due to their similarity to humans. There is an often-repeated statistic that humans share 98.5 percent of their DNA sequence with chimpanzees, although a 2002 study found that "a better estimate would be that 95% of the base pairs are exactly shared between chimpanzee and human DNA."[101] At the same time, many studies are conducted in mice, not only because they are extremely inexpensive as compared to nonhuman primates (e.g., a long-tailed macaque or rhesus monkey can cost over $55,000), but also because mice and humans share over 90 percent of the same genes.[102]

Gene editing is not the oldest method of genetic alteration. Farmers have been altering plant and animal species for many thousands of years through selective breeding.[103] Such crossbreeding has produced many well-known plant species, including the Carolina Reaper chili pepper.[104] Species created by crossbreeding are very different from the species that have been created through genetic modification, which the FDA identifies as "genetically modified organisms (GMOs)." Well-known GMOs include the "first GMO produce created through genetic engineering—a GMO tomato" which was approved by the FDA and available for sale in 1994.[105] Today there are many examples of GMO produce as well as genetically engineered salmon.[106]

In January 2008, the FDA "decided . . . that meat and milk from cloned animals, such as cattle, pigs and goats, are as safe as those from non-cloned animals."[107] The decisions by the FDA and USDA to permit food products resultant from cloned animals and genetically modified plants have led to significant opposition and disputes in the United States, with notable lawsuits between food makers and states like Vermont in opposition to labeling requirements and growing support for "organic" foods, which are not genetically modified.[108] Thus, the FDA has favored the genetic modification of animals and plants while opposing genetic modification of human embryos even when intended to prevent disease or improve fertility. At first glance, this may seem tenable, but the modification of animals and plants could affect far more individuals than the genetic modification of individual humans.[109]

Advanced Assisted Reproductive Technologies (AARTs)

Progress has been made in the development of AARTs. Mitochondrial transfer in particular has been progressing in the United Kingdom and Australia, which recently introduced a regulatory scheme to support eventual mitochondrial transfer trials.[110]

In 2016, a STAT News article noted, "The next great advance in fertility treatments may rest with five young monkeys in a lab outside of town."[111] That town was in Oregon and featured a lab run by Dr. Shoukhrat Mitalipov of the Oregon Health Sciences University. The five young rhesus macaques in Dr. Mitalipov's mitochondrial replacement therapy trials all have clever names: Mito, Tracker, Spindler, Spindy, and Chrysta.[112] In 2016, the animals were all 7 years old, with the exception of Chrysta, who was 4 years old at the time.[113] In terms of life span, "monkeys don't reproduce until they're 6 or 7—and they live 15 to 20 years in captivity."[114] Keith Campbell developed the technique that Dr. Mitalipov uses for mitochondrial transfer, nuclear transfer, in the process of cloning Dolly the sheep.[115] Dr. Mitalipov has noted, "My clinical goal was to use some of the basic knowledge to improve human reproduction. . . . The IVF platform can be used now to remanufacture gametes, to treat infertility, but also as a platform for gene therapy, which is probably where the future will go."[116]

In 2020, Hong Ma, Paula Amato, Shoukhrat Mitalipov, and other authors provided an update on Mito, Tracker, Spindler, Spindy, and Chrysta, as well as their offspring, in the journal *Human Reproduction*.[117] Funding sources for the work included the Burroughs Wellcome Fund, the National Institutes of Health, the National Research Foundation of Korea, and funds from the Oregon Health and Science University, where the macaques live.[118] In sum, the authors noted that the general health and fertility of the rhesus macaques created through mitochondrial transfer was "unremarkable and similar to controls."[119] The study noted paternal contribution to mitochondrial DNA, which was significant given the general belief that mitochondrial DNA is only transmitted maternally.[120] The study also showed that mitochondrial replacement is not completely effective; sometimes mutant mitochondria persist ("carry-over").[121] The study concluded that "clinical trials on children born after [mitochondrial replacement therapy (MRT)] will be required to fully determine safety and efficacy of MRT for humans."[122] The five monkeys created through mitochondrial transfer had their own offspring when mated with non-engineered monkeys, although at least one pregnancy ended in a miscarriage, possibly due to a bacterial infection."[123] Dr. Paula Amato noted, "We've done everything we can to show that it likely would be safe, but ultimately you never know until you do it," a statement that is reminiscent of the commentary of the former chief medical officer, Sally Davies, before she advocated for the legalization of human mitochondrial transfer trials in the United Kingdom.[124]

Conclusion

This chapter has provided background on genetic modification, with an emphasis on techniques that do not have human reproductive clinical uses. Such genetic innovations are nonetheless still relevant because (1) they illustrate concerns about new technologies that have significant genetic potential, and (2) they show how scientists have engaged in self-regulation of controversial genetic technologies. Advanced assisted reproductive technologies like cytoplasmic transfer and mitochondrial transfer are accompanied by a more intense ethical opposition than traditional ART like IVF and artificial insemination. AARTs, due to the small amount of genetic material that is implicated, are accompanied by the same ethical objections as ART as well as additional ones. Most importantly, the technologies that are the focus of this chapter are patented, unlike IVF and AARTs. The patents are significant because they have been awarded despite the controversial nature of these technologies. In contrast, US law denies patent protections to techniques used in nuclear weapons even though these meet the general requirements for patentability.[125] All the same, Congress has yet to pass substantive legislation that is clearly applicable to AARTs and human germline editing.

6

Self-Regulation, Techno-Anxiety, and the Growing Role of the Federal Government in the Regulation of Genetic Innovation and Embryonic Research

The topic of genetic engineering continued to arise in conversations about ethical objections to IVF. For instance, in testimony before a congressional subcommittee, an NIH ethicist observed that some may oppose IVF based on "an opposition to, the total objectification of reproduction . . . [as IVF] could be used as the opening technique in an effort to create optimum infants created from the sperm and ova of specially selected individuals and grown under carefully controlled circumstances, presumably laboratory conditions."[1] As we have seen, issues related to genetic diagnosis and genetic alteration continued to surface in congressional hearings and funding decisions.[2] Given the fact that, as far as we know, thus far there has been no human reproductive cloning, in spite of threats by researchers to do so, perhaps the legislation and administrative agency actions have had the desired effect.

Stem cell research and reproductive cloning are not usually seen as genetic technologies, but they are controversial scientific innovations that have routinely arisen in debates about genetic technologies. Fears of human reproductive cloning and personhood-based concerns about human embryos, scientific research, and medical research have shaped the regulation of reproductive genetic innovation. Namely, these fears have led to the subterranean regulation of reproductive genetic innovation by administrative agencies, budget riders precluding the use of funding related to embryo destruction, and agency interpretations of unclear congressional appropriations legislation in favor of obstructing the approval of techniques involving reproductive genetic innovation.

This chapter discusses medically and scientifically significant genetic technologies and techniques (recombinant DNA, stem cell research, reproductive cloning, somatic cell gene therapy, and human germline gene editing) as well as how the regulatory system addressed the legality of these technologies and techniques, including through patent law and self-regulation. The chapter also discusses external influences on the regulatory system like lobbyists and members of federal advisory committees.

Patent Law, ART, and Genetic Innovation

Various federal regulatory agencies, such as the FDA and the US Patent and Trademark Office, serve as gatekeepers in issues of intellectual property. The FDA has been characterized as the "global gold standard" of drug regulatory agencies, although it is often criticized.[3] The US patent system has also been characterized as "both broken and a failure."[4] These characterizations matter because patents are relevant to many aspects of everyday life.

Issues of patent law have arisen in conversations related to the cloning of humans and human embryonic stem cell research. Media coverage noted that the University of Missouri secured a patent that could be used for human cloning in the United States.[5] In a switch, however, the University of Missouri noted that it would not use the patent for human cloning and would refuse to license patents for human reproductive cloning.[6]

Patent law plays a role in the regulation of most of the innovations discussed in this chapter, and such law is connected to the private market. Patents can relate to the funding or lack of funding for ART innovation. There is a significant body of patent law scholarship related to genetic innovation. Genetic innovation has shifted over time but the traditional subjects of FDA regulation are patented products. The FDA, in general, has jurisdiction over small-molecule drugs (which are subject to patent protection), biologics (which are also generally patented), vaccines, another patented products. In 2009, after the FDA lost to the tobacco industry in *Brown & Williamson Tobacco v. FDA*, Congress added tobacco products to the FDA's regulated products.[7] Newer tobacco delivery products, like vape pens, are patented products, whereas cigarettes and tobacco (a naturally occurring plant, although there are genetically modified versions) are not subject to patent protection and have been a part of American history since the early settlers arrived.[8]

ART does not have significant coverage in patent law. IVF pioneers did not patent IVF, and discussion of patent law rarely surfaces in connection with traditional ART. Not only did the inventors of IVF not patent it, many others supported this decision, including scholars who opposed patenting the process of IVF.[9] One ART technique, "lavage," was patented, which led to negative reactions from fellow practitioners, industry groups like the American Medical Association, scholars, and politicians.[10] Because this was anomalous treatment of an ART technique, the practitioner associated with it, Dr. John Buster, faced questioning at a congressional subcommittee hearing as to why he would patent a method of assisted reproductive technology, especially when so many other medical procedures and their results "are always in the public domain."[11] Representative Al Gore noted, ""It's extremely rare to take a medical procedure and claim exclusive rights to that procedure. . . . That's wrong isn't it?"[12] Dr. Buster noted that the patent was related to the lack of governmental funding available at the time and how the investors that he was able to convince were interested in patenting these procedures.[13] Dr. Buster argued that he would not have received private funding from investors if those "investors stood no chance to profit from their investment via patenting and licensing the products and processes resulting from his research."[14] Ultimately, lavage was less effective than other fertility methods and "by the early 1990s, clinical trials of uterine lavage were abandoned in favor of the safer and more efficient IVF approach."[15]

Recombinant DNA innovations were a turning point in biological and medical innovations in many ways. A journal article co-authored by Drs. Paul Berg and Janet Mertz noted:

> None of the members of the Berg, Kaiser, or Davis groups ever considered patenting the reagents or procedures that were used for recombining DNA *in vitro*. Neither had the scientists who discovered TdT, DNA polymerases, DNA ligases, exonucleases, and restriction enzymes ever sought patents for their efforts. Indeed, few, if any, of the discoveries, reagents, and methods that constitute the foundations of molecular biology were ever patented.[16]

They also noted that, like some other academic institutions,

> the University of Wisconsin–Madison had a long history of patenting inventions in the biological and biochemical sciences (*e.g.*, vitamins, antibiotics), the sociology among most U. S. life scientists prior to the 1970s was to eschew patents, believing that they would restrict the free flow of information and reagents and impede the pace of discovery. However, that reticence disappeared in November, 1974 when Stanford University and the University of California at San Francisco jointly filed a United States patent application citing their respective faculty members, Stanley Cohen and Herbert Boyer, as the sole inventors of the recombinant DNA technology.[17]

UCSF and Stanford together later made over $300 million from the 1980 patent on recombinant DNA and two other related patents; Stanford's share was approximately $255 million.[18] Dr. Berg wrote, "In retrospect, Stanford's and UCSF's action set in motion an escalating cascade of patent claims by universities covering their faculties' respective discoveries that continues to this day."[19]

The notion of path dependence, we will see later, is relevant. "The claim for path dependence is that a minor or fleeting advantage or a seemingly inconsequential lead for some technology, product, or standard can have important and irreversible influences on the ultimate market allocation of resources, even in a world characterized by voluntary decisions and individually maximizing behavior."[20] In short, it is possible that individuals who developed IVF and other ART techniques did not seek patent protection because generally, innovators and investors considered the field not patent-worthy and thus not worthy of federal regulation. Once the industry started on that path, it simply continued on that path, and society and legislators had no incentive to change that path.[21] ART innovation has largely been a result of the free market—its research funding comes from private sources. Moreover, ART is even more exceptional because in many ways funding comes from the clients themselves. For example, while there has been a slow increase in insurance coverage of ART, for decades private institutions and private clinics funded ART innovation. Because ART often requires significant out-of-pocket costs, this funding system has led to many ineffective practices. Some ART providers were not concerned about health insurance coverage (or refusal to cover) because patients paid directly for the procedures and products. Additionally, ineffective practices persist because there is a lack of funding for research to determine the effectiveness of ART and its add-ons.[22] Patients who want a genetically related child might resort to treatments with especially low efficacy rates. The Dickey-Wicker Amendment continues to limit research on procedures that involve the destruction of embryos, so any ART innovation will likely remain in the private sector.[23]

Patents are routine in the world of FDA-regulated products. Notably, the FDA serves as a gatekeeper to the US drug market.[24] Federal law on prescription drugs prohibits manufacturers from marketing their drugs or biologics without an FDA-approved application.[25] There are various application types, including new drug applications (NDAs), investigational new drug applications (INDs, especially relevant to reproductive genetic innovation), biologic license applications (BLAs), and abbreviated new drug applications (ANDAs) for generic drugs.[26] Manufacturers are required to submit patent information to the FDA.[27]

Reactions to Dolly the Sheep and Their Lingering Influence on the Regulation of AARTs, Human Reproductive Cloning, and Stem Cell Research

Senator Dianne Feinstein noted at a 2002 hearing, "Cloning seems to be one of those words and concepts that seems to inspire a lot of dread in people, visions of an apocalyptic world marching lockstep."[28] Dolly, a sheep created from cloned cells from an adult sheep, was born on July 5, 1996.[29] Researchers did not publicize Dolly's birth until February 1997.[30] Before Dolly was born, legislators and scientists were aware of the possibility of "twinning," another word that individuals used to refer to cloning in the late 1970s and early 1980s.[31] Nevertheless, the issues raised in reaction to the cloning of Dolly highlight the fears that accompany both assisted reproduction and genetic modification.[32]

Similar to its responses to IVF and human reproductive cloning, Congress convened hearings related to animal cloning, but ultimately did not ban it in the United States. Both the House of Representatives and the Senate quickly convened hearings in relation to animal cloning.[33] Approximately two weeks after the announcement of Dolly's birth, the House Subcommittee on Science held a hearing on the somatic cell nuclear cloning that led to the creation of Dolly.[34] A few days later, a

Senate subcommittee considered the scientific and public policy issues (including bioethical concerns and legislative options) related to the cloning of mammals.[35] These hearings inevitably turned to many of the same issues that arose in hearings related to IVF: dignity, the limits of science, abortion, and embryos.[36]

Beyond animal cloning, many individuals announced they were planning to clone humans or had succeeded in doing so, including fringe groups like the Raelians.[37] Raelians believe that "humans are clones of God-like aliens destined to revisit Earth"; Dr. Brigitte Boisselier, "director of Clonaid, the scientific wing of the Swiss-headquartered Raelian Movement," announced that "implantations" of cloned embryos had occurred and that their next announcement would be the birth of a baby.[38] Later news reports indicated that Clonaid had moved its human cloning operations to another country after it was investigated by the Swiss government.[39] Agence France-Presse noted that in April 2002, Severino Antinori, an Italian physician, "told a Gulf News journalist at a genetics conference in Abu Dhabi that a woman on his programme was eight weeks pregnant with a cloned embryo" although he later refused to confirm that statement to journalists from other outlets.[40] Antinori also alleged that he had "overseen five pregnancies, with at least one birth expected in December [2002]."[41] Dr. Antinori was previously associated with Dr. Panayiotis (Panos) Zavos, and the two "appeared together before a panel at the National Academy of Sciences . . . to defend their plans" in August 2001, although Dr. Zavos later "broke away from" Antinori.[42] Others who announced intentions to clone human embryos included Dr. Zavos, who testified before Congress in a hearing titled "Medical Science and Bioethics: Attack of the Clones?"[43] At the beginning of that hearing, Representative Mark Souder noted,

> Opposition to human cloning is based upon both ethical and scientific considerations. All clones so far have been found to suffer from severe abnormalities, premature aging, and early death. In addition to these problems, cloning also poses significant health risks to the mother of a clone and to the women from whom the eggs necessary for cloning are harvested.
>
> These dangers have not, however, deterred some from attempting to produce cloned humans. We know scientists, such as Dr. Panos Zavos, who is with us today, are pursuing cloning as a means of producing live

> human offspring, while others seek to create cloned human embryos in order to destroy them for scientific research, with the hopes that such research may potentially yield treatments or cures.[44]

Representative Souder later noted that the "fact" was that "cloning, for whatever purpose, creates human life."[45] Representative Souder believed that a ban that permitted the creation of embryonic clones but that forbade their implantation in a uterus "legally requires the destruction of human life and criminalizes efforts to preserve and protect such life, once created."[46] Representative Souder cited concerns that the legalization of cloning could lead to the production, sale, and purchase of "stockpiles of embryonic human clones."[47] A complete ban on human cloning passed the House in July 2001 but did not pass the Senate.[48] Congress never passed substantive legislation related to human cloning, although various states did.[49]

In June 1997, the National Bioethics Advisory Commission (NBAC) issued a report, "Cloning Human Beings: Report and Recommendations of the National Bioethics Advisory Committee," which Congress subsequently discussed in several hearings.[50] The report highlighted the science of cloning as well as the "immediate and strong condemnation of any attempt to clone human beings" that arose after Dolly's creation was publicized.[51] The National Bioethics Commission opposed both human reproductive cloning and the financial funding of human reproductive cloning.[52] It also concluded that any legislative action should be careful to distinguish between a human child created using somatic cell nuclear transfer and other cloning used in scientific research.[53] In these hearings, Congress members were often similarly careful to distinguish between human reproductive cloning and other forms of cloning that were undertaken in order to further science, such as cloning DNA cells, tissues, and "non-human animals."[54]

Morality and religion appeared in conversations related to cloning, just as they did with ART and especially IVF. Moreover, ethical considerations formed a large portion of the NBAC publication, as well as an acknowledgment that for many individuals, "religious traditions influence and shape . . . moral views."[55] The NBAC report's third chapter, "Religious Perspectives," contained separate sections on themes in theological bioethics, many of which often arise in bioethics discussions in general, such as the idea of responsible human dominion over nature (not "playing God"), human destiny, human dignity, and concerns related to procreation and reproduction.[56] A June 1997 House subcommittee hearing titled "Ethics and Theology: A Continuation of the National Discussion on Human Cloning" included expert witnesses who provided religious perspectives on cloning, as well as legal and medical experts.[57] The fourth chapter of the NBAC report, "Ethical Considerations," addressed similar concerns, as well as concerns related to eugenics, personal autonomy, scientific inquiry, and reproductive choice.[58] The fifth chapter of the NBAC report, which covered legal considerations, including the potential for a moratorium, covered issues such as recombinant DNA and germline therapies, in addition to mentioning the Fertility Clinic Success Rate Act of 1992.[59] Recombinant DNA was discussed in subsequent congressional hearings related to human embryonic stem cell research. The *Chicago Tribune* quoted one of the expert witnesses, Dr. Irving Weissman, as saying, "As far as I'm concerned this technology is as important to opening the field as recombinant DNA was in the late 70s."[60] At a hearing on human cloning, Congresswoman Sheila Jackson Lee stated, "While you are in the midst of research to find better cures for diabetes or cancer or AIDS, there will be those who will be focusing on the question of abortion or anti-abortion."[61] Issues related to human embryos arose throughout hearings on human cloning, even though witnesses observed that "the unique and distinctive ethical issues raised by Dolly are really not related to the issues of embryos."[62]

The NBAC recommended that "one should consider a legislative ban that includes a sunset provision" because "it is notoriously difficult to draft legislation at any particular moment that can serve to both exploit and govern the rapid and unpredictable advances of science."[63] Many members of Congress introduced legislation to ban human reproductive cloning, the funding of human reproductive cloning, or both. State legislatures also introduced and passed legislation to ban human reproductive cloning.[64] Congress members introduced legislation to ban human cloning, in spite of declarations by the FDA that the agency had jurisdiction over human cloning technology through its authority under the Federal Food, Drug, and Cosmetic Act. The FDA declared that contentious reproductive technologies had to comply with the agency's onerous drug approval processes, and followed this up with public statements and documents indicating that the agency would not approve any such applications; this, along with its targeted communications with researchers, indicated agency hostility to those technologies. Hearings related to human cloning continued throughout the 2000s.[65] Ultimately, Congress never passed legislation banning human reproductive cloning.

Polls mentioned in congressional testimony led to differing interpretations. News articles included in the congressional record noted that "the public overwhelmingly opposes scientific experimentation on the cloning of human beings, says a new poll that also suggests public opinion is mixed on stem cell research. Nearly 4 out of 5 people opposed cloning, while one-third of those polled were against federal funding of stem cell research, according to the poll by the Pew Research Center for the People & the Press."[66] Results of Pew Research polls also were published in the *Congressional Record*.[67]

Senator Wicker noted that a 2010 Rasmussen poll revealed that "57 percent of Americans oppose taxpayer funding of embryonic stem cell research."[68] The prepared statement of the California Institute for Regenerative Medicine, submitted after that hearing, noted the opposite:

> Poll after poll since the early 2000's has unanimously demonstrated a majority support for [human embryonic stem cell] research and Federal funding of the research. . . . In the most recent poll on the subject conducted in August 2010 by Research!America, it was found that 70 percent of Americans favor expanded Federal funding of research using human embryonic stem cells. Gallup polls from 2005 to 2009 have shown support for fewer restrictions on [human embryonic stem cell] research to range between 52 [and] 60 percent.[69]

Congressional hearings mentioned safety concerns, although most of the focus was on ethical issues.[70] Senator Feinstein noted that, regarding human reproductive cloning, "there is broad agreement across our society, in Congress and in the scientific, medical and religious communities, that we should ban human cloning. Such cloning is scientifically unsafe, morally unacceptable, and ethically flawed."[71]

Not everyone agreed on just what "cloning" meant. Some members of Congress differentiated between reproductive and therapeutic cloning; others did not. Representative Souder, while chairing a hearing titled "Medical Science and Bioethics: Attack of the Clones?," said that "terminology in Washington changes based on kind of who wants to spin something for what period, we have seen a dramatic change in the argument toward research cloning from human cloning."[72] In his prepared statement before the hearing, he noted that "there is no difference between a cloned human embryo created for procreation or for research purposes."[73] Phyllis Schlafly, the conservative activist, similarly saw no difference between human reproductive cloning and therapeutic cloning.[74] She wrote: "The difference between reproductive cloning and cloning for research is not scientific; it is political and rhetorical. It's only the use of the embryo that is different."[75]

In 2002, Senator Dianne Feinstein referred to "good cloning" and "bad cloning": good cloning was "nuclear transplantation to produce stem cells," whereas bad cloning was human reproductive cloning.[76] Senator Hatch preferred the term "DNA regenerative therapy" to describe therapeutic cloning.[77] Later Senator Hatch remarked, "I hope that today's hearing will help the members of the committee gain a better understanding of the science, law, and ethics of cloning. It is my hope that this committee and the Congress will be able to arrive at a reasonable consensus on a policy that fully respects the dignity of humanity with respect to reproduction and research."[78]

Senator Hatch was thus in agreement with the American Society for Reproductive Medicine (ASRM), which had issued a statement in favor of somatic cell nuclear transfer for research but not for reproductive cloning.[79] Dr. Cowan, a professor of obstetrics and gynecology at the University of Mississippi Medical Center and a member of the board of the ASRM, testified that it was the view of the ASRM that the complete ban on cloning passed by the House "simply goes too far."[80]

Medical or research tourism surfaced in the testimony of Dr. Panos Zavos. Dr. Zavos noted that if infertile individuals were unable to avail themselves of human reproductive cloning in the United States, then they would "travel outside the [United States] to pursue their dream of creating a family."[81] Dr. Zavos also testified, on the topic of federal funding, that "in the words of a bioethicist, '[t]he best way to control this research is to fund it by the Federal Government, because then you create rules and regulate it."[82] Dr. Zavos did testify that his team would not "go forward with human cloning until the risks are comparable with other IVF procedures."[83]

Ultimately, statements of successfully cloning humans went unproven. Dr. Zavos claimed that a cloned human would be born in 2003, meaning that 2002 could be the "year of the clones," but no birth was confirmed.[84] Later, in 2002, Dr. Zavos alleged that he had identified couples who were willing to be the parents of "the first clones." Rekindling the debate over adoption as a substitute for assisted reproduction, a Scottish weekly newspaper noted that Bill and Kathy, an American couple who refused to give their surname but wanted to discuss their participation in Dr. Zavos's experiment with the *Sunday Herald*, "would . . . be considered too old to adopt in the US."[85]

Hearings debated the line between therapeutic cloning and reproductive cloning, suggesting there might be a "slippery slope" from therapeutic to reproductive cloning. Concerns were expressed that once a cloned embryo had been created, there would be no way of prohibiting a woman from carrying the embryo to term.[86] Part of this objection stemmed from the nature of the physician–patient relationship.[87] In answers submitted after her testimony, Professor R. Alta Charo, wrote, "I do not find the slippery slope arguments persuasive, because taken to their most logical conclusion, they would argue most strenuously for a ban on in vitro fertilization, as it is IVF that allows us to maintain and manipulate embryos outside the body. . . . Slippery slope arguments are for the timid."[88]

Human Embryonic Stem Cell Research

Dolly-related fears of cloning persisted. In a 2001 address on the topic of human embryonic stem cell research, President George W. Bush noted:

> The initial stem cell researcher was at first reluctant to begin his research, fearing it might be used for human cloning. Scientists have already cloned a sheep. Researchers are telling us the next step could be to clone human beings to create individual designer stem cells, essentially to grow another you, to be available in case you need another heart or lung or liver. I strongly oppose human cloning, as do most Americans. We recoil at the idea of growing human beings for spare body parts, or creating life for our

> convenience. And while we must devote enormous energy to conquering disease, it is equally important that we pay attention to the moral concerns raised by the new frontier of human embryo stem cell research.[89]

President Bush's statement shows how concerns related to human cloning often merged into discussions of regenerative medicine, a broad field that incorporates issues such as stem cell research.

Long after the furor over the cloning of Dolly the Sheep and discussions about efforts to clone humans, human embryonic stem cell research remained controversial. In 2010, Senator Tom Harkin opened the US Senate Subcommittee on Labor, Health and Human Services, and Education, and Related Agencies, Committee on Appropriations hearing, "The Promise of Human Embryonic Stem Cell Research," by noting that the September hearing was the twenty-first hearing the subcommittee had held on the matter since December 1998.[90] The first subcommittee hearing on human embryonic stem cells convened a month after Dr. Jamie Thompson announced that he had isolated human embryonic stem cells in 1998.[91] The 2010 hearing occurred during the multiyear debate over whether the Dickey-Wicker Amendment prohibited the use of federal taxpayer funds for research on embryonic stem cell lines. While the 2010 hearing specifically disclaimed any aspects of the legal debate, Senator Wicker (one of the authors of the Dickey-Wicker Amendment) noted that the "destruction or cloning of human embryos for research purposes raises profound moral and ethical challenges." Senator Wicker also characterized human embryonic stem cell research as "controversial life altering research" that taxpayer dollars should not be spent on, especially when there were other areas of health-related research that could be funded.[92]

President Bush also alluded to science fiction or techno-anxiety concerns by invoking the science fiction novel *A Brave New World*. "We have arrived at that brave new world that seemed so distant in 1932, when Aldous Huxley wrote about human beings created in test tubes in what he called a 'hatchery.'"[93] While President Bush was aware that stem cell lines are derived from existing human embryos, such as those left over from IVF, he noted that the public recently learned of scientists creating human embryos for the sole purpose of experimenting on them, which he found "deeply troubling."[94] Ultimately, President Bush announced that he would permit the use of federal funds for research on the 60 existing stem cell lines, in addition to creating a presidential council to monitor stem cell research that would be chaired by Dr. Leon Kass, a well-known conservative bioethicist.[95] Later, research indicated that there were 78 lines that qualified for federal funding, although only 19 of those 78 lines were available for research purposes.[96] Of course, not all conservatives were or are opposed to stem cell research. Nancy Reagan was well known for her support of stem cell research, and some note that her letter to President Bush "seemed to have made a difference," as he did not ban all stem-cell research, which was his original intention, and instead permitted some government funding for established cell lines.[97]

On March 5, 2002, the Senate Committee on Health, Education, Labor, and Pensions, held a hearing titled "The Dangers of Cloning and the Promise of Regenerative Medicine."[98] Although the title of the hearing juxtaposed the two techniques, some senators took care to ensure that one not "confuse human cloning with regenerative medicine," explaining that "one creates a person and should be banned; the other provides a cure and deserves our strong support."[99] Congressional hearings included scientists, advocates, and other stakeholders. For example, Christopher Reeve, the well-known actor and stem cell research activist, and Paul Berg, the Nobel Prize winner, testified in support of stem cell research and argued against legislation that would threaten stem cell research in the United States. Paul Berg's testimony was particularly useful as he specifically targeted misstatements that he heard in the news, including by members of Congress, thus providing important educational insight.[100]

Francis Collins, who was then the director of the NIH, was the first witness at the 2010 hearing titled "The Promise of Human Embryonic Stem Cell Research."[101] Dr. Collins discussed NIH funding for stem cell research—adult and embryonic—as well as the limitations of the stem cell lines permitted under President Bush's administration.[102] Dr. Collins offered some clarifying points in the questioning following his statement, including that: (1) the focus on the promise of human embryonic stem cells did not mean scientists were opposed to research on adult stem cells, (2) human embryonic stem cells research was unlikely to reach its full potential without federal support, and (3) the termination of federal funds could lead to scientists "moving into other research areas or moving overseas."[103]

Medical tourism and research being moved abroad continued to surface throughout congressional hearings. One expert, Dr. Jean Peduzzi-Nelson, whose testimony largely focused on adult stem cell research, noted, "We need more NIH funding so patients do not have to go to other countries and so these amazing results that I presented can go to clinical trials and become the standard of care for U.S. patients that need their support."[104] After President Bush's announcement limiting the availability of federal funding of human embryonic stem cell research, news coverage focused on an array of issues, including the work of scientists like Dr. Roger Pedersen, "a leading embryonic stem cell researcher who left [the University of California at San Francisco] for England because of fears his research would be restricted in the United States."[105] Dr. Collins's post-hearing responses to questions similarly emphasized the role of federal funding in innovation, the inability of states to replace federal funding, and the idea that the uncertainty of federal funding for human embryonic stem cells was "the most significant hurdle for American patients to remain competitive in the international stem cell arena."[106] Other witnesses included George Q. Daley, a well-known stem cell researcher who is now dean of Harvard Medical School, who also noted that "recent upheavals in Federal funding" were disrupting research and "dissuading scientists from entering the field."[107]

Beyond the moral perspectives of legislators, Dr. Collins's presence also raised issues of morality. Not only did senators invoke stories of individuals they knew in their personal lives, but they mentioned Dr. Collins's book, *The Language of God*.[108] Tom Harkin characterized it as "just one of the wonderful crossover books between science and faith. It is just a wonderful book."[109] There are many perspectives on the moral status of human embryos, including views that human embryos are potential life: akin to human tissue, human beings, babies, or occupiers of an intermediate moral status. Different states take different views in embryo disposition cases. For example, in *Davis v. Davis* the Tennessee Supreme Court dispelled the idea that the embryos were just property to be divided in the marriage or that they were human beings. The court in *Davis v. Davis* decided that human embryos occupied an "interim category that entitles them to special respect because of their potential for human life."[110] The view expressed by Judge Daughtrey in *Davis v. Davis* is similar to that of Dr. Collins, who noted that he believed "that the human embryo deserves moral respect. It is a potential human being" before discussing the leftover embryos that result from IVF and the choice in which the leftover embryos could be discarded or used in research. The Alabama Supreme Court decision that embryos were "unborn children" paused IVF treatment in Alabama until clarifying legislation was enacted.[111]

Moral and religious views on cloning, assisted reproduction, and stem cells abound. While the debate over embryonic stem cell research and cloning has often implicated IVF, at least one member of Congress noted that they did not think IVF should be prohibited.[112] Representative Richardson Preyer, for example, asked if there was "any danger" IVF would be a widespread form of reproduction before noting that the Catholic Church objects to IVF "because it is an unnatural form of reproduction. And others, not for religious reasons, object to it on the grounds that what they may be getting into is a form of making artificial life, as distinguished from natural reproduction."[113] For some legislators, like Orrin Hatch, who described himself as "an unabashed pro-life conservative . . . or should I say, to be more politically correct, I am a faith based conservative. In any event, I would be extremely hesitant to rewrite the Book of Genesis as the story of Adam or Eve."[114] Ultimately, Dr. Collins asked which, of discarding the embryos or performing research on them, was the "more ethical choice." He concluded that "putting the reality test here, I believe that most people who look carefully at the issues, whether from a faith perspective or a purely humanistic perspective, come up with a conclusion that what is potential here justifies what we are talking about in terms of Federal funding of human embryonic stem cell research."[115]

There was a disconnect between scientific and legislative perspectives like human cloning and human stem cell research. Sean Morrison of the University of Michigan noted that "stem cell scientists do not cluster into adult versus embryonic camps. The framing of the debate comes from political lobbyists," suggesting a disconnect between the perspectives and terms that existed in the scientific community and the conversations shepherded by legislators.[116] While legal commentary often focuses on the terminology used in the debate over the legality of federal funding of stem cell research, statutory interpretation, executive orders, and the lobbying that led to various presidents' positions, Dr. Morrison offered an account of those executive actions and litigation on his lab.[117]

For his work, Dr. Morrison noted that his NIH-funded research suffered multiple delays and setbacks because (1) the grant money itself "was delayed while NIH put in place its new embryonic stem cell policy," (2) the money was finally received but then the recipients were not allowed to "spend the money until NIH had the opportunity to review and approve new stem cell lines for funding" and (3) eight months after starting the research "the Federal injunction was issued."[118] Dr. Morrison noted in his testimony that he had brought Jack Mosher, a researcher in his laboratory, with him to Washington that day as "in those early days after the injunction, Jack did not know whether his work would survive the injunction, whether he would still have a salary, or what would happen to his career."[119] A prepared statement submitted by the California Institute for Regenerative Medicine (CIRM) similarly emphasized the importance of federal funding. CIRM also invoked morality: "We have a moral obligation as citizens of the United States to support the dedicated scientists, clinicians, and patient advocate organizations to pursue the best scientific approaches across the scientific field of stem cell research."[120]

President Bush later vetoed two bills to lift stem cell research restrictions that had passed the House and the Senate.[121] Reporting on his 2006 veto of a stem cell research funding bill noted that Bush had been urged not to veto it by many people, including Nancy Reagan, who was an advocate for stem-cell research.[122] Over the course of the Bush administration and the Obama administration, litigation and debate focused on these policies and the recurring moral and ethical debates that accompanied stem cell research.

Other Regulatory Influences: Advisory Committees and Lobbyists

There are a number of inputs into the legislative and regulatory processes that are not Congress, the president, or the judiciary. For example, federal administrative agencies, like the FDA and the NIH, often create advisory committees. Advisory committee members are often sourced from industry and academia. It is also worth noting that while universities are nonprofit institutions, academia is a particularly lucrative area for professors in the sciences and medicine, who may have commercial stakes in their innovations. Moreover, many universities own or partially own the intellectual property created by their employees and generate millions in revenue from those inventions as well as from their medical centers and research laboratories. The Federal Advisory Committee Act governs matters related to the establishment and operation of federal advisory committees.[123] There are an average of 1,000 federal advisory committees that advise executive branch agency members and the president.[124] Advisory committee meetings are sometimes open to the public.[125]

Lobbying has not received significant attention thus far because it is difficult to identify. Federal statutes requiring the registration of lobbyists have failed to define precisely what lobbyists are, and the penalties for noncompliance seem to lack a deterrent effect.[126] One source describes the role of lobbyists in this way: "In representing their organizations or clients, lobbyists aim to achieve two main objectives: gather intelligence about the policymaking process and sway policymakers and politicians and the public by providing relevant information and arguments."[127] Lobbyists are known to influence legislative perspectives in ways that are not visible to the general public. The literature has cited the work of lobbyists on behalf of the tobacco industry (in relation to lung cancer) and the fossil fuel industry (in relation to climate change) as work that is based on "bad science."[128] Campaign contributions are especially significant, especially after the Supreme Court's 2010 ruling in *Citizens United*, which increased the strength of corporate speech.[129]

Additionally, as states become more salient in the protection (or abolition) of reproductive rights, it is worth noting that lobbying occurs at the state level as well. Lobbying groups draft legislation and lobby for its passage, like the National Right to Life organization did for "trigger bans," which would automatically outlaw abortion in the states that used them, in the event *Roe v. Wade* was overturned, as it was.[130] Interestingly, some lawmakers have admitted that they viewed voting for such legislation as a statement instead of expecting it to actually be implemented, which has led them to reconsider what legislation should be in its place.[131] In the meantime, ProPublica found that after *Dobbs*, lobbying groups continued to "encourage" Republican legislators, through webinars and other outreach methods, to leave such laws as they are.[132]

Self-Regulation in Research and Medicine

Line drawing is important because it often dictates which form of oversight, if any, should apply. Scientific innovation and reproductive medicine both have many mechanisms for self-regulation. Medicine in particular is known for self-regulation, meaning that there is no oversight board that physicians apply to before putting innovations into practice. There is a general distinction between practice and products, where the practice of medicine is subject to state oversight and the products used in medicine, like surgical tools, medical devices, and pharmaceuticals fall within the realm of federal jurisdiction. There is also a distinction between clinical innovation and research. Definitions of research differ, but the Common Rule definition of research is useful:

> Research means a systematic investigation, including research development, testing, and evaluation, designed to develop or contribute to generalizable knowledge. Activities that meet this definition constitute research for purposes of this policy, whether or not they are conducted or supported under a program that is considered research for other purposes.[133]

Various activities are not defined as research under the Common Rule; these include legal research, public health surveillance, law enforcement agency specimen collections, and authorized national security missions.[134]

To a certain extent, the human subjects research regime in the United States is a hybrid of self-regulation and governmental oversight.[135] In 1974, Congress passed the National Research Act.[136] The FDA departs from certain Common Rule regulations, and regulated entities consult the regulations as necessary, in connection with research and licensing decisions.[137] The US Department of Health and Human Services promulgates regulations implementing the statute.[138] Individual institutions are responsible for ensuring compliance with those regulations (and the statute) through institutional review boards (IRBs).[139] Thus, many institutions, ranging from hospitals to universities (including liberal arts institutions) have institutional review boards.[140] The requirement that IRBs approve any human subjects research applies at institutions that receive federal funding, regardless of whether the specific project itself is federally funded.[141] Institutional review boards have at least five members, of varying backgrounds. Minimum IRB membership requirements have been established by the federal government for institutions receiving federal funding. IRBs must include individuals with scientific expertise, individuals whose primary concerns are in nonscientific areas, and at least one individual who is not affiliated with the institution and not an immediate family member of an institutional affiliate. There are also requirements related to conflicts of interest.[142]

Innovation, however, does not require institutional review board approval. In surgery, for example, many surgical innovations escape oversight because they are "intended to benefit an individual patient rather than systematically investigate a procedure."[143] Similarly, the distinction between clinical innovation and research is murky: research often leads to oversight, whereas clinical innovation is not subject to the restrictions that often accompany research, such as IRB approval, modification, or denial of a proposed research protocol.[144]

Some of the many aspects of the 1975 Asilomar Conference that were noteworthy and significant were (1) its discussion of a significant scientific innovation, (2) its discussion of the potential dangers of that innovation, and (3) its demonstration of (effective) self-regulation within a scientific field. Approximately 140 biomedical scientists attended the Asilomar Conference.[145]

Scientists at the conference debated assorted issues associated with recombinant DNA research, and "the conference recommended that the moratorium on the previously deferred experiments be lifted and replaced with guidelines governing such research."[146] After the conference, five individuals published the "Summary Statement of the Asilomar Conference on Recombinant DNA Molecules" in the *Proceedings of the National Academy of Sciences*.[147] The summary statement largely focused on the unknown risks of recombinant DNA research and methods of containing newly modified organisms. The statement characterized "free and open discussion" as "necessary" and noted that it was important to "undertake a continuing reassessment of the problems [of recombinant DNA research] in the light of new scientific knowledge."[148]

After publication of the 1975 Asilomar Conference summary statement, the NIH published the first set of Guidelines for Research Involving Recombinant DNA.[149] The NIH "was a major funding source for DNA research."[150] Even if the NIH did not directly fund research, NIH guidelines would be significant in practice. "Guidelines" do not have the force of law, but generally when any part of a university receives funding from the federal government for human subjects research, the rest of the university agrees to comply with those federal guidelines.[151] Moreover, the scientist-driven NIH guidelines stemmed from previous self-regulation.[152]

Human Gene (or Genome) Editing

Federal funding does not support heritable genetic modifications in humans. In 1985, the NIH issued for public comment various versions of a document titled "Points to Consider in the Design and Submission of Human Somatic-Cell Gene Therapy Protocols."[153] In that document, the NIH stated that the Recombinant DNA Advisory Committee (RAC) and its working group would entertain funding proposals for protocols involving somatic cell gene therapy but not for proposals involving germline genetic alterations.[154] This document and public comments were considered at the September 23, 1985, RAC meeting.[155] The document was revised several times, but each revision maintained the RAC's position that it would not fund human germline genetic alteration.[156]

Over time, many of the responsibilities of the RAC were transferred to the FDA.[157] In 2015, Congress added a recurring budget rider that prevented the FDA from considering any applications involving "heritable genetic modification."[158] The budget rider continues to remain in subsequent federal budgets even though the definition of "heritable" is contested. While the FDA has interpreted "heritable" to include mitochondrial and nuclear DNA, many others, including Dr. Eli Adashi, believe that the term "heritable" is not applicable to mitochondrial DNA but only to nuclear DNA. The FDA has not changed its interpretation, and Congress has not changed the language of the rider.

In addition to causing an international uproar, Dr. He was sentenced to three years in prison and a 3 million yuan fine ($445,000) in China for "illegal medical practices," although the trial and preceding investigation were not particularly transparent.[159] Dr. He is no longer in prison and is reportedly working on research proposals related to rare diseases and Alzheimer's disease.[160] In an interview after his release from prison he admitted that "I did it too quickly."[161] Meanwhile, scientists in the United States are prohibited from germline gene editing. Similarly, the National Institutes of Health will not provide federal funding for proposals involving human germline gene editing.[162]

In the United States, self-regulation of gene editing seems to be working. The condemnation of Dr. He Jiankui's use of CRISPR-Cas9 in humans in China was notably strong and swift, even though it is possible that before the announcement some individuals in the United States knew about Dr. He's plans to use CRISPR-Cas9 in human embryos.[163] So far, germline gene editing using technologies like CRISPR-Cas9 is already subject to various patent claims. In terms of human uses, the expectation is that CRISPR-Cas9 would be subject to the FDA's regulation. Nonetheless, calls for self-regulation seem to be effective. Many scientists, including leaders in the development of CRISPR-Cas9 technology, have published calls for moratoria or temporary pauses.[164] While the US House of Representatives passed a bill creating a Commission on Human Genetic Engineering, as advocated for by the House Subcommittee on Science and Technology, the US Senate did not enact a similar bill.[165] Chapter 7 explains why the FDA would be the expected regulator of human reproductive genetic innovation using CRISPR-Cas9 even if the jurisdictional support for that position is unclear.

Conclusion

Even when research is grant-funded, science and medicine often benefit from self-regulation. For example, recombinant DNA technology, the first controversial genetic technology discussed in this chapter, was largely managed through scientists' self-regulation. Although congressional hearings discussed ART, Congress did not enact legislation to draw it into its purview. Moreover, congressional hearings on ART tended to focus on federal funding (and the lack thereof) and access to ART as opposed to its legality. The chapter's discussion of embryonic stem cell research seemingly "detoured" to reproductive cloning and the fears that accompanied both animal reproductive cloning and the potential for human reproductive cloning, because these fears had significant impact on the regulation of human embryonic stem cell research funding as well as the regulation of forms of assisted reproduction involving genetic substitution, namely cytoplasmic transfer, and mitochondrial transfer. I use the word "detour" because cloning largely involves genetic "copying" as opposed to alteration, yet it is an issue that exacerbated fears of genetic engineering and reproductive genetic innovation. Moreover, discussions of embryonic stem cell research were often derailed by discussions of cloning.

As detailed in Chapter 7, the FDA sent letters to physician-researchers, informing them of the FDA's jurisdiction over forms of assisted reproduction like cytoplasmic transfer and mitochondrial transfer in the United States, like Dr. James Grifo. Thus, physician-researchers who received the FDA's untitled letters with the "subtle" threat of enforcement action would have reason to feel their communications from the FDA were "threatening" as Dr. Grifo characterized it: not only were violations of the Federal Food, Drug, and Cosmetic Act and Public Health Service Act recognized tools within the FDA's enforcement toolbox, but the Agency took the opportunity to remind members of Congress of other parts of the Federal Criminal Code that could be construed apply to proponents of human reproductive cloning.[166] This is notable not only from the criminal law and civil law perspectives, but also notable since again, the FDA failed to explain why it had jurisdiction over human cloning. This failure to explain is especially notable since members of Congress continued to introduce legislation related to human cloning despite her testimony. For example, Dr. Zoon's testimony was on March 28, 2001, but Congress members were still introducing legislation related to human cloning as late as 2005.[167] Continued efforts to introduce legislation related to human reproductive cloning are significant for at least 2 reasons: first, Congress members continued to introduce legislation related to an issue the FDA stated was within its jurisdiction, thus supporting the view that perhaps legislators did not think the FDA's jurisdiction was clear and second, the FDA's subterranean regulation of human reproductive cloning (and later reproductive genetic innovation more broadly), was as effective as the Congressional legislation that many tried to pass.

It is important to distinguish between moral "harms" and safety harms. The relationship between law and morality has developed over time and been the subject of many theories.[168] Without going into a lengthy discussion of political philosophy and legal theory, H. L. A. Hart and Lon L. Fuller's conversation on law and morality is still discussed in legal circles today. In that 1958 debate, Hart noted that utilitarians "certainly accepted many of the things that might be called 'the intersection of law and morals'" such as by not denying that "the development of legal systems had been powerfully influenced by moral opinion, and, conversely, that moral standards had been profoundly influenced by law."[169] There are various reasons why individuals argue that the law can or should be separated from morality and vice versa.[170] Nonetheless, in the area of reproduction, I argue in this book that (1) law and morality should be separated, and (2) in the realm of FDA regulation, it is important, at the very least, to signify when decisions are being made on the basis of law or safety as opposed to morality, fear, or techno-anxiety. Chapters 7 and 8 will focus on these matters more specifically.

Transparency is another issue. Yet, according to Lon L. Fuller "[t]he extent of the legislator's obligation to make his laws known to his subjects is, of course, a problem of legal morality that has been under active discussion at least since the Secession of the Plebs" in Ancient Rome.[171] Moreover, he notes, that this matter is

> most likely to arise in modern societies with respect to unpublished administrative directions. Often these are regarded in quite good faith by those who issue them as affecting only matters of internal organization. But since the procedures followed by an administrative agency, even in its "internal" actions, may seriously affect the rights and interests of the citizen, these unpublished, or "secret," regulations are often a subject for complaint.[172]

Modern versions of these complaints, including the implications of the possibility that morality was the reason for the delay in the switch of Plan B from prescription to over the counter, as well as issues related to the subterranean regulation of AARTs will be analyzed in the next chapters.

7

"Lost" FDA Files, Morality, and the Abortion Debate

The Influence of Politics on Regulation

Medication abortions, like surgical abortions, are an area of significant contention in the United States, as reflected in the US Supreme Court case *FDA v. Alliance for Hippocratic Medicine.*[1] In 2024, in a widely anticipated decision, the US Supreme Court held that an anti-abortion group, the Alliance for Hippocratic Medicine, did not have standing under Article III of the US Constitution to challenge the FDA's approval of the drug mifepristone.[2] Mifepristone is significant to abortion services, as medication abortions typically involve the use of mifepristone as well as another pill, misoprostol.[3] "Mifepristone blocks progesterone, the hormone needed to support a pregnancy. Misoprostol causes cramping and bleeding to empty [the] uterus."[4] In this chapter I focus on the role of abortion politics, especially in the area of reproductive medicine, to trace and explain the FDA's regulatory regimes. Significantly, this context shows why the FDA may have been motivated to regulate in a subterranean manner.

Historical Controversy: RU-486, Research Funding, and an Early US Importation Ban

FDA v. Alliance for Hippocratic Medicine was not the first time that mifepristone was the subject of a US Supreme Court decision. As emphasized by pro-mifepristone advocates, mifepristone has been on the market for decades. Early in its inception, mifepristone was called RU-486.[5] It was the subject of a Supreme Court case and congressional hearings due to one woman in particular, Leona Benten, who tried to import it in an attempt at a medication abortion at seven weeks of pregnancy. Benten's attempts to access the drug were deterred by an FDA-imposed importation ban on RU-486, which was issued after it received communications from certain legislators, including Representative Henry Hyde.[6] Benten obtained medication for herself in London. She notified federal agencies that she would arrive at John F. Kennedy International Airport with the drug, seeking to import it under an exception to a ban on "untested" drugs even though RU-486 had been approved and tested abroad. When Ms. Benten arrived at Customs, FDA and US Customs representatives seized the drug and provided her with a notice of detention.[7] She and other parties sued to access the drug. The US District Court judge noted, "It is, perhaps, unnecessary to note, given the prior history, that no notice and comment procedures preceded or followed this reversal by the agency."[8] Moreover, a Freedom of Information Act request issued in relation to the origins of the importation ban targeting RU-486 revealed that the FDA had no documents to provide, which, as I will note through other instances of subterranean regulation, seems unlikely and frankly unbelievable.[9] A judge from the Eastern District of New York ordered the RU-486 returned to Benten, but the government appealed to the Second Circuit Court of Appeals and obtained a stay of the injunction granting her the return of her RU-486 medication.[10] Ultimately, in a very short opinion, the US Supreme Court upheld the government's decision. Subsequent to this case, Representative Ron Wyden, when chairing a House subcommittee hearing convened to discuss the FDA's importation ban, noted that "when the FDA issued its import alert without any evidence that RU 486 presented a safety problem each of [the FDA's] principles was dumped in the trash can. In the Chair's opinion RU 486 has now been effectively blocked for all uses in this country because one use does not pass the administration's antiabortion political litmus test."[11] Throughout the hearing there was emphasis on "the political monkey wrench that's being thrown into the RU 486 debate."[12] Experts at the hearing discussed the many non-obstetric uses for RU-486. Some of this evidence was presented through personal stories of individuals who tried to access the drug in efforts to save their lives from aggressive recurring meningiomas, testimony of researchers detailing comparative disadvantages, and of course repeated mentions of the impact of the United States' abortion debate on access to the drug.[13]

Years later, in 2000, the FDA approved Mifeprex, the brand-name version of mifepristone, "for use as recommended in the agreed upon labeling text" for abortions in the United States.[14] Mifepristone "blocks a hormone called progesterone that is needed for a pregnancy to continue."[15] Because mifepristone is most effective when combined with misoprostol, a drug that "empties" the uterus, health care providers generally prescribe this two-drug protocol for medication abortions in the United States.[16] Health care providers prescribe mifepristone and misoprostol to patients for non-obstetric reasons, sometimes with different dosing regimens.[17]

As of 2023, 63 percent of abortions that took place within the formal health care system, as opposed to other types of abortions such as self-managed medication abortions outside of the formal health care system, were medication abortions.[18] Unlike mifepristone, which the FDA approved as an abortifacient, the FDA approved misoprostol "as a stomach ulcer medication in 1988," although health care providers use it off-label "for obstetric uses, including miscarriage management, and abortion."[19]

The history of mifepristone merits a brief examination because it emphasizes the depth of the effect of the federal regulatory regime and many societal actors on reproductive autonomy. Volumes have been written about the development of contraception and mifepristone, some more accurate than others, but these are also the subject of a broader literature in sociology, history of science and medicine, chemistry, and law.[20] Gregory Pincus, the "inventor" of the oral contraceptive pill, mentored Étienne-Émile Baulieu, the "father of the abortion pill."[21] A *New Yorker* profile noted that Baulieu chose to focus on sex hormones "expressly because of their social implications, hoping that they would yield new possibilities for reproductive autonomy and for alleviating the 'pain and punishment' that had long been the lot of those who chose to end a pregnancy. ('Teach her a lesson she'll remember,' he'd once heard a surgeon say, instructing his assistant to forgo an abortion patient's anesthesia.)"[22] In September 1988, French regulators approved RU-486 for sale in France, and international and national opposition followed.[23] The pope referred to the drug as "the 'pill of Cain'—the monster that cynically kills its brothers."[24]

After notable opposition to RU-486 in France, Roussel-Uclaf, the pharmaceutical manufacturer, decided to pull the pill from the market and reversed previous promises to supply the product abroad.[25] The French government, which held a minority stake of 36 percent in the company, threatened to force the company to cede its patent to another company.[26] After applying pressure on Roussel-Uclaf to reintroduce the drug into the French market, the French minister of health, Claude Evin, stated "I could not permit the abortion debate to deprive women of a product that represents medical progress. From the moment Government approval for the drug was granted, RU-486 became the moral property of women, not just the property of the drug company."[27] As a result of this potential business threat, Roussel-Uclaf put the drug back on the French market but slowed its expansion to other countries.[28]

In the United States, lobbyists targeted not only Roussel-Uclaf but also its German parent company Hoescht AG.[29] Planned Parenthood tried to obtain the product from Roussel-Uclaf for clinical trials but the company declined to provide it to them.[30] In the United States, Republican efforts to pass legislation preventing the expenditure of federal funds on research related to RU-486 failed, so Republicans turned to an importation ban.[31] Even though some drugs could be imported for personal use, the FDA concluded that "the drug was not safe enough for importation, even under supervision of a physician," a decision that "was so controversial that it sparked Congressional hearings."[32] Ultimately this also led to "a slowdown in drug supplies to American researchers examining it for treatment of breast cancer and endometriosis."[33]

Mifepristone Today

Reportedly, several major pharmaceutical companies refused to distribute or manufacture the drug in the United States.[34] Eventually, "in 1994, Roussel-Uclaf . . . donated the rights to sell mifepristone in the United States to the Population Council, a large nonprofit group in New York City that conducts international research on reproductive health."[35] Through various business arrangements, the rights to sell the drug were transferred to Danco Laboratories, which contracted with another company to manufacture the drug.[36] In 1999, Danco Laboratories announced that it planned to manufacture and market RU-486 in the United States.[37] Danco decided "to distribute mifepristone directly to doctors and clinics, rather than to pharmacists," because, according to a Danco spokesperson, "it's a medical procedure and proper counseling is really important."[38] In 2019, the FDA approved a generic version of Mifeprex; both the brand-name version and the generic version of the drug are legally marketed in the United States.[39]

Law and Cloning: Ethical Debates, Subterranean Regulation, and Failed Legislation

Cloning does not fit neatly into the main topics of discussion in this book. Cloning is not reproduction, it is replication. All the same, fears about cloning impacted matters of assisted reproduction and stem cell research. Cloning technology is also worth discussing because the FDA's approach to the regulation of human reproductive cloning, in the absence of a clear congressional prohibition, is similar to the approach the FDA took to preclude the use of cytoplasmic and mitochondrial transfer in the United States. The FDA continues to use this regulatory approach for techniques like germline gene editing and other forms of reproductive genetic innovation. Additionally, opponents of AARTs, especially mitochondrial transfer, routinely reference cloning in their arguments against using AARTs. For example, some opponents of therapeutic cloning noted that to permit therapeutic cloning would permit human reproductive cloning, because one could not order the abortion of a fetus created from a cloned embryo.[40]

The use of ART and AARTs especially can often lead to public distaste. Cloning similarly evokes strong reactions, some of which are stronger than reactions to ART. Hearings focused on cloning featured witnesses from various walks of life: faith leaders (including rabbis, archbishops, and priests), members of Congress who were not on the commissioning committees but asked their colleagues to be heard, representatives of industry organizations, and researchers and professors of various disciplines, including law, theology, medicine, and other life sciences.[41]

In the debate over cloning, some, including members of the National Academies' Panel on Scientific and Medical Aspects of Human Reproductive Cloning, called for a "legally enforceable ban" that would be reviewed within five years. We might ask, though, what a legally enforceable and reviewable ban looks like at the federal level.[42] In the context of human germline gene editing, many within the scientific community have called for a moratorium, yet scientists and lawyers can differ in what they consider to be a ban. For example, what many scientists refer to as "bans" are really agreed-to moratoria—self-regulatory bans as opposed to legislatively arranged bans. Another option in the world of "banning" is to go the route of criminal law and to implement criminal penalties for an action.

Cloning has elicited various regulatory reactions. The US Congress failed to pass a statute banning human reproductive cloning, despite repeated efforts to do so. These repeated efforts occurred even though FDA employees assured politicians that it already had jurisdiction over human cloning. Various states also passed legislation on cloning, some with more nuance than others.[43] In an opinion piece about cloning, Professor Jack Balkin wrote, "Congress can use lawyers' tricks to get around these new federalism doctrines. It can withhold federal funds from hospitals that perform cloning, or require proof that the doctors or the tools they use have moved in interstate commerce."[44]

After the FDA's Kathryn Zoon testified in Congress that the FDA had jurisdiction over cloning and would not permit an IND application for human reproductive cloning to go forward, the subcommittee chair, Mark Souder, praised her testimony in a letter to the acting principal deputy commissioner of the FDA.[45] In his letter—in which he cc'd Tommy Thompson, who at that time was secretary of the Department of Health and Human Services—Souder specifically cited Zoon's testimony that the "'FDA views the use of cloning technology to clone a human being as a cause for public health concern' and that 'FDA would not permit the use of cloning technology to clone a human being at this time.' Dr. Zoon further stated that 'the Administration is unequivocally opposed to the cloning of human beings.'"[46] Later in the letter Souder asked what the meaning of "human beings" was and whether "the FDA considers an embryo to be a human being."[47] He also asked about the unresolved safety concerns that were mentioned in Dr. Zoon's testimony:

> Could you elaborate as to what safety questions would have to be resolved in order for the FDA to approve human cloning investigations or research to begin?
>
> Because the FDA has outlined its authority under law to regulate cloning, and clinical research cannot legally be conducted without an investigational new drug application (IND) in effect, what penalties would be levied by the agency against an individual or entity found to be either attempting human cloning or found to have cloned a human being without FDA approval?[48]

Melinda K. Plaisier, associate commissioner for legislation, replied to Souder's letter, restating that the administration was unequivocally opposed to "the use of cloning technology to clone a human being."[49] She also noted that the FDA had "not published or otherwise announced a definition of 'human being'" and noted that the FDA "did not believe it [was] necessary to define the term human being to establish whether or not human cloning has taken place . . . [or] to establish or exercise its jurisdiction over the use of cloning technology to clone a human being."[50] Plaisier repeated the "refrain" found in other conversations between the agency and innovators of reproductive technologies that the agency found objectionable: "FDA . . . would not allow clinical trials to proceed unless and until the Agency received sufficient evidence from the sponsor that the trial could proceed safely."[51]

Regarding the issue of safety, Plaisier said that "the FDA would consider the safety of the surrogate mother and the safety of any child born from the procedure."[52] This statement is interesting for several reasons. First, the agency did not explain why the surrogate mother of a human reproductive clone would be any different from the surrogate mother of a noncloned embryo. Second, the agency referred to "the procedure" which is presumably the cloning procedure, but Plaisier did not explain why a "child born from the procedure" would be different from any other child born as a result of ART, such as IVF or artificial insemination, which the agency does not regulate. Moreover, the reference to "procedure" is alarming because in the standard view of the divide between practice and products, which FDA representatives often reference on their website and in congressional testimony, a "procedure" would fall within the practice of medicine and thus outside of the FDA's jurisdiction.

As the FDA's enabling statutes, documents revealed through responses to the author's FOIA requests, and media accounts of recipients of the FDA's letters indicate, the FDA can impose criminal and civil penalties on violators of the Public Health Service Act and the Federal Food, Drug, and Cosmetic Act. These penalties were specifically mentioned by Associate Commissioner Plaisier in her letter to Chairman Souder, as well as other criminal violations outside of the agency's enabling statutes:

> FDA may seek to restrain and enjoin individuals who fail to adhere to laws administered by FDA, including the [Federal Food Drug & Cosmetic (FD&C)] and the [Public Health Service] Acts. The maximum penalty that could be imposed on an individual for a criminal violation

of the [Public Health Service] Act or a misdemeanor violation of the FD&C Act is one year imprisonment and/or a fine of up to $100,000 (for a misdemeanor not resulting in death) or an alternative fine of twice the amount of gross pecuniary gain or loss. The maximum penalty that could be imposed on an individual for such a felony violation of the FD&C Act 'with the Intent to defraud and mislead' is three years imprisonment and/or a fine of up to $250,000, or the alternative fine described above.

It is possible that fraudulent conduct involving cloning could also violate provisions of the Federal criminal code (Title 18) such as the conspiracy, mail fraud, wire fraud, or false statement laws. The maximum penalty for such crimes is five years imprisonment and/or the fines set forth above.[53]

Cloning and the Early History of Subterranean Regulation

With regard to letters received by US physician-researchers regarding regulatory matters, I am mostly interested in those related to AARTs and not cloning. But cloning and the legislative and regulatory responses to cloning form part of the context associated with executive responses to cloning in the United States. In 1998, the FDA issued a "Dear Colleague" letter on human reproductive cloning, which this chapter will discuss. While there is little reason to believe the announcements of the Raelians related to human cloning, Dr. Brigitte Boisselier "told a House energy and commerce subcommittee in March [2001] that her lab had received a letter from FDA warning that it would be against the law to proceed with cloning without permission."[54] Similarly, the Associate Press reported that an FDA spokesperson stated that the FDA "had inspected a lab set up by Brigitte Boisselier in an effort to attempt human cloning."[55] According to the FDA spokesperson, Dr. Boisselier allegedly signed a statement "committing not to attempt human cloning and not to do research using human eggs until the legality of human cloning is determined."[56]

Documents included in the "attack of the clones" hearing included a letter by Representative Souder alleging that Advanced Cell Technology (ACT), a Massachusetts company, had engaged in human cloning, in violation of the FDA's stated policy.[57] Souder sent an email to ACT providing a number of (pointed) questions that the representative wanted answered.[58] The next document in the hearing file was a *Boston Globe* article related to ACT, indicating that "the FDA officials [including Kathryn Zoon], along with getting ACT to promise not to allow any cloned embryos to become fully formed humans, also offered encouragement."[59] ACT received congressional and media attention, and media coverage noted that ACT's president and CEO, Michael West, declared that the company "was not interested in cloning human beings and did not create the embryos for reproductive purposes."[60]

Later, lawyers and professors debated whether the FDA had jurisdiction over human reproductive cloning, with some finding it "questionable," some finding it outside of the agency's jurisdiction, and others noting that it was "unproblematic, although certainly Congress could help by making that easier to understand."[61] Arguably, it was equally unclear to members of Congress, who proceeded to introduce statutes banning cloning in spite of FDA assertions that cloning fell under FDA jurisdiction. Ultimately, Congress failed to pass a statute on human cloning, although it did ban human cloning in the United States through other means, as I have described. Moreover, a ban could suffer from the same lack of clarity as other legislation, which led to concern among some legislators, like Senator Maria Cantwell, that a "unilateral ban [on cloning] could be read to prohibit DNA replication, which is necessary for important biotechnology research."[62]

Abortion Politics, ART, and Reproductive Genetic Innovation

The impact of morality, including religious conservatism, on the law and regulation is of concern.[63] Abortion politics affects scientific research, reproductive medicine, health insurance coverage decisions, and access to pharmaceuticals, especially pharmaceuticals related to reproduction. There are clear ways in which the law can compel individuals and companies to respect religious views, but it is concerning that religious views, especially conservative religious views, can impact regulation in ways that are outside of defined, clearly accessible public channels. We can expect more to come, as the Supreme Court has shifted significantly in a conservative direction.[64]

As I have described, religious views often underlie abortion politics. Abortion politics routinely deter scientific research in the United States. Federal funding is a significant portion of research funding. Yet presidential administrations continue to waver on support for scientific research that may have a connection to abortion, such as research on stem cells or fetal tissue transplantation. In 1991, Representative Henry Waxman (one of the namesakes of the Hatch-Waxman Act) participated in a subcommittee hearing titled "Federal Ban on Research on Fetal Tissue Transplantation."[65] Waxman's opening statement emphasized that fetal tissue transplantation research was not research on abortion.[66] At the hearing, patient family members, including the "parents of the first fetus to receive a fetal transplant in the history of the United States," the physician who performed that first fetal tissue transplant, and other interested parties, testified to the importance of fetal tissue transplantation research.[67] One of those parents, Guy Walden, was the pastor of the Broadway Baptist Temple in Houston, Texas.[68] Reverend Walden mentioned his support for the Hyde Amendment in his testimony and noted that both he and his wife wished for abortion to "become illegal" in the United States, "but until it is we must make decisions about the use of fetal tissue."[69] Reverend Walden then urged the passage of legislation and "proper guidelines."[70] At that same 1991 hearing, Representative Wyden mentioned RU-486 and his hope that it would "be possible to finally get some specificity as to NIH policy on non-abortion research on the drug RU-486."[71]

The FDA did not assert jurisdiction over artificial insemination or in vitro fertilization, but it has increasingly asserted its authority over reproduction, especially assisted reproduction. In 1992, Congress passed the Fertility Clinic Success Rate Act.[72] This act requires fertility clinics to report success rates on an annual basis to the Centers for Disease Control and Prevention (CDC), although the statute provides no enforcement mechanism.[73] The CDC publishes this information in annual reports. The FDA is not involved in issuing these reports and was not even mentioned in the legislative debate that led to the Fertility Clinic Success Rate Act, nor is it mentioned in the statute.[74] In 1997, the FDA embarked on a project to regulate laboratories, including those involved in the fertility industry. In beginning this project, the agency observed that it "[had] not previously regulated reproductive tissues." At that time in 1997, the agency recommended communicable disease testing for individuals undertaking assisted reproduction in the laboratory, but did not require it. In 1998, the FDA issued its "Dear Colleague" letter on cloning (see Appendix B). In 1999, the FDA published a proposed rule, "Suitability Determination for Donors of Human Cellular and Tissue-Based Products," in the *Federal Register*. This rule, sometimes referred to as the HCT/P rule, was issued on the basis of section 361 of Public Health Service Act, which allows the FDA, by delegation, to make regulations to prohibit the transmission or spread of communicable diseases. The Final Rule, published in 2001, contains a "minimal manipulation" standard.[75] According to the rule, "minimal manipulation" is "processing that does not alter the original relevant characteristics of the tissue relating to the tissue's utility for reconstruction, repair, or replacement . . . [or] the relevant biological characteristics of cells or tissues."[76] Under the framework created by the rule, tissues that are "minimally manipulated" are "lightly regulated" by the agency. The FDA regulates "more-than-minimally manipulated human cells and tissue products" as "drugs . . . and/or biological products,'" rendering them subject to the agency's substantial approval process.[77]

Abortion-Related Federal Statutory Funding Restrictions: The Hyde Amendment and the Helms Amendment

Funding restrictions are a useful tool for legislators who aim to restrict access to certain procedures or products when the legislators cannot successfully obtain support from a majority of Congress. Representative Hyde is known for his association with the Hyde Amendment, as well as his motivation for the amendment: "I would certainly like to prevent, if I could legally, anybody having an abortion, a rich woman, a middle class woman, or a poor woman. Unfortunately, the only vehicle available is the [Medicaid] bill."[78] The Hyde Amendment was upheld by the Supreme Court in *Harris v. McRae* and continues to recur in congressional budgets.[79] A similar funding restriction applies to American foreign aid, which also cannot be used to fund abortion.[80] Views on the origins of life influenced not only the Dickey-Wicker Amendment and the Hyde Amendment, but also international policy and funding subsidies. The Helms Amendment, named for Senator Jesse Helms, of Title X similarly prohibits the use of American funds abroad for abortions, involuntary sterilization, and certain forms of associated research.[81]

Those who provide ART services and genetic testing were concerned by and opposed to legislation that attempted to codify the Hyde

Amendment. For example, the American Medical Association (AMA) and American College of Obstetricians and Gynecologists (ACOG) opposed legislation that aimed to restrict "established and accepted medical care [including abortion] to any segment of the population."[82] Moreover, a representative of both the AMA and ACOG referred to their position in opposition to appropriations and funding restrictions aimed at reducing abortion access as "longstanding."[83] They also noted that even legislation like S. 522, an attempt to codify the Hyde Amendment, would cause contraception to "become suspect."[84]

Plan B or the "Morning After Pill"

Today, Plan B One-Step emergency contraception is available at drugstores across America as an over-the-counter (OTC) product, although some stores lock up the drug on shelves or behind a pharmacy counter, even though no prescription is necessary, which requires customers to have more interactions with drugstore personnel in order to purchase it.[85] On December 7, 2011, Kathleen Sebelius, the secretary of the US Department of Health and Human Services in the Obama administration, ignored recommendations from the FDA that Plan B One-Step be available over the counter in the United States for those below age 16. She justified her decision by saying, "Today's action reflects my conclusion that the data provided as part of the actual use study and the label comprehension study are not sufficient to support making Plan B One-Step available to all girls 16 and younger, without talking to a health care professional."[86] Even though the evidence before Margaret Hamburg, commissioner of the FDA at that time, indicated that the drug was safe and effective for women of all ages, Kathleen Sibelius "directed" her to ignore this evidence.[87]

Sebelius's action drew the ire of many, including physicians and proponents of women's reproductive rights. Depositions undertaken during the litigation related to this switch revealed that Sebelius, secretary of the HHS, an executive branch agency, and the White House were meddling in the approval process in ways the public would not notice. This should give us all pause, because (1) apparently federal agencies that oversee scientific research are not always motivated only by science, and (2) this meddling occurred during a Democratic administration, meaning that reproductive rights may not be particularly safe under any administration.[88]

Professor Lisa Heinzerling's 63-page article, "The FDA's Plan B Fiasco: Lessons for Administrative Law," detailed the many deliberate actions the FDA undertook to reduce reproductive autonomy and delay the approval of Plan B as an over-the-counter medicine instead of a prescription-only drug.[89] Her article traces the FDA's actions over years and focuses on

> at least five major decision points: the refusal to approve OTC status for Plan B (May 2004); the decision to make Plan B available over-the-counter for women and girls eighteen and older but not for younger girls (August 2006); the decision to accede to the district court's order to make Plan B and its cousins available to girls seventeen and older (April 2009); the decision not to allow nonprescription access to Plan B or Plan B One-Step for girls under seventeen (December 2011); and last, the decision to make Plan B One-Step (but not Plan B) available over-the-counter to all women and girls (May 2013).[90]

These actions were revealed partially due to litigation related to the FDA's failure to approve the switch in spite of compelling scientific evidence about its safety. As a result of litigation, it became clear that the FDA was acting in accordance with reasons that were unrelated to the safety or efficacy of the drug. At one point the director of the FDA's Office of Women's Health resigned in response to the politicization of the approval and noted in her resignation letter,

> Sadly, your recent decision to not approve Plan B emergency contraception, overturning the clear scientific and clinical evidence, contradicts both the FDA mission and my commitment to women's health. The rationale offered is not convincing, and is in fact a denial of access to a product clearly established as safe and effective for all women who need it.[91]

In addition to litigation, 48 members of Congress asked the Government Accountability Office (GAO) to investigate the FDA's actions in relation to the conversion of Plan B availability from prescription to over-the-counter.[92] The GAO also outlined the many ways in which the FDA diverted from its usual decision-making process. The GAO report is similarly extensive but notes that the FDA's decision-making process differed from the "the other 67 proposed prescription-to-OTC switch decisions made by FDA from 1994 through 2004. The Plan B OTC switch application was the only one during this period that was not approved after the advisory committees recommended approval."[93] Sebelius's decision was notable for many reasons, including the reminder that reproductive rights do not enjoy unparalleled support from Democratic presidencies.

Subterranean Regulation and Reproductive Genetic Innovation

Subterranean regulation is characterized primarily by four factors:

1. Letters as assertions of wrongdoing
2. Lack of jurisdiction
3. Obfuscation of the evidence of agency action
4. "Chilling" effects[94]

The next four subsections address these aspects of subterranean regulation.

1. Letters as Assertions of Wrongdoing

The FDA's regulation of cloning was a precursor to subterranean regulation of reproductive genetic innovation. In response to reports that various groups were "contemplating" cloning human beings using reproductive cloning, the FDA sent, and posted on its website, the 1998 "Dear Colleague" letter related to cloning.[95] This October 26, 1998, "Letter about Human Cloning," reproduced in Appendix B, began by stating, "The purpose of this letter is to confirm to institutional review boards (IRBs) that the Food and Drug Administration (FDA) has jurisdiction over clinical research using cloning technology to create a human being, and to inform IRBs of the FDA regulatory process that is required before any investigator can proceed with such a clinical investigation."[96] The next paragraph of the letter ended by noting that "since FDA believes that there are major unresolved safety questions pertaining to the use of cloning technology to create a human being, until those questions are appropriately addressed in the IND, FDA would not permit any such investigation to proceed."[97] This statement is significant because it is unclear what the FDA would consider "safe," and it is likely that the FDA would never deem human reproductive cloning safe in the United States. No entities, including groups that received significant media coverage like the Raelians, submitted IND applications for human reproductive cloning. The hurdle of "safety questions" surfaced in conversations between physicians and the FDA related to cytoplasmic transfer. The result of these FDA communications was that the use of these techniques was prohibited in the United States.

Approximately two and a half years later, on July 6, 2001, FDA employee Dr. Kathryn Zoon sent an "untitled" letter to sponsors/researchers working with cytoplasmic transfer.[98] This letter, like the FDA's "Letter About Human Cloning," began with a jurisdictional advisory: "We want to advise you that the Food and Drug Administration (FDA) has jurisdiction over human cells used in therapy involving the transfer of genetic material by means other than the union of gamete nuclei."[99] The FDA then provided examples of "such genetic material," which included but was not limited to, "cell nuclei (e.g., for cloning), oocyte nuclei, [and] ooplasm, which contains mitochondrial genetic material."[100] Due to the FDA's asserted jurisdiction, the letter then said that such transfers required submission of an IND to the FDA. Thus, physicians who provided fertility treatment to US patients would suddenly need to submit investigational new drug applications to the FDA.

2. *Lack of Jurisdiction*

Without jurisdiction, an agency action is unlawful. The FDA's letters mention the Public Health Service Act in passing, with an emphasis on communicable disease regulation, but they do not cite statutory provisions. The FDA's letter cited many regulations that did not clearly apply but missed the more important jurisdictional questions: If in vitro fertilization is not a new drug, then how is cytoplasmic transfer a drug? How are AARTs "drugs and/or biologics," in the FDA's regulatory view?[101] What is the regulated "article"? The discussion farther below of the FDA's treatment of OvaScience's technique, AUGMENT, will expand upon these issues.

Members of Congress continued to introduce statutes related to human reproductive cloning as well as therapeutic cloning, even though FDA employees testified that the agency already had jurisdiction over the technique.[102] While there are various reasons members of Congress might try to pass legislation in an area that an agency already regulates, this seems redundant.

3. *Obfuscation of the Evidence of Agency Action*

The FDA's system for recordkeeping is not particularly transparent. In a conversation with an employee in relation to FOIA 2016-4883, the employee stated that the agency did not have a system for recordkeeping when an application was not active.[103] Furthermore, the FDA does not confirm an application unless the applicant publicly confirms it.

In addition to "failing to locate" files for letters, the FDA also does not routinely post untitled letters on its website, even when they are significant. Part of this is due to the agency's general secrecy. The agency's regulations state that the agency will not acknowledge the existence of an IND for a biological product or a biological product file "unless it has previously been publicly disclosed or acknowledged," notwithstanding certain FOIA requirements.[104] As a result, members of the public would need to (1) know to request the information on their own and (2) be willing to submit a FOIA request because they will not be able to easily search for and access this information through publicly available portals.

4. *Chilling Effects*

The chilling effects of the FDA's subterranean regulation of reproductive genetic innovation were apparent at an advisory committee meeting in 2002. While a list of the recipients of the letter are not available through a FOIA request, several participants at the FDA advisory committee meeting, including providers from the Jones Institute for Reproductive Medicine, noted that they had been providing the technique to patients until they received the FDA's letter.[105] One physician who received the letter noted, ""What was threatening was they couldn't give me a sense of what the consequences would be . . . if I continued. They made

it sound as if there would be recourse without saying it. I was very threatened."[106]

The FDA does not automatically post untitled letters to an agency website, such as the website for the Center for Drug Evaluation and Research (CDER) or the Center for Biologics Evaluation and Research (CBER). It does post such letters, though, when the FDA determines that posting the letter would:

> (1) respond to 3 or more received or anticipated requests for the letter under the Freedom of Information Act (FOIA); (2) inform the public about violative practices and conditions that may pose a risk to their health; (3) deter future violations and allow similarly situated regulated entities to determine what activities and practices FDA finds violative and use the information to increase compliance with the law.[107]

In this way, deterring future action is one goal of posting the letters on the agency's website. By reducing the public availability of the letters, entities that the FDA has wrongfully targeted for potential enforcement action or simply the threat of enforcement through letters, would have trouble identifying similarly situated entities, making it harder for them to serve as a "check" on the agency.

Since then, the agency has begun to maintain a list on its website of interventions requiring FDA approval, including germline gene editing. This list does not explain how any of the featured techniques fit within the agency's statutory mandate. In 2017, the FDA sent a letter to Dr. John Zhang, who submitted an investigational new drug application to the FDA for his work on mitochondrial transfer in Mexico. The FDA's three-page letter discussed Dr. Zhang's article, "Live Birth Derived from Oocyte Spindle Transfer to Prevent Mitochondrial Disease," as well as his request for "a pre-investigational new drug (IND) meeting for a clinical investigation of a 'spindle transfer for assisted pregnancy in patients with mitochondrial disease.'"[108] The FDA's letter ended: "This letter is not intended to be an all-inclusive list of violations. It is your responsibility to ensure full compliance with the [Food Drug & Cosmetic] Act and the [Public Health Service] Act and their implementing regulations. We request that you notify this office, in writing, of the steps you have taken or will take to address the violation noted above and to prevent recurrence."[109]

OvaScience and AUGMENT

Scientists and physician-researchers continue to try to improve fertility outcomes. Some individuals who had difficulty conceiving via IVF had successful pregnancies via cytoplasmic transfer. Mitochondrial transfer, which sometimes involves the same technique as cytoplasmic transfer, is another option that can improve fertility outcomes or help commissioning parents avoid transmitting mitochondrial disease to their offspring. A Massachusetts-based company, OvaScience, marketed a technique called AUGMENT to individuals seeking improved fertility outcomes. AUGMENT was a technique that removed mitochondria from a woman's ogonial stem cells and then injected them "into that same woman's oocytes at the time of intracytoplasmic sperm injection (ICSI) to restore bioenergetic potential and enhance IVF success."[110] According to the CEO, the company "commenced a clinical study" of the technique in 2012, but it did so without an investigational new drug application because company employees believed that the technique did not constitute more-than-minimal manipulation under the FDA's Human Cellular and Tissue-Based Rule framework.[111] The FDA disagreed with this characterization and sent an untitled letter to the company, which company representatives then had to reveal to their shareholders on a call as well as in securities filings.[112] I obtained a copy of this letter through a FOIA request, reportedly after other entities had also requested the letter as well. In its letter the FDA stated, "The removal of mitochondria and introduction into other reproductive tissue appears to be more than minimal manipulation. This is based on the limited information available; please note that the addition of mitochondrial DNA to other reproductive tissue may raise additional regulatory concerns."[113] While I do not know who those other entities might have been, after news of the untitled letter surfaced, shareholders commenced a lawsuit.[114] Moreover, the company stopped providing the technique in the United States, although it reportedly did offer it to patients in Canada as well as some other countries. A filing submitted by the company to the US Securities and Exchange Commission (SEC) stated that the company might "re-examine our strategy with the United States after we have gained more experience with our fertility treatments," but the company no longer exists.[115] Similarly, an OvaScience

spokesperson once told the *MIT Technology Review* that "OvaScience was still 'exploring a potential US market entry strategy with the FDA,'" but the technique was not later offered in the United States, and the company was sold to Millendo Therapeutics.[116] After Millendo Therapeutics purchased OvaScience in 2018, the merged company went by the name "Millendo Therapeutics."[117] In 2020, the SEC announced that "the CEO of the now defunct OvaScience, Inc., agreed to settle fraud charges for misleading investors about the availability and commercial prospects for the company's fertility treatments [namely AUGMENT] that were in development."[118] The SEC's announcement noted that Michelle Dipp, while CEO of OvaScience, made several false and misleading statements to investors, including her false claim that "the company was on track to meet its goal of performing 1,000 commercial AUGMENT treatments in 2015, when just a few treatments had been done and there was little demand for treatment."[119] In 2021, Tempest Therapeutics closed its merger with Millendo Therapeutics.[120]

Criticism of Subterranean Regulation

Critics of subterranean regulation would naturally ask: Why don't the subjects of subterranean regulation push back against the agency? Individual FDA guidance documents contain disclaimers that they are not binding on the public or the FDA. Similarly, the agency's own regulations contain a provision, § 10.115 Good guidance practices, that explains the same along with the availability of alternative approaches, among other matters.[121] Yet, as Daniel J. Kenney and Professor Catherine Sharkey note in an article, "the FDA has largely avoided scrutiny compared to other agencies likely because the FDA's regulatory interests are typically aligned with the business interests of drug and device manufacturers."[122] Professor Nicholas R. Parrillo published an article, "Federal Agency Guidance and the Power to Bind: An Empirical Study of Agencies and Industries," based on a report he wrote for the Administrative Conference of the United States.[123] His article focused on the binding nature of agency guidance and highlighted the practices of certain administrative agencies more than others, including the FDA. Professor Parrillo noted that, in general, regulated parties facing preapproval requirements, like those before the FDA, have a stronger incentive to

comply with guidance that is not legally binding but that can be practically binding.[124] Parillo's study included many anonymous participants as well as some regulated parties' representatives who were identified by name in the article. A theme of "folly" persisted. One food and drug industry attorney noted that "it would be 'foolish' to proceed with an application without following the agency's guidance."[125] A former FDA senior official stated, "If a new drug applicant asks to proceed differently than the guidance suggests . . . the agency will often reply, 'you can, but it will be a review issue'—that is only after you invest large sums in certain studies and submit the application will we decide whether those studies are acceptable."[126] Regulated entities aim to maintain a "good relationship" with the FDA, especially if they must repeatedly appear before the agency for other pre-marketing approvals or other action, including potential enforcement action.[127] At the same time, some of the study subjects thought that FDA-compliance due to fears of punishment from the agency for failing to comply with guidance documents were "overblown."[128] Within that analysis, some noticed that while attorneys understood the difference between legally binding regulations and nonbinding guidance documents, most of the decision-makers at various companies were not attorneys but instead were scientists, compliance officers, or regulatory affairs professionals, who see their mission as "maintaining relations with the FDA."[129] Agency attorneys might acknowledge that guidance was nonbinding, even if they were reluctant to grant departures from that guidance; other agency personnel often had difficulty differentiating between legislative rules and guidance, which required special training.[130] Others noted that the FDA was more flexible on matters of science than policy.[131] Reputational cost is also an issue for some regulated entities, as agencies "often . . . announce their enforcement activities to the public."[132]

Administrative agencies are a larger threat to smaller entities than to larger ones, although pharmaceutical companies still seem to have concerns about their reputations in front of the FDA. Moreover, while personalized medicine is increasing in its prevalence in the United States, most physicians do not interact with the FDA. After receiving the letters from the FDA for his use of cytoplasmic transfer, Dr. Grifo noted that he was "very threatened."[133] Large companies fare better against the FDA but still feel a need to defer to the agency. "A former senior official

at the FDA Office of Chief Counsel said, regarding consumer protection suits against the food industry premised on FDA warning letters that in turn rested on noncompliance with guidance, that 'the Chobanis of the world can handle these lawsuits,' but 'they hurt small companies.'"[134] Interestingly, trade associations provide a way for individual companies to influence agencies like the FDA—entities that are fearful of the FDA can use their trade association to anonymously "urge the agency to rethink the guidance's application."[135]

Outside of the food context, it can be expected that certain large entities, such as the tobacco industry, can handle lawsuits after enforcement actions. One question that arises is why regulated entities and entities that have unexpectedly been subjected to the FDA's jurisdiction do not fight back in court.[136] Part of my answer is that (1) litigation is expensive and (2) for entities that have "repeat" business in front of the FDA, they might want FDA employees to have a positive impression of them. Another answer is that some entities are very good "gamblers" and the companies and their lawyers may have concluded that they are likely to lose. There may also be a cost–benefit analysis where the plaintiffs have so much money that they are undeterred by litigation, as indicated by the *Brown & Williamson* case. *Brown & Williamson* was a US Supreme Court case that stemmed from the FDA's unexpected assertion of jurisdiction over cigarettes under the regulatory theory that nicotine is a drug and cigarettes are the devices used to deliver that drug.[137] After not regulating the tobacco industry for years, the FDA asserted jurisdiction over cigarettes using this regulatory theory. This was notable not only due to the prior absence of regulation but also because cigarettes are very different from other FDA-regulated products as they are dangerous items with no health benefit. The US Supreme Court agreed with the tobacco industry and held that the FDA exceeded its jurisdiction. The case was significant and continues to be cited in major US Supreme Court decisions related to administrative law, like *West Virginia v. EPA* and *King v. Burwell*.[138] Congress later enacted substantive legislation, the Family Smoking Prevention and Tobacco Control Act, specifically giving the FDA jurisdiction over tobacco products.[139]

AARTs are not the only procedures that have been targeted for FDA enforcement action. In the late 2010s, the FDA targeted many stem cell clinics throughout the United States for enforcement action, culminating

in litigation (and an FDA win), in one of those well-publicized cases: *U.S. v. Regenerative Sciences*.[140] In this instance, there was a court case because the clinic decided to litigate the matter, instead of accepting the FDA's declaration of jurisdiction. Unlike the tobacco industry; however, Regenerative Sciences lost in its legal fight over the FDA's jurisdiction.[141]

Various external parties can influence the FDA. The FDA is made of supervisory employees and nonsupervisory employees. It is also staffed by political appointees and civil service members. Professor Dan Carpenter, whose work on the FDA and its "gold standard" reputation has been characterized as "canonical," noted that Dr. Janet Woodcock, a long-serving FDA employee who briefly served as the FDA's principal deputy commissioner, "began to 'think about the drug review process as one in which the incentives and culture for future innovations had to be protected,' taking into account the implications of one drug's approval for innovation incentives more broadly."[142]

Carpenter presented a laudatory view of the FDA, but FDA and CDC responses to the COVID-19 pandemic severely reduced public trust in those agencies.[143] An article by Professor Daniel G. Aaron highlighted the many ways the FDA is racing to approve certain products, especially outside of the clinical trial context, by using other forms of evidence. He also emphasized that the FDA has been significantly captured by the pharmaceutical and medical device industries, among others.[144]

Professor Aaron's article also noted proposals by seven former FDA commissioners to transform the FDA into an "independent regulatory agency," even when some of those commissioners were notably "captured" in various ways and made use of the revolving door between government and industry.[145] Industries that are accustomed to being before the FDA in a more "traditional" practice might have an easier time capturing agency officials than would individuals who do not have a history of interacting with the FDA, such as reproductive endocrinologists.

Subterranean regulation may have similar issues. In the example of reproductive genetic innovation, 17 years after cloning was regulated by letter in 1998, in 2015 Congress passed a recurring budget rider, applicable to the FDA.[146] The rider states:

> None of the funds made available by this Act may be used to notify a sponsor or otherwise acknowledge receipt of a submission for an

> exemption for investigational use of a drug or biological product . . . in research in which a human embryo is intentionally created or modified to include a heritable genetic modification. Any such submission shall be deemed to have not been received by the Secretary, and the exemption may not go into effect (emphasis added).[147]

This rider was almost removed from the congressional budget in 2019, but as of 2024, Congress continues to include the rider in the federal budgets that the president signs into law annually.[148]

In a reminder of Congress's "inartful drafting"—a term that came up in the US Supreme Court's decision in *King v. Burwell*, addressing the constitutionality of the Patient Protection and Affordable Care Act (PPACA), with an emphasis on the PPACA's health insurance reforms—even this appropriations rider is not without ambiguity.[149] The term "heritable genetic modification" is in dispute. The FDA interprets it to include techniques like mitochondrial transfer, even though many scientists and physicians do not view mitochondrial transfer as "heritable genetic modification."[150] Moreover, unlike Congress's response to *Brown & Williamson*, Congress has not passed comprehensive substantive legislation on issues like AARTs and germline gene editing; instead, one subcommittee has met to discuss gene editing, and an appropriations rider has been continually enacted. One possible explanation could be that Congress wants to ban reproductive genetic innovation and germline gene editing but does not feel the need to do so through substantive legislation, given the success of subterranean regulation in essentially banning human reproductive cloning (ignoring the likelihood that the technology still likely does not exist).

Subterranean regulation persists until Congress takes firm action, which it seems unlikely to do in the field of reproduction because funding restrictions on reproduction tend to be renewed. Alternatively, if the potential targets of subterranean regulation have enough political capital, they can band together against the agency. Academic medical centers, for example, did so in response to the FDA's attempt to regulate fetal microbiota transplants in a burdensome fashion. After pushback, the FDA announced that the guidance document would continue to exist but that the agency would exercise enforcement discretion, meaning that the FDA maintained that fetal microbiota transplants were within its jurisdiction, but it would not enforce the laws and regulations against entities that met certain conditions, such as academic medical centers.

Subterranean regulation provides a way for federal agency employees to eventually influence Congress to act, thus introducing another influence on legislation and legislative decisions, along with lobbyists, patient groups, and the general citizenry. More concerning is the possibility that agency regulation takes place without a congressional response, either because members of Congress did not notice or prioritized other matters, potentially allowing agency employees to operate unchecked.

Conclusion

If individuals are able to ascertain administrative agencies' efforts to regulate outside of their authority, the judiciary can help preserve the integrity of the regulatory state, such as when it facilitates transparency in the public administrative record, especially when there is evidence that an agency is behaving inappropriately.[151] When administrative agencies engage in subterranean regulation, it is detrimental to the goals of administrative law, which include transparency, accountability, and public input.[152] Moreover, even though the Freedom of Information Act enables access to some documents, there are many sources that are not available to the public by way of FOIA request. This fact was highlighted during the GAO's report on the FDA's actions when it failed to facilitate access to emergency contraception in the United States.[153] As noted by Professor Heinzerling, the sources the GAO referenced in its report "would not be the kinds of sources that an outsider could have obtained in a Freedom of Information Act request nor the kinds of sources that a reviewing court would normally have access to in evaluating an agency's decision."[154] Moreover, "the Plan B saga should stand as a lesson that unless courts are sometimes willing to depart from the usual plotline for judicial review, they will be unlikely to uncover and remedy the most serious violations of administrative law."[155]

Similarly, as emphasized by the FDA's enabling statutes, its responses to FOIA requests, and media accounts of recipients of the FDA's letters, the FDA can impose criminal and civil penalties on violators of the Public Health Service Act and the Federal Food, Drug, and Cosmetic Act. The FDA's communications emphasize these potential financial penalties and prison sentences, and this deters many physicians and researchers from continuing to provide reproductive genetic innovation in the United States. Moreover, in 2017 Dr. John Zhang traveled to Mexico to provide mitochondrial transfer to US-based patients due to the comparatively less onerous regulatory system in Mexico. Criminal and civil penalties were specifically mentioned by Associate Commissioner Plaisier in her letter to Chairman Souder, as well as "other criminal violations outside of the agency's enabling statutes."

Abortion, contraception, and emergency contraception have all been subject to legal disputes and will likely continue to be, as politics influence legislation and regulation. Reproduction continues to be an area of societal and legal contention, and ethical and moral views can impact the actions of administrative agencies. The regulatory hostility toward AARTs and germline gene editing is part of a long history of efforts by legislators, lobbyists, and regulators to reduce reproductive autonomy and access to abortifacients, contraception, and assisted reproduction. Examples of this include the debate related to the switch from prescription-only to OTC status for Plan B (and accompanying regulatory shortcomings and litigation) and access to abortion and abortifacients in general and particularly during the COVID-19 pandemic, where public health decision-making has highlighted the impact of politics over scientific and medical decision-making.

8

Reproductive Genetic Innovation, Subterranean Regulation, and Ways to Reduce Political Influence on Reproduction

Congressional hearings, administrative agency decisions, and executive branch statements related to stem cell research, abortion, contraception, and in vitro fertilization have shown how moral, social, and political views can impact regulation. Religious or moral views guide many legislators in their decisions in relation to legislation, whether substantive legislation or appropriations legislation. These views may stem from the legislators' own personal beliefs, the beliefs of their constituents, and, perhaps more influentially, the views of lobbyists. One issue underlying the discussion in previous chapters is whether moral views should guide scientific legislation, which connects to a second, implicit question of this book: Do assisted reproduction and reproductive genetic regulation have to be regulated in the way they currently are? I would argue that religious and moral views should not impact research related to reproduction, in order to foster and facilitate reproductive autonomy, a value that is even more important in today's post-*Dobbs* United States. While the United States is a leader in many medical, scientific, and technological innovations, it has trailed other countries in the area of reproductive medicine. For example, the United States was the third country, behind England and Australia, to be the birthplace of a child born via IVF.

The United Kingdom and many other countries created centralized regimes to regulate assisted reproduction. In the United States, on the other hand, a largely reactionary regulatory regime governs assisted reproduction, including even cytoplasmic transfer, an AART that physicians briefly provided in the United States. This reactionary, *ex post* approach to traditional ART and (briefly) one form of AART, is notable in light of the regulatory system's robust, subterranean opposition to mitochondrial transfer and germline gene editing. Nevertheless, I am not recommending a centralized regulatory system like that of the United Kingdom and other countries.

Instead, I am arguing for hands-off regulation of both ART and AARTs in the United States. In this realm, "hands-off" means the same form of regulation as we have for the practice of medicine in general. Medicine is the subject of state oversight, notably through state licensure requirements and state malpractice regimes, as opposed to premarket clearance by the federal government. Notably, this decision to treat reproduction like medicine is interesting because the effective availability of certain medical treatments is, for most of the individuals in the United States, limited by health insurance coverage.

This chapter begins by outlining the advantages of the hands-off approach in terms of regulatory choices, the path to innovation (including funding decisions), and administrative agencies' deliberate inaction in the realm of IVF in an effort to avoid controversy.

Advantages of the Preferred Hands-Off Regime

The less regulation there is of ART or AARTs, the more the regulatory regime supports reproductive and parental autonomy. There are lessons to glean from other countries, including the United Kingdom. The UK is well-known for its regulatory approach to assisted reproduction, which involves a centralized regulatory body, the Human Fertilisation and Embryology Authority (HFEA).[1] The HFEA was authorized by the Human Fertility and Embryology Act of 1990 and established in 1991.[2] In 2013 the United Kingdom undertook a public consultation, which considered, among other matters, whether the HFEA should be retained: 75 percent of respondents indicated that it should be. In a prior article, I outlined the process that led up to the legalization of mitochondrial transfer.[3] The HFEA's public consultation on the topic of mitochondrial transfer/donation had five strands:

1. Deliberative public workshops
2. Nearly 1,000 face-to-face interviews with members of the public on topics related to mitochondrial disease, treatment of genetic disease, and assisted reproductive technology
3. Open consultation meetings

4. Open consultation questionnaire (website combined with mail/ online questionnaire)
5. Patient focus group

Various academics have argued for an American system of regulating ART that is far more strenuous than the current regime, which I do not agree with because the history of regulation in the United States, especially the regulation of reproductive technologies, tends to reduce reproductive autonomy.[4] Moreover, conservative groups have exhibited a particular exceptionalism at capturing the regulatory system when matters involving reproduction are at issue, so a state-based approach would at least permit those who inhabit the United States the chance to engage in a domestic reproductive tourism and would focus on the relationship between patients and their health care providers.

Increased regulation often corresponds with increased time from innovation to market, a marker that has been the target of FDA and congressional goals outside of the reproductive context. For this reason, some companies like OvaScience developing AARTs specifically aim to introduce their products in markets without premarket review or approval.[5] While some isolate ART for being an industry with many untested products and techniques, the field of medicine, especially surgery, is known for the lack of premarket approval of techniques. OvaScience characterized the "traditional pre-market approval clinical trials" required for pharmaceutical companies as "additional risk," as it considered the economic impacts of regulatory requirements.[6] OvaScience also noted in a required filing with the SEC that "clinical testing is expensive, difficult to design and implement, can take many years to complete, and is uncertain as to outcome."[7] Similarly, Dr. John Zhang provided mitochondrial transfer to patients in Mexico instead of the United States in order to avoid onerous requirements in the United States.[8] A hands-off regime means that risk is sited after the product or surgery is used, which allows a company more time to recoup potential costs. If the product or technology harms the patient, then the company could be subject to tort lawsuits under product liability or malpractice regimes.[9] Additionally, because there are significant age-based constraints, for women in particular, a hands-off regime enables individuals to obtain fertility treatment more quickly, even though the risk of unscrupulous actors continues.

The FDA is not transparent. Moreover, its jurisdictional grabs are often surprising, leading to significant criticism and outcry in various areas. For example, the FDA's plan to regulate laboratory testing services, through a scheme provided through guidance documents, led to opposition.[10] As indicated by the litigation related to the switch of Plan B from prescription-only to OTC status, FDA employees can be motivated by politics, going so far as to ignore proof of safety due to political concerns. During the resistance to approving OTC access to Plan B, attempts were made to couch those political concerns in the language of sex and public health, such as concerns about a potential increase in teenage promiscuity. At a 2002 advisory committee meeting convened after the FDA sent letters to providers of cytoplasmic transfer, an FDA employee noted that "the FDA recognizes [that there are] moral, ethical, and social policy issues related to genetic modification of eggs and embryos, and that these issues have the potential to affect regulatory decisions."[11] Similarly, at a 2014 FDA advisory committee meeting on cellular, tissue, and gene therapies, convened for purposes of discussing "oocyte modification in assisted reproduction for the prevention of transmission of mitochondrial disease or treatment of infertility," an FDA employee noted that the "FDA is [cognizant] that there are ethical, legal, and social policy issues raised by such heritable genetic modification of gametes, but these [a]re outside of FDA's delegated authority, and will not be discussed at this meeting."[12] There are two perspectives on this. Either the decision of agency employees to "limit . . . discussion to the science behind [cytoplasmic] transfer and not extend that discussion to FDA's jurisdiction in general, FDA's proposed rules for the regulation of human cells and tissues and other assisted reproductive technologies" was an effective way to organize a meeting and to focus on the task at hand, or the agency was aware of these potential controversial issues and wanted to preclude any discussion of them.

The current regime encourages reproductive tourism and inequality in access to AARTs (as well as ART). ART is often not fully covered by health insurance plans or not covered at all. As a result, individuals seeking ART must pay out of pocket. When techniques are unavailable in the United States or even in one's state, as with abortion in certain US states currently, individuals seeking those treatments must travel, and not all have the resources to do so. Examples of medical tourism that have been covered in the literature include travel to access stem cell treatment, surrogacy, and cytoplasmic transfer. For example, Senator (and Chairperson) Dianne Feinstein said, in reference to the congressional response to cloning: "Let's say we ban therapeutic cloning and it was available in Europe. Ms. Gulden, would you go to Europe? Of course you would. I don't know how you effectively stop people from looking for hope when they have a condition or disease or a problem that might otherwise be changed."[13] Feinstein also noted that she was aware of individuals leaving universities in the United States and going to Europe due to feelings that there were more opportunities in Europe. Thus, the current regulatory regime led not only to medical tourism but also to the potential "drain" of promising researchers.[14] Senator Feinstein's questions during the hearing, as well as after, indicate that there is a reproductive exceptionalism occurring in the United States. As she noted in a question, "few people would argue that we should ban organ transplantation even though we are concerned about the sales of human organs or the transplant of organs from executed prisoners. Still there are those who would completely ban somatic cell nuclear transplantation. This is in spite of the fact that the overwhelming majority of the scientific, medical, and patients' advocacy community opposes such a complete ban."[15] Of course, just because something will always be available abroad does not mean we cannot render it safer in the United States. A hands-off regime fosters transparency and openness as opposed to clandestine regulation or clandestine trips abroad. A hands-off regime also facilitates access because medical tourism often requires that an individual pay out-of-pocket for the medical services sought as well as the travel to obtain that service. Moreover, accessing medical care abroad generally requires more sophistication, not only in terms of ascertaining the quality of care available and success rates but also in navigating potential language barriers, than it would in the United States, which can make accessing reproductive care more difficult. In light of the multiple steps required for assisted reproduction and stories of individuals whose access to their gametes was restricted during the COVID-19 pandemic restrictions, facilitating access to ART and reproductive genetic innovation in the United States could minimize disparities in access to and use of ART in the United States.[16]

Disadvantages of Subterranean Regulation: Science, Politics, and Reproductive Medicine's Preferred Hands-off Regime

As noted in Chapter 1, increased regulation or the placement of a funding source in the government can foster access by subsidizing the development of a technique, but it can also reduce autonomy by introducing further regulatory hurdles. Moreover, it is not sufficient to obtain federal funding, which is notoriously hard to qualify for, even when controversial matters are not at issue. For those who do obtain federal funding, it is possible that later inquiries might lead Congress to rescind that funding, as illustrated in Chapter 4 by the experience of the company ACT after it had received NIH funding.[17] Moreover, ART providers often have difficulty obtaining subjects for follow-up studies because many parents do not wish to subject their apparently healthy children to medical interventions.[18]

In 2023, the *Washington Post* published an article titled "How a Renowned Fertility Doctor Profits from an Unproven Supplement."[19] The article discussed fertility doctor Norbert Gleicher, who owned the company that sells an unproven "fertility booster."[20] The article mostly focused on the potential conflict of interest, but also noted that "reproductive and women's health are infrequent and underfunded subjects of research, in part due to long-standing stigmas and gender biases, as well as restrictions on federal funding for research involving embryos. As a result, droves of people seeking to start families in later years are left struggling."[21] This fertility doctor is one of many who have provided unproven supplements or treatments in the fertility industry.[22] In the absence of scientific studies, individuals seek answers on websites like Reddit and Mumsnet, a UK website.[23]

The current regulatory regime for ART and AARTs reveals the shortcomings of the hands-off approach, which can exacerbate disparities. For example, there are significant disparities in access to ART based on income, employer, race, and sexual orientation.[24] These disparities, especially the socioeconomic and racial disparities, also accompany health care in general in the United States. Due to the general lack of health insurance coverage of ART, individuals who aim to use ART must often pay out of pocket, although the list of insurance companies and employers that subsidize ART is increasing; even the Department of Defense and Department of Veterans Affairs are now increasing ART coverage and availability.[25] For those who must or choose to travel abroad in order to avail themselves of ART or AART, travel costs and a lack of insurance coverage will add to the cost of accessing those techniques. Others may not be able to access the technique at all.

There have been many criticisms of the system of regulating drugs in the United States.[26] These criticisms often focus on the resource constraints that face a well-funded FDA. The FDA has faced criticism for the slow pace at which it approves drugs, leading to various expedited pathways for certain products and devices.[27] Yet those expedited approvals target mainstream pharmaceuticals, therapies, and medical devices, but not techniques involving reproductive genetic innovation in the United States. The slow increase in employer-based subsidies of assisted reproduction in the United States can expand access to ART with a focus on the health insurance market, subsidies, and expanded patient choice. But without the suggested hands-off, market-based approach, even if ART is subsidized by health insurance coverage, it will remain difficult to access techniques of reproductive genetic innovation. Moreover, the longer it takes for those techniques to enter into clinical practice, the longer they will be "experimental," a disadvantage because health insurance generally does not cover experimental procedures.

In its majority opinion in *Wyeth v. Levine*, a case related to a woman who was substantially harmed by a brand-name drug, the Supreme Court cited a report by the US GAO that noted the resource constraints faced by the FDA.[28] In the decision, Justice Stevens wrote, "The FDA has limited resources to monitor the 11,000 drugs on the market, and manufacturers have superior access to information about their drugs, especially in the postmarketing phase as new risks emerge. State tort suits uncover unknown drug hazards and provide incentives for drug manufacturers to disclose safety risks promptly."[29] In the United States, without a central regulator, it is even more difficult to monitor adverse events in the realm of IVF. By contrast, the United Kingdom, with its centralized regulator, has a "rigorous process for reporting, handling, and investigating adverse incidents and near misses. There, reporting adverse incidents in IVF is a statutory requirement [that] . . . allows clinics to learn from incidents and ensure changes can be made to prevent reoccurrence."[30] At the same time, however, tort law operates *after* a harm has occurred, whether this relates to unknown drug hazards or physician malpractice, which is disadvantageous for those who have suffered harm. Nonetheless, without discussing the broader goals of the tort system, which include deterrence and compensation for actual harms, the nature of the regulation of medicine is such that the regime generally compensates patients after they have suffered a harm. This means that after a successful suit, which can take several years, patients could continue to be harmed by dangerous techniques or products, and afterward, even in the case of a patient's success in a malpractice suit, the general pool of patients will have to wait for the industry to "self-correct" after a successful verdict. Even though this is a disadvantage, treating ART in the same way as the practice of medicine, more broadly, helps to reduce the targeting of reproduction for a burdensome regulatory system.

Societal Discourse and Separating Politics and Religion from Science and Medicine

In the aftermath of the use of (and unexpected regulation of) cytoplasmic transfer, some individuals argued that there should be public discussions of ART.[31] Many felt mitochondrial transfer should also be subject to a societal discourse.[32] The same calls in relation to germline gene editing have come from many well-recognized individuals, including the former director of the NIH, Dr. Francis Collins, and Francoise Baylis, a Canadian bioethicist.[33] Others simply say that these techniques should not go forward "at this time," which was the position of the Obama administration.[34]

Currently the FDA's subterranean regulation has served as an obstacle to the clinical use of AARTs and germline gene editing. Moreover, there has been a very limited national conversation about the topic. The National Academies of Science and Medicine issued a report in 2016 titled "Mitochondrial Replacement Techniques: Ethical, Social, and Policy Considerations."[35] The panel recommended that any initial clinical investigation involving mitochondrial transfer should only involve the transfer of male embryos, "to avoid introducing heritable genetic modification during initial clinical investigations," although the work of Professor Mitalipov and others indicates that the commonly held view that mitochondria are transmitted only maternally may not be accurate.[36] Nevertheless, international conversations about germline gene editing continue.

In the United States, the closest we have come to a societal discourse on germline gene editing was a 2015 subcommittee hearing that focused on improvements in human germline gene editing, gene drives, and preimplantation genetic diagnosis.[37] In 2015, Congress added a now-recurring budget rider (which was not the subject of the 2015 subcommittee hearing) that prohibits the FDA from using its agency funding on any application involving "heritable genetic modification." The FDA interpreted this to mean that mitochondrial transfer is a heritable genetic modification, meaning that AARTs cannot obtain FDA approval in the United States. During the drafting process for the 2020 spending bill, the provision was removed, according to an unidentified "Democratic aide speaking on background" to *Science Insider* in May 2023, "because it was inserted in private 3 years ago and has never been subject to public debate. We believe this provision could limit important scientific research and, if Congress chooses to prohibit such research, that should be done in the light of day."[38] The decision-making process is unclear. Yet by June 2024 the rider had been restored by voice vote by the full Appropriations Committee of the US House of Representatives.[39] A news article covering the rider noted in its update that "several Democrats said they were reluctantly supporting the request from Republicans to restore the rider, and lawmakers from both parties suggested congressional health committees that shape agency policies need to address the issue comprehensively, rather than have it debated annually during the appropriations process."[40] Representative Debbie Wasserman Schultz (Democrat–Florida) reportedly voted against restoring the rider in the voice vote, but she was outvoted by her colleagues.[41]

In prior works, I have asked what the purpose of a public consultation might be, and have expressed some concerns that it may be an effort to create a (possibly insurmountable) regulatory hurdle to the use of reproductive genetic innovation.[42] A public consensus on ART would be impossible and an absolute hurdle if required before the clinical use of reproductive genetic innovation, whether domestically or internationally. Medical innovations, especially medical innovations related to reproduction, should not be subject to public consultations that have a regulatory impact. In other words, it is good to inform the public of scientific and medical innovations, but the public, whatever that is, should not be allowed to determine whether individuals will have access to those techniques.

Dangers of the Current Regime Where Administrative Agencies Can Engage in the Subterranean Regulation of Reproductive Genetic Innovation

Subterranean regulation is an obstacle to the clinical use of various innovative forms of assisted reproductive technology. Subterranean regulation also reduces the system's ability to "check" political concerns that may affect science-related decision-making, especially when the public and scientists expect, without legal protection, agency decisions based on objective criteria.

In 2004 Paul Berg, recipient of the Nobel Prize for Chemistry in 1980 for his work on recombinant DNA, wrote an article related to the Asilomar Conference in which he posed the question, "Are the deep divisions about fetal tissue and embryonic stem cell research, somatic and germ-line gene therapy and directed genetic modification of food crops amenable to deliberation and resolution?"[43] He concluded that they were not, citing economic self-interest and "nearly irreconcilable ethical and religious conflicts and challenges to deeply held social values."[44] He also noted that the Asilomar Conference occurred before the development of "an entrenched, intransigent and chronic opposition" to the technology.[45] Because of this, Berg wrote, "attempts to prohibit the research or reverse the actions recommended by the conference threatened but never generated sufficient traction to succeed."[46] Berg argued that an Asilomar-style conference to address issues related to somatic and germline genetic engineering, fetal tissue research, and genetically modified plants and animals would be "doomed to acrimony and policy stagnation, neither of which advances the cause of finding a solution."[47] Stanford's news release announcing Paul Berg's death noted that "as part of his effort to separate science from politics, Berg was one of 20 Nobel laureates who signed a 2004 open letter accusing the Bush administration of citing bad science to support policy decisions."[48]

It is worth acknowledging that smaller funding grants to do exist. In 2022, the CDC awarded a grant to Charles River Analytics and

Massachusetts General Hospital for APRICOT (ART Provider and Patient Resources to Improve Communication about Outcomes and Treatment), a health information tool that would "facilitate the electronic transmission of pregnancy outcomes from ART patients to ART clinics."[49] This tool, though, while federally funded, would focus on data related to ART as opposed to the safety and efficacy of various treatments. This tool invokes a potential shortcoming of the Fertility Clinic Success Rate Act of 1992, which is that clinics that provide ART treatments report outcomes to the CDC, but they "only monitor ART pregnancies through the first ten weeks, after which patients receive ongoing prenatal care from their obstetricians," who are not the subjects of the Fertility Clinic Success Rate Act.[50] Moreover, in spite of stigmas related to funding reproductive research, some biotechnology receives millions of dollars in grants for the development of fertility drugs through programs such as Small Business Innovation Research Awards.[51]

There is a robust scientific funding regime, although the United States is lagging previous records. In 2005, the United States funded 57 percent of the world's biomedical research; a decade later, it funded only 44 percent of that research.[52] For example, in the United States there can be funding for ART research, including research related to drugs and novel techniques, but the federal funding tends to be for animal models as opposed to human models.[53] Beyond the National Institutes of Health, defense funding can be significant. For example, the Defense Advanced Research Projects Agency (DARPA) spent three times as much as the National Science Foundation on synthetic biology.[54] Counterarguments related to federal funding of reproductive genetic innovation could focus on the nature of CRISPR. In 2016 James Clapper, when he was director of national intelligence, included genome editing on the US intelligence community's list of global threats, in the category of "weapons of mass destruction and proliferation."[55] This might lead to increased research funding for CRISPR.

Moreover, just because fertility clinics are not as motivated to spend money on research studies does not mean that they or their practitioners never do. Dehydroepiandrosterone (DHEA), a drug advertised by a fertility doctor for improved outcomes, has been the subject of human clinical studies in Egypt, Hong Kong, and Israel, some of which have involved university grant funding.[56]

Federal advisory committees provide expert input to regulators but they do not resolve the issue of transparency. Federal advisory committee meetings vary in terms of openness and can range from fully open, to partially open, to closed. There are certainly justifiable reasons for a partially open meeting, such as discussion of proprietary information. Meetings' transcripts and agendas do not always explain why part or all of a meeting is closed. Agencies tend to be captured by their regulated entities. In the realm of drug approval, FDA regulator actions "aligned with 262 of 298 advisory committee votes [88 percent] on initial approvals, supplemental approvals, withdrawals of approval, and safety action" from 2010 to 2021.[57]

The history of the FDA in the area of reproduction, however, tells a far more complicated story of capture. In this area there is potentially "political capture" or, as characterized by Professor Daniel G. Aaron, "ideological capture" with a pro-innovation perspective for certain industries.[58] Moreover, the more ART is subject to intellectual property regimes, whether regarding patent solutions or trade secrets, the greater the diminishment of transparency and access. For example, CooperSurgical has been sued for the shortcomings of its embryo cultivation solution.[59] The embryo that became Louise Brown was cultivated in a salt solution with additional ingredients. Today, IVF clinics use commercialized solutions, the ingredients of which, and their proportions, are not fully disclosed. Physicians have complained that they are unable to conduct quality checks on the solutions because they do not know all the ingredients or their proportions, so they do not know what to check for to determine the viability of the solution.[60] Some practitioners have called for a disclosure of the ingredients in order to monitor the influence of embryo culture media on IVF outcomes, a call that has been strengthened by the CooperSurgical experience.[61]

Separating Politics and Societal Debate from Medicine and Scientific Research

One of the concerns addressed in this book is the influence of politics over regulation. This includes the growing role of partisanship and personal views in judicial decision-making, especially at the level of the US Supreme Court. Many argue that it is impossible to separate politics from regulation. Yet, one goal is to identify situations where partisanship or political concerns have influenced regulation, especially when this occurs in a scientific or medical area where the public might expect objectivity. We have seen the circumstances surrounding the switch of Plan B to OTC, as well as the extensive history of subterranean regulation of reproductive genetic innovation and the targeting of reproduction with burdensome regulations across both Democratic and Republican administrations. It is reasonable to conclude that a reduction in federal regulation of reproduction will foster reproductive autonomy.

We can ask what would have happened if legislators allowed morality or religion to curtail other innovations. Issues regarding organ transplantation also arose in congressional hearings. Bryan Cowan, MD, who testified as a representative of the American Society for Reproductive Medicine, argued: "Organ transplantation and IVF were hugely controversial upon their introduction, and we were greeted with the same objections raised here against cloning. Thankfully, this knowledge was not made illegal, and today we can successfully use these advances to help patients every single day."[62]

Politicization of issues related to reproduction has long been a concern. In a 1989 hearing on the never-reconstituted Ethics Advisory Board, which would have reviewed research related to IVF if federally funded, Representative Nancy Pelosi noted that she was "concerned that an Ethics Advisory Board appointed by any Secretary of HHS, a political appointee, will always be somewhat politicized."[63] When in 1989 the FDA placed an importation ban on RU-486, a district court judge noted that the ban followed letters to the FDA from legislators who were opposed to abortion. "A request made pursuant to the Freedom of Information Act for documents that would support such a factual finding was answered with the statement that no such documents exist in FDA's files."[64] Instead of waiting for FOIA requests, the FDA should practice a more open decision-making process and aim to provide as much information to the public as possible. Doing so will not harm the public, and it will foster transparency and accountability.

There is rarely a clear statement or acknowledgment of the influence of morality on the law. In the UK, Mary Warnock wrote of her committee's deliberations: "As soon as a committee (or more generally its chairman) begins to think in terms of what would be realistic as a proposal to turn into law, it becomes clear that the relation between morality and the law is not simple. Still less is it easy to say what is the relation between very strongly held but not universally shared moral views and legislation, which must be binding on everyone whatever their views."[65] Thus, I recommend a regulatory approach that minimizes the ability of anyone, especially those in a politically powerful majority, to impose their views on anyone else to the detriment of those individuals' reproductive autonomy.

Conclusion

The US Department of Health and Human Services is an executive branch agency. As indicated in Chapter 7, executive branch agencies not only fall within the control of the president but are often directly influenced by the White House. The public is often unaware of external influences like this, and without costly and unpredictable litigation, the public might never know. One could interpret the FDA's efforts to regulate cellular and gene therapy as a noble effort to quickly adapt to unforeseen technologies in the absence of clear congressional legislation until the enactment of the 21st Century Cures Act in 2016. But the FDA's regulation of gene therapy has resulted in a permissive scheme, in contrast to the FDA's regulation of reproductive genetic innovation, which has led to a preclusive regime. Ultimately the FDA has treated reproductive genetic innovation, such as mitochondrial transfer and cytoplasmic transfer, with significant hostility, and this has basically eliminated their availability in the United States.

Historically, in the realm of reproduction, individuals use assisted reproduction methods to create their families, and the law addresses the implications of these actions after children are born. Science, morality, and public opinion are often intertwined. The judiciary is supposed to be impartial, but the US Supreme Court has shifted in a notably conservative direction, as have many judicial federal court judges and many other members of the judiciary as well as the executive branch. In *Dobbs*, the Supreme Court noted that its opinion did not threaten contraception because contraception did not involve the "destruction of what Roe called 'potential life,'" but many disagree.[1] Similarly, those interested in assisted reproduction were particularly (and justifiably) worried post-*Dobbs*. While the majority decision denied that it was motivated by a personhood theory or a theory of life, many ART advocates feared it was, and the Alabama Supreme Court's decision that embryos were "unborn children" under the Wrongful Death of a Minor Act led to the halt of IVF in Alabama in the immediate aftermath of the decision. Post-*Dobbs*, as I have argued recently, it will be important that legislation protect access to IVF so that access to ART is not denied due to the implied theory of personhood that underpinned the majority's decision.[2]

Before introducing the concept of subterranean regulation, I examined other instances in which the FDA and other operating divisions of the US Department of Health and Human Services behaved in a biased way, including the well-known switch of Plan B from prescription-only to OTC availability as well as prior regulatory and legislative hostility to access to RU-486, even for research purposes, as well as to research involving reproductive genetic innovation. Chapter 7 outlined the origins of subterranean regulation, which, insofar as it could be ascertained, lay with human reproductive cloning, but could possibly extend to as far back as access to RU-486, the abortifacient now commonly referred to as Mifeprex (brand name) or mifepristone (generic drug). Moreover, Chapter 7 traced subterranean regulation in the realm of reproductive genetic innovation. Going forward, legislators and even agency employees should aim to improve the transparency of the FDA, with an emphasis on publishing more agency documents, a matter that will become more pertinent in the wake of the US Supreme Court's decision in *Dobbs*, which has made reproduction even more obviously politicized than it was in 1973 before *Roe v. Wade*.[3]

Reproductive genetic innovation could improve fertility outcomes and lead to the birth of more children.[4] The high costs of egg freezing are a particular deterrent for many. Of those employers that are known for providing egg freezing as an employee perk, many of their corporate employees are college graduates who may be delaying childbirth and marriage.[5] Statistics show that women with bachelor's degrees are more likely to marry later in life than women without those degrees.[6] Marriage factors into statistical analysis, as many women would prefer to have, or would only consider having, children if married.[7] In terms of egg freezing, while it is more effective to freeze eggs between ages 30 and 34, egg freezing is most cost-effective at age 37.[8] Further, for those who lack independent financial means, freezing eggs later in life likely corresponds with the financial stability that comes from working (and saving) for years, in order to afford personal goals like homeownership and, these days, biological or genetic parental status. For those whose employers do not cover these services, startups are increasingly targeting women who are of reproductive age and may be seeking to access ART techniques.[9] Some of those individuals could benefit from AARTs and germline gene editing for improved fertility outcomes but will be unable to access those technologies in the United States.

Many external influences can be separated from scientific decision-making. Without going too far afield from the issues of reproductive autonomy, I will note that "genetically engineered children," just like children born via IVF, have no genetic impact on the rest of us, but genetically modified organisms certainly do. There are several developments that may be impacted by this book's analysis and the political economy of reproduction. Scholars have been spending more time discussing the possibilities of in vitro gametogenesis (IVG), a technique that could use somatic cells, like skin cells, to create sex cells ("germ cells")—sperm or eggs.[10] These possibilities are characterized as being a "long way off" now, but the technology could eventually have revolutionary impacts on reproduction.[11] It could also meet with the same hurdles to funding and FDA licensing as mitochondrial transfer.[12] Individuals continue to debate when public consultation should occur in connection with technologies like in vitro gametogenesis. While IVG is not a focus of the book, it could involve very difficult issues, were it to ever come to fruition, such as the possibility that individuals' genetic material could be obtained against their will and turned into sex cells.[13]

Similarly, in utero gene editing could positively impact lives. While many, including the program manager of the NIH's Somatic Cell Genome Editing Consortium, have expressed support for clinical trials in the future, it would be wise not to forget how easily moral or religious views can diminish support for scientific research and innovation.[14]

As new forms of reproductive genetic innovation—including germline gene editing, in vitro gametogenesis, and new testing methods—develop, significant impediments arise when society and the FDA assume that the federal government is the proper and best regulator of techniques involving reproductive genetic innovation. It should not be. The chilling of domestic research, and the resultant offshoring of fertility innovation, is harmful to patients (and the opposite of the usual way in which medical innovation unfolds). It also increases disparities in access to medicine and innovation. The current regulatory regime requires patients seeking reproductive genetic innovation to be sophisticated enough to find and evaluate fertility treatments abroad, to have the resources to do so (both financial and intellectual), and to exercise this sophistication without the benefit of domestic consumer and patient protection.

ACKNOWLEDGMENTS

Thank you for reading this work. I very much appreciate the opportunity to have workshopped drafts of the manuscript at various scholarly colloquia. I thank participants at the following workshops for their constructive comments, questions, and feedback: Baby Markets Roundtable; Biolawlapalooza; Family Law Scholars and Teachers Conference; 45th Annual Health Law Professors Conference; Health Law Policy, Bioethics, and Biotechnology Workshop at Harvard Law School; Law & Society Association Annual Meeting; Lutie A. Lytle Black Women Law Faculty Workshop; Penn Bioethics Seminar; Sturm College of Law Faculty Workshop; Thirteenth Annual Constitutional Law Colloquium; University of California Los Angeles Health Law Scholarship Workshop; University of Texas Health, Innovation, and the Law Colloquium; and the University of Toronto Health Law, Policy, and Ethics Seminar. Thank you to the many people who gave me advice on the book proposal and writing process over the years, including Lisa Benjamin, Hank Greely, Browne Lewis, Theodosia Stavroulaki, and Tim Zick. I would also like to thank the following individuals for their research assistance: Isabelle Auble, Emily Buttolph, Christopher Byrne, Susanna Clark, Michaela Cotton, Shay Crotty, Rebecca Fox, Kelsey Huckins, Majesta-Doré Legnini, Miah Lynch, Christian Marsh, Kim Nguyen, Zulekha Tasneem, Katharine von Schaumburg, Shane Vaughn, and Chelsea Yedinak. Lastly, there is not enough space to provide adequate appreciation for Dr. Cali Slair.

APPENDIX A

Letter to Sponsors / Researchers

HUMAN CELLS USED IN THERAPY INVOLVING THE TRANSFER OF GENETIC MATERIAL BY MEANS OTHER THAN THE UNION OF GAMETE NUCLEI[1]

Department of Health and Human Services
Public Health Service
Food and Drug Administration
1401 Rockville Pike
Rockville, MD 20852-1448

July 6, 2001

Dear Sponsor / Researcher:
We want to advise you that the Food and Drug Administration (FDA) has jurisdiction over human cells used in therapy involving the transfer of genetic material by means other than the union of gamete nuclei.

Examples of such genetic material include, but are not limited to:

cell nuclei (e.g., for cloning),
oocyte nuclei,
ooplasm, which contains mitochondrial genetic material, and
genetic material contained in a genetic vector, transferred into gametes or other cells.

The use of such genetically manipulated cells (and/or their derivatives) in humans constitutes a clinical investigation and requires submission of an Investigational New Drug application (IND) to FDA. We wish to inform you of the FDA regulatory process governing clinical investigations, which includes requirements applicable to manufacturing processes, the study of the safety and efficacy of such cells, and the protection of human participants in such studies. We can advise you whether or not your activities require submission of an IND. If what you are doing or plan to do does require an IND, we would be pleased to provide you with information and guidance regarding filing such an application.

FDA's regulations on investigational new drugs, including those for the submission and review of an IND are described in Title 21 of the Code of Federal Regulations (CFR), Parts 50, 56, and 312. The agency has provided notice of the applicability of these requirements to cellular and tissue-based products in many public forums and in various published documents available at http://www.fda.gov/cber/, including the following:

A Federal Register (FR) notice describing FDA's authority over cell and gene therapy products ("Application of Current Statutory Authorities to Human Somatic Cell Therapy Products and Gene Therapy Products," October 14, 1993, 58 FR 53248) (PDF-489 KB).

A comprehensive regulatory program for the regulation of human cellular and tissue-based products, based on a tiered, risk-based assessment ("A Proposed Approach to the Regulation of Cellular and Tissue-Based Products," March 4, 1997, 62 FR 9721).

A final rule that establishes the criteria for regulation of human cells, tissues, and cellular and tissue-based products (HCT/Ps), including reproductive cells and tissues, published on January 19, 2001 (66 FR 5447). This rule also describes which HCT/Ps will be regulated solely under 21 CFR Part 1271, the regulations to prevent communicable disease transmission authorized by section 361 of the Public Health Service Act. HCT/Ps that do not meet the criteria under Part 1271 will be regulated as biological products, drugs, or devices under section 351 of the Public Health Service Act and/or the Food Drug and Cosmetic Act.

"Suitability Determination for Donors of Human Cellular and Tissue-Based Products; Proposed Rule." September 30, 1999 (64 FR 52696).

"Current Good Tissue Practice for Manufacture of Human Cellular and Tissue-Based Products; Inspection and Enforcement; Proposed Rule" January 8, 2001 (66 FR 1508).

If you are unable to access the internet to obtain information on submitting an IND to the FDA, please call or write and we'll supply you with the needed information:

Center for Biologics Evaluation and Research
Office of Communication, Training & Manufacturers Assistance
Manufacturers Assistance and Technical Training Branch
1401 Rockville Pike, HFM-44
Rockville, MD 20852-1448
800-835-4709 or 301-827-1800
matt@cber.fda.gov

The specific information required in an IND will depend upon the cells under investigation and on the phase of study. For assistance in determining whether you need to file an IND submission and in preparation of a submission, please contact Wendy Aaronson, Application Administration Branch Chief, Division of Application Review and Policy, at 301-827-5101.

Sincerely,
—signature—
Kathryn C. Zoon, Ph.D.
Director
Center for Biologics Evaluation and Research
Food and Drug Administration

APPENDIX B

Letter About Human Cloning[1]

October 26, 1998

Dear Colleague:
The purpose of this letter is to confirm to institutional review boards (IRBs) that the Food and Drug Administration (FDA) has jurisdiction over clinical research using cloning technology to create a human being, and to inform IRBs of the FDA regulatory process that is required before any investigator can proceed with such a clinical investigation. This letter is being sent to IRBs at this time because of reports in the media that scientists are contemplating the use of cloning technology to create human beings. As described more fully below, the appropriate mechanism to pursue a clinical investigation using cloning technology is the submission of an investigational new drug application (IND) to FDA.

Clinical research using cloning technology to create a human being is subject to FDA regulation under the Public Health Service Act and the Federal Food, Drug, and Cosmetic Act. Under these statutes and FDA's implementing regulations, before such research may begin, the sponsor of the research is required to submit to FDA an IND describing the proposed research plan; to obtain authorization from a properly constituted and functioning IRB; and to obtain a commitment from the investigators to obtain informed consent from all human subjects of the research. Such research may proceed only when an IND is in effect. Since FDA believes that there are major unresolved safety questions pertaining to the use of cloning technology to create a human being, until those questions are appropriately addressed in the IND, FDA would not permit any such investigation to proceed.

FDA may prohibit a sponsor from conducting a study proposed in an IND application (often referred to as placing the study on "clinical hold") for a variety of reasons. If the Agency finds that "human subjects are or would be exposed to an unreasonable and significant risk of illness or injury," that would be sufficient reason to put a study on clinical hold. Other reasons listed in the regulations include "the IND does not contain sufficient information required . . . to address the risks to subjects of the proposed studies," or "the clinical investigators . . . are not qualified by reason of their scientific training and experience to conduct the investigation."

The procedures and requirements governing the use of investigational new drugs, including those for the submission and review of INDs, are set forth in Title 21 of the Code of Federal Regulations (CFR), Part 312. Additional responsibilities of the sponsor of an IND include: selecting qualified investigators and overseeing the conduct of the investigators; ensuring that the investigations are performed in accordance with the protocols of the IND; submitting adverse experience reports and annual reports; and other duties as outlined in the regulations. The responsibilities of an investigator include: ensuring that the study is conducted in accordance with the protocols; obtaining informed consent from study subjects; and ensuring that an IRB that complies with the requirements of 21 CFR Part 56 reviews and approves the proposed clinical study and the informed consent form and procedures for obtaining informed consent, among other requirements specified in the regulations. IRBs and clinical investigators may obtain a copy of the current "Information Sheets for IRBs and Clinical Investigators" by contacting FDA's Office of Health Affairs (301-827-1685), through the world wide web (http://www.fda.gov/oha/IRB/toc.html*) or through a Fax-on-demand system (1-800-993-0098).

We hope the above information is useful to you. Please feel free to share this information with others at your institution.

Sincerely yours,
—signature—
Stuart L. Nightingale, M.D.
Associate Commissioner

NOTES

INTRODUCTION

1 *Prize Announcement*, The Nobel Prize, www.nobelprize.org.

2 *IVF Pioneer Patrick Steptoe Gets Blue Plaque*, BBC News (May 4, 2019), www.bbc.com/.

3 Madeline Holcombe, *About 2% of Babies Born in the US Are from IVF. Here's What You Need to Know About It*, CNN (Feb. 21, 2024, 1:01 PM), www.cnn.com.

4 Gretchen Livingston, *A Third of U.S. Adults Say They Have Used Fertility Treatments or Know Someone Who Has*, Pew Rsch. Ctr. (July 17, 2018), www.pewresearch.org; Maggie Fox, *A Million Babies Have Been Born in the U.S. with Fertility Help*, NBC News, www.nbcnews.com.

5 Michelle Obama, Becoming, 188–90 (Crown, 2018).

6 *Id.* at 199; James Crowley, *Amy Schumer & 6 Other Celebrities Who Have Used IVF to Start Their Families*, Newsweek (Aug. 14, 2020, 12:30 PM), www.newsweek.com; Marianne Garvey, *More and More Older, Single Men Are Becoming Dads Now (Like Andy Cohen)*, Bravo (Dec. 27, 2018, 11:35 AM), www.bravotv.com; Jen Juneau, *Andy Cohen Reveals He Has at "Least One Embryo" Left and Is "Thinking About" Second Child*, People (Dec. 19, 2019, 11:10 AM), https://people.com.

7 Gabriela Weigel et al., *Coverage and Use of Fertility Services in the U.S.*, KFF (Sept. 15, 2020), www.kff.org.

8 Livingston, *supra* note 4.

9 *Parenting in America*, Pew Rsch. Ctr. (Dec. 17, 2015), www.pewresearch.org.

10 *What Is Assisted Reproductive Technology?*, Ctrs. for Disease Control & Prevention (Feb. 7, 2017), www.cdc.gov; Nat'l Health Service England, Clinical Commissioning Policy: Assisted Conception (2014), Reference: N-SC/037, at 5–6, www.england.nhs.uk.

11 Genesis 16:1–16, 17:5–6.

12 Chapter 3 *infra*.

13 *See, e.g.*, Naina Bajekal, *Why So Many Women Travel to Denmark for Fertility Treatments*, Time (Jan. 3, 2019), https://time.com.

14 *See* Asia Grace, *I Found Out My Gynecologist Was My Secret Dad—and He Knew It*, N.Y. Post (Apr. 1, 2022, 5:34 PM), https://nypost.com; Baby God (HBO Documentary Films 2020); Kerri O'Brien, *Who's Your Daddy? Woman Sues Glen Allen Fertility Doctor for Using His Own Sperm to Impregnate Her*, ABC News (Nov. 20, 2020, 12:06 PM), www.wric.com.

15 *See, e.g.*, Kate Brumback, *Georgia Court Allows Lawsuit Against Sperm Bank to Proceed*, WASH. POST (Sept. 28, 2020), www.washingtonpost.com.
16 Tummino v. Hamburg, F. Supp. 2d 162, 166–69 (E.D.N.Y. 2013).
17 Myrisha S. Lewis, *Innovating Federalism in the Life Sciences*, 92 TEMP. L. REV. 391–401 (2020).
18 *Id.* at 397–99.
19 Rebecca S. Eisenberg, *The Role of the FDA in Innovation Policy*, 13 MICH. TELECOMM. & TECH. L. REV. 345, 347–50 (2007).
20 *Hard Law/Soft Law*, EUROPEAN CTR. FOR CONST. & HUM. RTS., www.ecchr.eu.
21 Transcript of Center for Biologics Evaluation and Research, Food and Drug Administration, Biological Response Modifiers Advisory Committee Open Session Meeting #32, 46 (May 9, 2002, 8:00 AM), www.fda.gov.
22 Nat'l Acad. of Scis., Insts. of Med., HUMAN GENOME EDITING: SCIENCE, ETHICS, AND GOVERNANCE, 188 (National Academies Press 2017); Nat'l Acads. of Sci., HERITABLE HUMAN GENOME EDITING, 88–89 (2020); Nuffield Council on Bioethics, NOVEL TECHNIQUES FOR THE PREVENTION OF MITOCHONDRIAL DNA DISORDERS: AN ETHICAL REVIEW (Springer 2012).
23 Myrisha S. Lewis, *How Analogizing Socio-Legal Responses to Organ Transplantation Can Further the Legalization of Reproductive Genetic Innovation*, 74 SMU L. REV. 665 (2021).
24 Myrisha S. Lewis, *How Subterranean Regulation Hinders Innovation in Assisted Reproductive Technology*, 39 CARDOZO L. REV. 1239 (2018).
25 Lewis, *supra* note 23; Myrisha S. Lewis, *Normalizing Reproductive Genetic Innovation*, 74 ADMIN. L. REV. 481 (2022).
26 Derek Hawkins, *Jury Awards $15 Million in Landmark Case over Embryos, Eggs Destroyed in Clinic Tank Failure*, WASH. POST (June 11, 2021, 7:25 PM), www.washingtonpost.com.
27 Adam Popescu, *The Octomom Has Proved Us All Wrong*, N.Y. TIMES (Dec. 15, 2018), www.nytimes.com.
28 *Sofia Vergara: US Actress Faces Lawsuit "from Own Embryos,"* BBC NEWS (Dec. 8, 2016), www.bbc.com.
29 Neil Vigdor, *"We Had Their Baby, and They Had Our Baby": Couple Sues over Embryo "Mix-Up,"* N.Y. TIMES (Nov. 9, 2021), www.nytimes.com/2021/11/09/us/fertility-clinic-embryo-mixup.html.
30 Sarah Zhang, *One Sperm Donor. 36 Children. A Mess of Lawsuits*, THE ATLANTIC (Sept. 11, 2020), www.theatlantic.com.
31 Laurel Wamsley, *Ohio Fertility Clinic Says 4,000 Eggs and Embryos Destroyed when Freezer Failed*, NPR (Mar. 28, 2018, 11:19 AM), www.npr.org; LePage v. Ctr. for Reprod. Med., P.C., No. SC-2022-0515, 2024 WL 656591 (Ala., Feb. 16, 2024).
32 *President Discusses Embryo Adoption and Ethical Stem Cell Research*, THE WHITE HOUSE: PRESIDENT GEORGE W. BUSH (May 24, 2005, 2:07 PM), https://georgewbush-whitehouse.archives.gov.

33 *White Paper: Access to Care Summit*, AM. SOC'Y REPROD. MED. (Sept. 2015), www.asrm.org.
34 *Id.*
35 Weigel et al., *supra* note 7.
36 *See, e.g.*, Obama, *supra* note 5 at 188.
37 *State Laws Related to Insurance Coverage for Infertility Treatment*, NAT'L CONF. STATE LEGISLATURES (Mar. 12, 2021), www.ncsl.org; Amy Klein, *I.V.F. Is Expensive. Here's How to Bring Down the Cost*, N.Y. TIMES (Apr. 18, 2020), www.nytimes.com.
38 Crystal Martin, *How Much Infertility Treatments Actually Cost 8 Different Women*, WOMEN'S HEALTH (Oct. 29, 2018), www.womenshealthmag.com; Korin Miller, *American Women Are Traveling Abroad to Get IVF Treatment*, SELF (Apr. 5, 2016), www.self.com; Naina Bajekal, *Why So Many Women Travel to Denmark for Fertility Treatments*, TIME (Jan. 3, 2019), https://time.com.
39 Lauren Lyons Cole, *A Single Round of Fertility Treatments Can Cost over $2,000—A Couple Who Did It Breaks Down Where the Money Went*, BUSINESS INSIDER (June 25, 2017, 9:45 AM), www.businessinsider.com; Marissa Conrad, *How Much Does IVF Cost?*, FORBES HEALTH (Sept. 28, 2021, 9:44 AM), www.forbes.com; Martin, *supra* note 38; A.D.A.C. Smith et al., *Live-Birth Rate Associated with Repeat in Vitro Fertilization Treatment Cycles*, 314 J. OF AMER. MED. ASSOC. 2654–62.
40 Martin, *supra* note 38.
41 *The Fertility Market Overview*, HARRIS WILLIAMS, www.harriswilliams.com; Cyrus Abbassi, *The State of the Fertility Industry*, 12 THE NAT'L L. REV. (Aug. 18, 2021).
42 Jena McGregor, *The New Silicon Valley Perk? Freezing Your Eggs*, WASH. POST (Oct. 14, 2014), www.washingtonpost.com. *See also Introducing Meta: A Social Technology Company*, META (Oct. 28, 2021), https://about.fb.com; *2015 Founders' Letter*, ALPHABET INVESTORS RELATIONS (Aug. 10, 2015) (explaining the decision to change the company name from Google to Alphabet), https://abc.xyz.
43 Luz Pena, *Bay Area Woman Travels to Spain to Freeze Eggs*, ABC NEWS (July 20, 2019), https://abc7news.com.
44 Anna Louise Sussman, *I Froze My Eggs in Europe to Save Money. Then, the Pandemic Hit*, ELLE (Nov. 23, 2020), www.elle.com; *Covid Restrictions Postpone Woman's IVF Treatments Abroad*, BBC NEWS (Nov. 3, 2020), www.bbc.com.
45 Mary Pflum, *Egg Freezing Has Boomed During the Pandemic, as Women Opt to Wait Out Family Life*, NBC NEWS (Apr. 24, 2021, 6:00 AM), www.nbcnews.com/.
46 *Pregnancy After 35: Healthy Moms, Healthy Babies*, MAYO CLINIC (Feb. 10, 2022), www.mayoclinic.org.
47 Am. Soc'y for Reprod. Med., *Age and Fertility* (2012), 4, www.asrm.org.
48 *United States Government Handbook*, LIBR. CONGR. (2021), www.govinfo.gov.
49 Kirti Datla & Richard L. Revesz, *Deconstructing Independent Agencies (and Executive Agencies)*, 98 CORNELL L. REV. 769 (2013).

50 Jonathan Kim, *Administrative Law*, CORNELL LEGAL INFO. INST. (June 2017), www.law.cornell.edu; *An Overview of Federal Regulations and the Rulemaking Process*, CONGR. RSCH. SERV. (Mar. 19, 2021), https://sgp.fas.org.

51 *HHS Agencies & Offices*, US DEP'T HEALTH & HUM. SERVS. (Jan. 5, 2022), www.hhs.gov.

52 Later, after the 2018 summit, the birth of a third child via gene-editing technology was announced.

53 *See* FDA Response to FOIA Request 2016-4883 (on file with author).

54 *Id.*

CHAPTER 1. A RANGE OF REGULATORY OPTIONS

1 Jessica Bulman-Pozen, *From Sovereignty and Process to Administration and Politics: The Afterlife of American Federalism*, 123 YALE L.J. 1920, 1922 (2014) ("We cannot understand today's federalism without considering the separation of powers, and we likewise cannot understand the separation of powers without considering federalism. Our federal government is really a federalist government").

2 For more on the scholarly debates and analyses related to federalism, *see generally* Bulman-Pozen, *supra* note 1; Jessica Bulman-Pozen, *Federalism as a Safeguard of the Separation of Powers*, 112 COLUM. L. REV. 459 (2012); Jessica Bulman-Pozen & Heather K. Gerken, *Uncooperative Federalism*, 118 YALE L.J. 1256 (2009).

3 Heather Gerken, *The Supreme Court, 2009 Term: Foreword: Federalism All the Way Down*, 124 HARV. L. REV. 4, 9 (2010); Janel George et al., *The Federal Role and School Integration: Brown's Promise and Present Challenges*, LEARNING POLICY INSTITUTE (Feb. 2019), https://learningpolicyinstitute.org.

4 Alexis Clark, *Black Americans Who Served in WWII Faced Segregation Abroad and at Home*, HISTORY (Aug. 3, 2023), www.history.com; Suyin Hanes, *You've Probably Heard of the Red Scare, but the Lesser-Known, Anti-Gay "Lavender Scare" Is Rarely Taught in Schools*, TIME (Dec. 22, 2020, 9:11 AM), https://time.com.

5 *Using Local Ordinances, Resolutions, and Non-Prosecution Measures to Protect Reproductive Health*, THE NETWORK FOR PUBLIC HEALTH LAW (Sept. 1, 2022), www.networkforphl.org; *Frequently Asked Question—Sanctuary Cities*, CITY OF CHICAGO, www.networkforphl.org.

6 *See, e.g., Using Local Ordinances, supra* note 5.

7 *See, e.g., Dental Licensure and CE Requirements Maps*, AM. DENTAL ASS'N (2022), www.ada.org; *Board for Barbers and Cosmetology*, DEP'T OF PRO. AND OCCUPATIONAL REGUL. (2022), www.dpor.virginia.gov/.

8 Barry Furrow et al., HEALTH LAW: CASES, MATERIALS, AND PROBLEMS 1117 (8th ed. 2022).

9 Sara K. Hayden, *The Business of Birth: Obstacles Facing Low-Income Women in Choosing Midwifery Care After the Licensed Midwifery Practice Act of 1993*, 19 BERKELEY WOMEN'S L. J. 257, 259–64 (2004). For more on expanding coverage of doula services, *see* Taylor Platt & Neva Kaye, *Four State Strategies to Employ*

Doulas to Improve Maternal Health and Birth Outcomes in Medicaid, NATIONAL ACADEMY FOR STATE HEALTH POLICY (July 13, 2020), www.nashp.org; Chasity Maxie, *Midwives, Doulas Say They Want Their Voices Considered in ADPH's Birth Center Regulations*, WBRC (Aug. 22, 2022), www.wbrc.com; see *Doula Medicaid Project*, NATIONAL HEALTH LAW PROGRAM, https://healthlaw.org.

10 *See, e.g.*, Astrue v. Capato ex rel. B.N.C., 566 U.S. 541, 545–46 (2012); Woodward v. Comm'r of Soc. Sec., 760 N.E.2d 257, 257–62 (Mass. 2002).

11 Bridget A. Fahey, *Coordinated Rulemaking and Cooperative Federalism's Administrative Law*, 132 YALE L.J. 1213 (2022–2023).

12 15 U.S.C. § 1 ("Every contract, combination in the form of trust or otherwise, or conspiracy, in restraint of trade or commerce among the several States, or with foreign nations, is hereby declared to be illegal"); 15 U.S.C.A. §77a–77mm (West 1934); *Securities Act of 1933*, U.S. GOV'T PUBLISHING OFC. (Jan. 24, 2023), www.govinfo.gov/; 15 U.S.C. § 1051; U.S. Trademark Law, UNITED STATES PATENT AND TRADEMARK OFFICE (Nov. 25, 2013), www.uspto.gov.

13 21 U.S.C. § 355 (2022) ("No person shall introduce or deliver for introduction into interstate commerce any new drug, unless an approval of an application filed pursuant to subsection (b) or (j) is effective with respect to such drug."); 15 U.S.C.A. § 1331 ("(2) commerce and the national economy may be (A) protected to the maximum extent consistent with this declared policy and (B) not impeded by diverse, nonuniform, and confusing cigarette labeling and advertising regulations with respect to any relationship between smoking and health").

14 *See* United States v. Rutherford, 442 U.S. 544, 552 (1979).

15 *See* Weinberger v. Hynson, Westcott & Dunning, Inc., 412 U.S. 609, 612 (1973).

16 *See* Rutherford, *supra* note 14 at 552.

17 *See* Rutherford, *supra* note 14 at 555 (1979) (citing Weinberger v. Hynson, Westcott & Dunning, Inc., 412 U.S. 609 (1973)).

18 *See* Rutherford, *supra* note 14 at 555.

19 *Id.*

20 Cong. Research Svc., CENTERS FOR DISEASE CONTROL AND PREVENTION (CDC): HISTORY, OVERVIEW OF DOMESTIC PROGRAMS, AND SELECTED ISSUES 2 (Mar. 22, 2024) https://crsreports.congress.gov (noting that "CDC does not have a single, overarching statute that defines its overall mission, structure, and programs."); Cong. Research Svc., THE NATIONAL INSTITUTES OF HEALTH (NIH): BACKGROUND AND CONGRESSIONAL ISSUES 2 (April 19, 2019), https://crsreports.congress.gov (noting that "Congress designated the [Hygienic Laboratory] the National Institute of Health in 1930 (P.L. 71-251). . . . By 1948, several new institutes and divisions had been created, and the agency became the National Institutes of Health (P.L. 80-655)"); Irena Hwang et al., *The Gutting of America's Research: Here Is Every Canceled or Delayed N.I.H. Grant*, N.Y. TIMES (June 4, 2025), www.nytimes.com.

21 OvaScience, Inc., ANNUAL REPORT (FORM 10-K), 11-3 (Mar. 16, 2015). OvaScience licensed the right to use certain patents from Massachusetts General Hospital and Harvard University. *Id.* at 11.

22 *See* U.S. Food and Drug Admin., *Warning Letter* 3 (May 20, 2021), www.ftc.gov/system/files/warning-letters/fda-fertility-nutraceuticals.pdf.

23 *See, e.g.*, Fed. Trade Comm'n v. Ruberoid Co., 343 U.S. 470, 487 (1952) (J. Jackson Dissent); Peter L. Strauss, *The Place of Agencies in Government: Separation of Powers and the Fourth Branch*, 84 COLUM. L. REV. 573, 578 (1984).

24 *See generally* Cary Coglianese, *Administrative Law: Governing Economic and Social Governance,* in OXFORD RESEARCH ENCYCLOPEDIA OF ECONOMICS AND FINANCE (Jonathan H. Hamilton et al., eds.) (Oxford University Press 2022).

25 *About FDA Product Approval*, U.S. FOOD & DRUG ADMINISTRATION, www.fda.gov; *Occupational Safety and Health Administration (OSHA) Inspections*, OSHA, www.osha.gov; Rebecca S. Eisenberg, *The Role of the FDA in Innovation Policy*, 13 MICH. TELECOMM. & TECH. L. REV. 345 (2007).

26 *See, e.g.*, Nicholas R. Parrillo, *Federal Agency Guidance and the Power to Bind: An Empirical Study of Agencies and Industries*, 36 YALE J. ON REG. 165, 210 (2016). *See* 5 U.S.C. § 551 (8)-(10) (defining "license," "licensing," and "sanction"). *See also* 21 U.S.C. § 301; 21 C.F.R. § 10.1.

27 *See, e.g.*, Nick Oberheiden, *I Received a Federal Target Letter, Now What?*, THE NAT'L L. REV. (Nov. 23, 2022), https://natlawreview.com. *See also* Chapter 7 *infra* (discussing the penalties for violations of the Public Health Service Act).

28 FDA, *supra* note 22.

29 *Id.*

30 *Id.*

31 *See, e.g.*, 21 U.S.C. § 301; 21 C.F.R. § 10.1. *See* discussion *infra* in Chapters 4–8 *infra*.

32 *See, e.g.*, Marcy E. Gallo et al., Cong. Research Serv., R44824, ADVANCED GENE EDITING: CRISPR-CAS9, 17–18 (2018); Jordan Paradise, *U.S. Regulatory Challenges for Gene Editing*, 13 SCI.TECH. LAWYER 10, 12 (2016).

33 *The Promise of Human Embryonic Stem Cell Research*, H. before the Subcomm. on Labor, HHS, Education, and Related Agencies, 111th Cong., Sept. 16, 2010 at 25; National Institutes of Health Loan Repayment Programs (LRPs), USAGOV, www.govloans.gov.

34 U.S. Gov't Accountability Off., GAO-23-105396, FEDERAL RESEARCH AND DEVELOPMENT: FUNDING HAS GROWN SINCE 2012 AND IS CONCENTRATED WITHIN A FEW AGENCIES (2022), www.gao.gov.

35 *The Federal Budget in Fiscal Year 2023: An Infographic*, CONGRESSIONAL BUDGET OFFICE (Mar. 5, 2024) www.cbo.gov; Todd Kuiken, *U.S. Trends in Synthetic Biology Research Funding*, WILSON CENTER, www.wilsoncenter.org; Devon L. Suits, *CSA Discusses Impact of Technology at Military Invention Day*, U.S. ARMY, www.army.mil.

36 Dan Ready, Jorge Salazar, and Caitlin Verboon, *A Closer Look at Discretionary Spending, 2022*, CONGRESSIONAL BUDGET OFFICE (Mar. 2023), https://cbo.gov.

37 Mike Lauer, *FY 2022 by the Numbers: Extramural Grant Investments in Research*, NATIONAL INSTITUTES OF HEALTH (Mar. 1, 2023), https://nexus.od.nih.gov/.

38 *Id.*

39 *See* Nat'l Insts. of Health, GRANTS AND FUNDING, www.nih.gov/grants-funding; Hwang et al., *supra* note 20.
40 Gillian E. Metzger, *Taking Appropriations Seriously*, 121 COLUM. L. REV. 1075 (2021); I. Glenn Cohen & Eli Y. Adashi, *The FDA Is Prohibited from Going Germline*, 353 SCIENCE 545, 545 (Aug. 2016).
41 *See, e.g.*, Further Consolidated Appropriations Act 2024, P.L. 118-47, Mar. 23, 2024, 138 Stat 460, www.congress.gov. *See also The Hyde Amendment: An Overview*, CONGRESSIONAL RESEARCH SERVICE, https://crsreports.congress.gov/.
42 Marlene Fried, *Hyde Amendment: The Opening Wedge to Abolish Abortion*, NEW POLITICS 82, 84 (2007).
43 *The Mexico City Policy: An Explainer*, KFF (Jan. 28, 2021), www.kff.org.
44 *See, e.g.*, Sherley v. Sebelius, 689 F.3d 776, 779 (D.C. Cir. 2012) (citing Consolidated Appropriations Act, 2012, Pub. L. No. 112-74, § 508).
45 *See id.*
46 *But see* Ann Laquer Estin, *Sharing Governance: Family Law in Congress and the States*, 18 CORNELL J. L. & PUB. POL'Y. 267, 269–71 (2009) (challenging the "traditional view that family law belongs to the states").
47 *Id.*
48 25 U.S.C. § 1901.
49 *Id.*
50 28 U.S.C. § 1738A. Full faith and credit given to child custody determinations; Parental Kidnapping Prevention Act, H.R. 8406, 96th Cong. (1980) (enacted), 94 Stat. 3566 at 3568–3569.
51 *The Impact of Federal Policy on Global Competition in Stem Cell Research*, HARVARD STEM CELL RESEARCH, https://hsci.harvard.edu.
52 *History*, CAL. INST. FOR REGENERATIVE MED., www.cirm.ca.gov.
53 Kirstin R. W. Matthews & Daniel Morali, *Can We Do That Here? An Analysis of U.S. Federal and State Policies Guiding Human Embryo and Embryoid Research*, 9 J.L. & BIOSCIENCES 1, 9 (2022).
54 *Id.* at 10 (2022) (citing Andrew Karch, *Vertical Diffusion and the Policy-Making Process: The Politics of Embryonic Stem Cell Research*, 65 POLIT. RES. QUART. 48 (2010)).
55 David M. Studdert, Michelle M. Mello, and Troyen A. Brennan, *Medical Malpractice*, 350 THE NEW ENGLAND JOURNAL OF MEDICINE 283 (2004).
56 Mary Broughman, *How Long Does a Medical Malpractice Suit Take?*, BROWN & CROUPPEN, Feb. 28, 2022, www.brownandcrouppen.com.
57 *Id.*
58 Jacqueline Landess, *State Medical Boards, Licensure, and Discipline in the United States*, 17 J. LIFELONG LEARNING IN PSYCHIATRY 337 (2019); John Fauber & Matt Wynn, *7 Takeaways from Our Year-Long Investigation into the Country's Broken Medical License System*, USA TODAY, Nov. 30, 2018, www.usatoday.com; James M. DuBois et al., *Preventing Egregious Ethical Violations in Medical Practice:*

Evidence-Informed Recommendations from a Multidisciplinary Working Group, 104 J. of Med. Regul. 23, 23–24 (2018), https://doi.org/10.30770/2572-1852-104.4.23.

59 *See* Michelle M. Mello & Troyen A. Brennan, *Deterrence of Medical Errors: Theory and Evidence for Malpractice Reform*, 80 Tex. L. Rev. 1595, 1616, 1621 (2002).

60 OvaScience, Inc., Annual Report (Form 10-K), at 35 (Mar. 16, 2015).

61 Catherine M. Sharkey, *Drug Advertising Claims: Preemption's New Frontier*, 41 Loy. of L.A. L. Rev. 1625, 1651 (2008).

62 *See* Chapter 3 *infra*.

63 The Indian Child Welfare Act is a notable exception. *See, e.g.*, Miss. Band of Choctaw Indians v. Holyfield, 490 U.S. 30 (1989); Adoptive Couple v. Baby Girl, 570 U.S. 637 (2013); Haaland v. Brackeen, 599 U.S. 255 (2023).

64 *See* Troxel v. Granville, 530 U.S. 57 (2000); Obergefell v. Hodges, 576 U.S. 644 (2015). But see Dobbs v. Jackson Women's Health Organization, 597 U.S. 215 (2022) (Thomas, J. concurring).

65 Joseph S. Kass & Rachel V. Rose, *Medical Malpractice Reform: Historical Approaches, Alternative Models, and Communication and Resolution Programs*, 18 Amer. Med. Assoc. J. of Ethics 299 (2016).

66 *See, e.g.*, Virginia State Bar, *Preamble to the Rules of Professional Conduct, Part Six, Section II of the Rules of the Supreme Court of Virginia*, https://vsb.org.

67 Paul Berg, *Asilomar 1975: DNA Modification Secured*, 455 Nature 290 (2008).

68 Alexander Capron, *The Lessons of Asilomar for Today's Science*, N.Y. Times (May 28, 2015), www.nytimes.com.

69 Amer. Soc'y for Reprod. Med., *About Us—Mission Statement*, www.reproductivefacts.org; Soc'y for Assisted Reproductive Technology, *About Us*, www.sart.org.

70 Micah R. Onixt et al., *Institutional Review Board Liability for Adverse Outcomes*, AMA J. of Ethics (Apr. 2009), https://journalofethics.ama-assn.org.

71 *Self-Regulation: A False Promise for Public Health?*, European Public Health Alliance (Dec. 2016), https://epha.org.

72 Amer. Soc'y for Reprod. Med., *Guidance on the Limits to the Number of Embryos to Transfer: A Committee Opinion*, 116 Fertility and Sterility 651, 651–52 (2021) (recommending the number of embryos implanted based on the patient's characteristics); Adam Popescu, *The Octomom Has Proved Us All Wrong*, N.Y. Times (Dec. 15, 2018), www.nytimes.com.

73 *See The Regulation of Private Health Insurance*, KFF (last updated July 29, 2024), www.kff.org.

74 Sana Loue, *The New Wallet Biopsy and Involuntary Patient Transfers Abroad: How Physicians Can Help Protect Patients*, 50 The Hastings Center Report 19 (2020).

75 *What Is a Copay?*, Blue Cross Blue Shield Minnesota, www.bluecrossmn.com.

76 *IVF Access in Nations and Regions*, Stonewall (last accessed July 13, 2023), www.stonewall.org.uk/ivf-access-nations-and-regions.

77 Vanessa Grigoriadis, *I.V.F. Coverage Is the Benefit Everyone Wants*, N.Y. Times (Jan. 30, 2019), www.nytimes.com.

78 Nat'l Soc'y of Genetic Counselors, *Demystifying Insurance to Unlock Genetic Counseling and Genetic Testing Opportunities*, www.aboutgeneticcounselors.com.
79 *See* Naomi Cahn and June Carbone, *Uncoupling*, 53 ARIZ. ST. L.J. 1, 1, 18–23 (2021).
80 Burwell v. Hobby Lobby Stores, Inc., 573 U.S. 682, 697–98. *See generally id.*; Zubik v. Burwell, 578 U. S. 403 (2016); Little Sisters of the Poor, 591 U. S. 657 (2020); *Clinical Preventive Services for Women: Closing the Gaps*, INST. OF MED., 109–10 (2011), https://nap.nationalacademies.org; *Women's Preventive Services Guidelines*, HEALTH RES. & SERVS. ADMIN., www.hrsa.gov.
81 *See* Myrisha S. Lewis, *Reproductive Innovation and Reproductive Exceptionalism: How Private Health Insurance Coverage of Fertility Treatment Complements Hostile Governmental Action and Expands Access to Assisted Reproduction in the United States*, in HEALTH LAW AS PRIVATE LAW (I. Glenn Cohen, Wendy Netter Epstein, Christopher Robertson, Carmel Shachar, & Susannah Baruch eds.) (Cambridge University Press 2025). For more on how federal insurance law can preempt state health insurance mandates, especially in relation to reproduction, *see* Valarie Blake & Elizabeth McCuskey, *Privatized Abortion Benefits*, in HEALTH LAW AS PRIVATE LAW (I. Glenn Cohen, Wendy Netter Epstein, Christopher Robertson, Carmel Shachar, & Susannah Baruch eds.) (Cambridge University Press, 2025); Valarie Blake & Elizabeth McCuskey, *Employer-Sponsored Reproduction*, 124 COLUM. L. REV. 273 (2024).
82 *See* Lewis, *supra* note 81.
83 Michelle Obama, BECOMING, 188 (Crown, 2018).
84 *See* Lewis, *supra* note 81.
85 Olivia Rockwell, *A New Benefit Is Born to Help Companies Find and Keep Workers*, BLOOMBERG (Apr. 22, 2022), www.bloomberg.com/news/articles/2022. *See generally* Lewis, *supra* note 81.
86 *See Employers Enhanced Health Benefits in 2024, Adding Coverage for Weight-Loss Medications and IVF Despite Growing Health Costs, Mercer Survey Finds*, MERCER (Nov. 20, 2024), www.mercer.com.
87 Wendy Funk et al., *Military Health System Basics*, VETERANS AFFAIRS, www.hsrd.research.va.gov; *The Federal Employees Health Benefits (FEHB) Program*, U.S. OFF. OF PERS. MGMT., www.opm.gov/healthcare-insurance/healthcare/; *Health Coverage Options for American Indians and Alaska Natives*, U.S. CTR. FOR MEDICARE AND MEDICAID SERVICES 1, 2–3 (2024), www.cms.gov; *Basic Medical Benefits Package for Veterans*, USA.GOV, www.benefits.gov (last visited July 21, 2024).
88 *Congress Passes Bill to Help Wounded Veterans Start Families*, PR NEWSWIRE (Sept. 29, 2016, 10:52 AM), www.prnewswire.com; *Community Care: In Vitro Fertilization Treatment*, U.S. DEP'T OF VETERANS AFFAIRS (Dec. 21, 2022), www.va.gov/.
89 TRICARE, *Covered Services* (Apr. 4, 2024), www.tricare.mil; *see also* TRICARE, *Infertility Diagnosis and Treatment* (Mar. 7, 2024), https://tricare.mil/CoveredServices/IsItCovered/InfertilityTreatment.
90 Pallas A. Wahl, *In Vitro Fertilization/Assisted Reproductive Program Helped This Couple's Dream Come True*, U.S. DEP'T VETERANS AFF.: VANTAGE POINT (May 3,

2021, 6:00 PM), https://blogs.va.gov; *In Vitro Fertilization Treatment*, U.S. DEP'T VETERANS AFF. (Mar. 10, 2022), www.va.gov; *Infertility and IVF*, U.S. DEP'T VETERANS AFF. (May 25, 2022), www.womenshealth.va.gov; *Service-Connected Infertility Treatment*, U.S. DEP'T VETERANS AFF. (2018), www.va.gov.

91 *See generally* Lewis, *supra* note 81.

92 *Id.*

93 For more on the issues raised in this table, *see* Anshu Siripurapu & Noah Berman, *What Does the U.S. National Guard Do?*, COUNCIL ON FOREIGN RELATIONS, www.cfr.org/; *Our Forces*, U.S. DEP'T OF DEF., www.defense.gov; *Guide to Medical Regulation in the United States: Introduction*, FEDERATION OF STATE MEDICAL BOARDS, www.fsmb.org; 26 U.S.C. §§ 1–9834; Rebecca S. Eisenberg, *The Role of the FDA in Innovation Policy*, 13 MICH. TELECOMM. & TECH. L. REV. 345 (2007); *About Us*, U.S. PATENT AND TRADEMARK OFFICE, www.uspto.gov/; *Protecting & Strengthening Abortion Rights*, N.Y. STATE, www.ny.gov/; Jonathan Mattise, *District Attorneys Refuse to Prosecute Some GOP-Led Laws*, AP NEWS (Oct. 19, 2021, 10:40 AM), https://apnews.com; Oberheiden, *supra* note 27; *Guidance for Industry: Enforcement Policy Regarding Investigational New Drug Requirements for Use of Fecal Microbiota for Transplantation to Treat* Clostridium difficile *Infection Not Responsive to Standard Therapies*, U.S. FOOD AND DRUG ADMIN. (Nov. 2022), www.fda.gov; Bureau of Just. Stat., *Law Enforcement*, U.S. DEP'T OF JUST., https://bjs.ojp.gov; U.S. Dep't of Just., *Just. Manual* § 9-27.230 (2023); *What Is an Executive Order?*, AM. BAR. ASS'N., www.americanbar.org/; *Governors: Power and Authority*, NAT'L GOVERNORS ASS'N, www.nga.org; Carol S. Weissert et al., *Governors in Control: Executive Orders, State-Local Preemption, and the COVID-19 Pandemic*, 51 PUBLIUS 396 (2021); I. Glenn Cohen & Eli Y. Adashi, *The FDA Is Prohibited from Going Germline*, 353 SCIENCE 545, 545–46 (Aug. 2016); Consolidated Appropriations Act of 2016, Pub. L. No. 114-92, § 749, 129 Stat. 2242, 2283 (2015); California Institute for Regenerative Medicine, *Funding Opportunities*, www.cirm.ca.gov/; Cornell Law School, *Criminal Code—by State*, www.law.cornell.edu; Title 18 of U.S. Code. Comparatively, some countries have decided to ban certain actions such as assisted reproduction in general, illicit substances, and same-sex marriage. *See* Susan L. Crockin et al., *Costa Rica's Absolute Ban on In Vitro Fertilization Deemed a Human Rights Violation: Implications for U.S. Assisted Reproductive Technology Policy and "Personhood" Initiatives*, 100 FERTILITY & STERILITY 330 (2013); *Marriage Equality: Global Comparisons*, COUNCIL ON FOREIGN RELATIONS (updated Dec. 10, 2021), www.cfr.org; *A New Atlas of Fertility Treatment Policies in Europe Exposes Inconsistencies in Regulation and Funding*, ESHRE NEWS (Dec. 17, 2021), www.focusonreproduction.eu; Patrick Präg & Melinda C. Mills, *Assisted Reproductive Technology in Europe: Usage and Regulation in the Context of Cross-Border Reproductive Care*, in CHILDLESSNESS IN EUROPE: CONTEXTS, CAUSES, AND CONSEQUENCES (Micheala Kreyenfeld & Dirk Konietzka eds.) (Springer 2017), 289; Daphna Birenbaum-Carmeli, *Thirty-Five Years of Assisted Reproductive Technologies in Israel*, 2 REPROD. BIOMEDICINE

& Soc'y Online 16 (2016); Chokri Kooli, *Review of Assisted Reproduction Techniques, Laws, and Regulations in Muslim Countries*, 24 Middle East Fertility Soc'y J. 8 (2020); Rachel Savage, *Long Road to Motherhood: Lesbians Fight for IVF in Europe*, Reuters (Apr. 26, 2021), www.reuters.com. For a discussion of the intersection of state and federal law in the realm of health insurance coverage of fertility treatment, *see* Myrisha S. Lewis, *Reproductive Innovation and Reproductive Exceptionalism: How Private Health Insurance Coverage of Fertility Treatment Complements Hostile Governmental Action and Expands Access to Assisted Reproduction in the United States*, in Health Law as Private Law (I. Glenn Cohen, Wendy Netter Epstein, Christopher Robertson, Carmel Shachar, & Susannah Baruch eds.) (Cambridge University Press, 2025).

CHAPTER 2. THE DEVELOPMENT OF TRADITIONAL AND ADVANCED ASSISTED REPRODUCTIVE TECHNOLOGIES

1 Esme Mazzeo, *Kerry Washington Learned the Truth About Her Biological Father After She Told Her Parents She Wanted to Appear on "Finding Your Roots,"* Bus. Insider (Sept. 25, 2023, 4:53 PM), www.insider.com.

2 *See* I. Glenn Cohen et al., *Sperm Donor Anonymity and Compensation: An Experiment with American Sperm Donors*, 3 J. L. & Biosciences 468, 469 (2016); Kate Silver, *Sperm Donors May Not Be as Anonymous as They Think*, WebMD (Feb. 5, 2024), www.webmd.com.

3 *See State-Specific ART Surveillance*, U.S. Ctrs. for Disease Control & Prevention (Oct. 9, 2024), www.cdc.gov.

4 E. Chronopoulou et al., *Elective Oocyte Cryopreservation for Age-Related Fertility Decline*, 38 J. Assist. Reprod. & Genetics 1177, 1177–79 (2021).

5 Bat-Sheva L. Maslow et al., *Likelihood of Achieving a 50%, 60%, or 70% Estimated Live Birth Rate Threshold with 1 or 2 Cycles of Planned Oocyte Cryopreservation*, 37 J. Assisted Reprod. & Genetics 1637, 1641 (2020).

6 Gerard Letterie, *In re: The Disposition of Frozen Embryos: 2022*, 117 Fertility & Sterility 477, 479 (2022).

7 Gabriela Weigel et al., *Coverage and Use of Fertility Services in the U.S.*, KFF (Sept. 15, 2020), www.kff.org.

8 Isabel Goddard & Carolina Aragão, *A Growing Share of Americans Say They've Had Fertility Treatments or Know Someone Who Has*, Pew Rsch. Ctr. (Sept. 14, 2023), www.pewresearch.org/short-reads/2023/09/14/a-growing-share-of-americans-say-theyve-had-fertility-treatments-or-know-someone-who-has/.

9 Weigel et al., *supra* note 7.

10 *See ART Success Rates*, U.S. Ctrs. for Disease Control & Prevention (Jan. 8, 2024), www.cdc.gov; *see also Fact Sheet: In Vitro Fertilization (IVF) Use Across the United States*, U.S. Dep't of Health & Hum. Servs. (Mar. 13, 2024), www.hhs.gov.

11 Goddard & Aragão, *supra* note 8.

12 Myrisha S. Lewis, *Reproductive Innovation and Reproductive Exceptionalism: How Private Health Insurance Coverage of Fertility Treatment Complements Hostile*

Governmental Action and Expands Access to Assisted Reproduction in the United States, *in* HEALTH LAW AS PRIVATE LAW (I. Glenn Cohen et al. eds.) (Cambridge University Press 2025).

13 *ART Surveillance*, U.S. CTRS. FOR DISEASE CONTROL & PREVENTION (Dec. 10, 2024), https://www.cdc.gov/art/php/surveillance/index.html; *ART Success Rates*, *supra* note 10.

14 *See Assisted Reproductive Technology (ART)*, EUNICE KENNEDY SHRIVER NAT'L INSTITUTE OF CHILD HEALTH & DEV. (June 18, 2024), www.nichd.nih.gov; *Assisted Reproductive Technology (ART): Commonly Asked Questions*, U.S. CTRS FOR DISEASE CONTROL & PREVENTION, www.cdc.gov (Feb. 21, 2023); Uniform Parentage Act § 102 (2017) ("'Assisted reproduction' means a method of causing pregnancy other than sexual intercourse. The term includes: (A) intrauterine or intracervical insemination; (B) donation of gametes; (C) donation of embryos; (D) in-vitro fertilization and transfer of embryos; and (E) intracytoplasmic sperm injection").

15 *See* 42 U.S.C. § 263a-7 (1992) ("Assisted reproductive technology. The term 'assisted reproductive technology' means all treatments or procedures which include the handling of human oocytes or embryos, including in vitro fertilization, gamete intrafallopian transfer, zygote intrafallopian transfer, and such other specific technologies as the Secretary may include in this definition, after making public any proposed definition in such manner as to facilitate comment from any person (including any Federal or other public agency)").

16 Willem Ombelet & Johan Van Robays, *History of Human Artificial Insemination*, FACTS, VIEWS & VISION IN OBGYN 1, 1, 5 (2010).

17 *See, e.g.*, Steve Almasy, *Mother Loses Appeal in Turkey Baster Pregnancy Case*, CNN (Apr. 22, 2015, 2:22 AM), www.cnn.com/2015/04/21/us/turkey-baster-pregnancy-legal-ruling/index.html.

18 Elizabeth Yuko, *The First Artificial Insemination Was an Ethical Nightmare*, THE ATLANTIC (Jan. 8, 2016), www.theatlantic.com; *Antonie van Leewenhoek*, BBC, www.bbc.co.uk/ (last visited July 11, 2024).

19 Meghana Keshavan, *"There's No Such Thing as Anonymity": With Consumer DNA Tests, Sperm Banks Reconsider Long-Held Promises to Donors*, STAT NEWS (Sept. 11, 2019), www.statnews.com.

20 Alex C. Varghese et al., *Human Sperm Cryopreservation*, in Kamini A. Rao et al., ANDROLOGY LABORATORY MANUAL 196 (Jaypee Brothers Medical Publishers 2010).

21 Rachel Arocho et al., *Estimates of Donated Sperm Use in the United States: National Survey of Family Growth 1995–2017*, 112 FERTILITY & STERILITY 718, 718 (2019).

22 *What Is IUI?*, PLANNED PARENTHOOD, www.plannedparenthood.org/learn/pregnancy/fertility-treatments/what-iui; Kristen V. Brown, *DIY Artificial Insemination Kit for $129 Just Got Cleared by the FDA*, BLOOMBERG, www.bloomberg.com.

23 Charles P. Kindregan, Jr. & Maureen McBrien, *Assisted Reproductive Technology: A Lawyer's Guide to Emerging Law and Science* 91 (American Bar Association 2011).

24 *See, e.g.*, D.C. Code § 16-401 (1993) ("'Gestational surrogate' means an individual who is not the intended parent, who has not provided the egg used to form any embryo that is transferred to the gestational surrogate's uterus, and who agrees to become pregnant, gestate, and deliver, through collaborative reproduction, the intended parent's child on behalf of the intended parent").

25 *See* Susan L. Crockin & Howard W. Jones Jr., *Legal Conceptions: The Evolving Law and Policy of Assisted Reproductive Technologies* 1 (Hopkins Press 2010).

26 Walter Sullivan, *"Test-Tube" Baby Born in U.S., Joining Successes Around the World*, N.Y. Times (Dec. 29, 1981), www.nytimes.com; *This Day in History: July 25, 1975*, Hist., www.history.com; Aina Hunter, *U.S. First Test Tube Baby Elizabeth Carr Gives Birth, Tells Her Story*, CBS News (Aug. 9, 2010, 10:14 AM), www.cbsnews.com.

27 *Prize Announcement*, The Nobel Prize, www.nobelprize.org; Susan J. Fisher & Linda C. Giudice, *Robert Edwards (1925–2013)*, 340 Sci., 825, 825 (2013).

28 *IVF Pioneer Patrick Steptoe Gets Blue Plaque*, BBC (May 4, 2019), www.bbc.com; Iliana Magra, *Three Created a Fertility Revolution with I.V.F., but One, a Woman, Went Unrecognized*, N.Y. Times (June 20, 2019), www.nytimes.com.

29 *IVF Pioneer, supra* note 28.

30 *See The Warnock Committee*, 289 Brit. Med. J. 238, 238 (1984).

31 *See* Dep't of Health & Soc. Sec., *Report of the Committee of Inquiry into Human Fertilisation and Embryology* (1984), in Hum. Fertilisation & Embryology Auth. i (June 24, 2008), www.hfea.gov.uk.

32 *See id.* at 80–86; *The Warnock Committee, supra* note 30, at 238–39.

33 *See Warnock Committee, supra* note 30, at 238–39.

34 *State of the Fertility Sector 2023/24*, Hum. Fertilisation & Embryology Auth. (Oct. 1, 2024), www.hfea.gov.uk.

35 NHS England, www.england.nhs.uk/; Nat'l Servs. Scotland, www.nss.nhs.scot/; NHS Wales, www.nhs.wales/; *Health and Social Care in Northern Ireland (HSC)*, N. Health & Soc. Care Tr., www.northerntrust.hscni.net.

36 *Eligibility for HSC Funded IVF and Related Treatments Effective from 1st June 2019*, Belfast Health & Soc. Care Tr. (Jan. 13, 2020), https://belfasttrust.hscni.net.

37 *Publicly Funded Treatment*, Belfast Health & Soc. Care Tr., https://belfasttrust.hscni.net/services/rfc/first-steps/nhs-funded-treatment.

38 *See, e.g., Eligibility for HSC Funded IVF, supra* note 36; *IVF Availability*, NHS (Oct. 18, 2021), www.nhs.uk/conditions/ivf/availability/.

39 *IVF*, NHS 111 Wales (May 26, 2023, 9:00 AM), https://111.wales.nhs.uk/ivf/.

40 *See Fertility Clinic Search*, Human Fertilisation & Embryology Auth., www.hfea.gov.uk.

41 Rosie Taylor, *Long NHS Waiting Lists Cutting Chances of Pregnancy, Fertility Chief Warns*, The Guardian (Jan. 22, 2023, 2:00 AM), www.theguardian.com; *IVF Waiting Times in Scotland: Quarter Ending 31 March 2023*, Pub. Health Scotland (May 30, 2023), https://publichealthscotland.scot.

42 M. Chetty, *Access Criteria for NHS IVF Treatment in Scotland*, NHS Lothian 1 (Jan. 3, 2022), https://services.nhslothian.scot.

43 *IVF Availability*, *supra* note 38.
44 *Id.*
45 *NHS Funding*, FERTILITYNETWORKUK, https://fertilitynetworkuk.org.
46 Ian Sample, *England Lagging Behind Rest of UK in IVF Cycles Funded by the NHS*, THE GUARDIAN (May 9, 2019, 1:00 PM), www.theguardian.com.
47 *State of the Fertility Sector*, *supra* note 34.
48 *See generally Reality Check: Does UK Spend Half as Much on Health as US?*, BBC (Feb. 6, 2018), www.bbc.com.
49 Joe Holley, *Georgeanna Jones Dies at 92: In Vitro Fertilization Pioneer*, WASH. POST (Mar. 28, 2005), www.washingtonpost.com.
50 *Id.*
51 *Id.*
52 Crockin & Jones Jr., *supra* note 25, at 1, 3–6 (discussing certificate-of-need proceedings).
53 *Reproductive Endocrinology and Infertility Fellowship*, EASTERN VIRGINIA MEDICAL SCHOOL, www.evms.edu.
54 *ART Success Rates*, *supra* note 10.
55 *Fact Sheet*, *supra* note 10.
56 *New Fertility Procedures May Make It Possible for Older Women to Give Birth to Their Biological Children*, NBC NIGHTLY NEWS (Oct. 17, 1997, 10:40 AM), NBC News Transcripts; Lucy van de Wiel, FREEZING FERTILITY: OOCYTE CRYOPRESERVATION AND THE GENDER POLITICS OF AGING, eds. Monica J. Casper and Lisa Jean Moore, (New York University Press 2020) 5–7.
57 *New Fertility Procedures*, *supra* note 56.
58 *New Fertility Procedures*, *supra* note 56.
59 R. Alta Charo, *Back to the Future in Alabama*, 390 NEW ENG. J. MED. 1253 (Mar. 6, 2024).
60 Ethics Comm. of the Am. Soc'y for Reprod. Med., *Planned Oocyte Cryopreservation to Preserve Future Reproductive Potential: An Ethics Committee Opinion*, 121 FERTILITY & STERILITY 604, 606 (2024).
61 Lewis, *supra* note 12.
62 Prac. Comm. of the Am. Soc'y for Reprod. Med., *Guidance on the Limits to the Number of Embryos to Transfer: A Committee Opinion*, 116 FERTILITY & STERILITY 651, 651 (2021).
63 Letterie, *supra* note 6 at 479.
64 *See generally* Lewis, *supra* note 12.
65 *See* Mark G. Larman et al., *Cryopreservation in ART and Concerns with Contamination During Cryobanking*, 13 REPROD. MED. & BIOLOGY 107, 107–8 (2014); *Freezing Embryos*, JOHNS HOPKINS MED., www.hopkinsmedicine.org.
66 Harriet Taylor, *Egg Freezing Has Become the Go-To for Delayed Parenthood—and Companies Are Popping Up to Provide More Cost-Effective Solutions*, CNBC (May 9, 2019), www.cnbc.com.
67 *IVF by the Numbers*, PENN MED. (Mar. 14, 2018), www.pennmedicine.org.

68 *Id.*
69 *Id.*
70 *Id.* (dropping to 5.7 percent for women 41–42 years old, and to 2.3 percent for women 43–44 years old).
71 *See generally* Liat Lerner-Geva et al., *The Possible Association between* in Vitro *Fertilization Treatments and Cancer Development*, 13 INT'L J. GYNECOLOGICAL CANCER 23 (2003); Lindsay Kroener et al., *Use of Fertility Medications and Cancer Risk: A Review and Update*, 29 CURRENT OP. IN OBSTETRICS & GYNECOLOGY 195 (2017).
72 Pam Belluck, *What Fertility Patients Should Know About Egg Freezing*, N.Y. TIMES (Mar. 13, 2018), www.nytimes.com.
73 Elkin V. Lemos et al., *Healthcare Expenses Associated with Multiple vs Singleton Pregnancies in the United States*, 209 AM. J. OBSTETRICS & GYNECOLOGY 586.e1, 586.e4 (2013); Elsevier, *Multiple Birth Pregnancies Can Cost 20 Times More than Singletons*, SCIENCEDAILY (Nov. 11, 2013), www.sciencedaily.com.
74 *See, e.g.*, *ART and Multiple Births*, U.S. CTRS. FOR DISEASE CONTROL & PREVENTION (Apr. 1, 2016), www.cdc.gov.
75 *Guidance on the Limits*, *supra* note 62; Jane E. Brody, *Some I.V.F. Experts Discourage Multiple Births*, N.Y. TIMES (Oct. 10, 2016), www.nytimes.com.
76 Bob Kronemyer, *Impact of State Mandatory IVF Insurance Coverage*, CONTEMP. OB/GYN J. (Dec. 6, 2022), www.contemporaryobgyn.net.
77 Robert H. Shmerling, *First, Do No Harm*, HARVARD HEALTH BLOG, www.health.harvard.edu.
78 Keith Alan Byers, *Infertility and In Vitro Fertilization: A Growing Need for Consumer-Oriented Regulation of the In Vitro Fertilization Industry*, 18 J. LEGAL MED., 265, 273–74 (1997).
79 *Prize Announcement*, *supra* note 27.
80 *Id.*
81 *Id.*
82 *Id. See generally* Martin H. Johnson et al., *Why the Medical Research Council Refused Robert Edwards and Patrick Steptoe Support for Research on Human Conception in 1971*, 25 HUM. REPROD. 2157, 2157 (2010).
83 *Prize Announcement*, *supra* note 27.
84 Myrisha S. Lewis, *Is Germline Gene Editing Exceptional?*, 51 SETON HALL L. REV. 735, 735 (2021).
85 *Mitochondrial Replacement Techniques: Ethical, Social, and Policy Considerations*, NAT'L ACADS. OF SCI., ENG'G, & MED., 90–91 (2016).
86 Mary Warnock, *Moral Thinking and Government Policy: The Warnock Committee on Human Embryology*, 63 MILBANK MEM'L FUND Q. HEALTH & SOC'Y, 504, 506 (1985).
87 *See, e.g.*, Filipa Carvalho et al., *ESHRE PGT Consortium Good Practice Recommendations for the Organisation of PGT*, HUM. REPROD. OPEN, 1, 2 (2020). ("The previous terms of preimplantation genetic diagnosis (PGD) and preimplantation genetic screening (PGS) have been replaced by the term preimplantation

genetic testing (PGT), following a revision of terminology used in infertility care.")

88 *See also* Joris Robert Vermeesch et al., *Prenatal and Pre-Implantation Genetic Diagnosis*, 17 NATURE REVS. GENETICS 643, 648–49 (2016); *PGT Q&A*, CTR. FOR ADVANCED REPROD. SERVS. (2025), www.uconnfertility.com; Shoukhrat Mitalipov et al., *Limitations of Preimplantation Genetic Diagnosis for Mitochondrial DNA Diseases*, 7 CELL REP. 935, 935–37 (2014); Sozos J. Fasouliotis & Joseph G. Schenker, *Preimplantation Genetic Diagnosis Principles and Ethics*, 13 HUM. REPROD. 2238, 2239 (1998).

89 *See, e.g.*, Jeff McMahan & Julian Savulescu, *Reasons and Reproduction: Gene Editing and Genetic Selection*, AM. J. BIOETHICS, 1, 3–4 (2023).

90 *Consumer Protection Issues Involving In Vitro Fertilization Clinics,* Hearing Before the Subcommittee on Regulation and Business Opportunities of the Committee on Small Business, House of Representatives, 100th Cong. 17 (1988). *See* U.S. Congress, Office of Technology Assessment, INFERTILITY: MEDICAL AND SOCIAL CHOICES, OTA-BA-358 (US Government Printing Office, May 1988), https://ota.fas.org/reports/8822.pdf.

91 The Ethics Comm. of the Am. Soc'y for Reprod. Med., *Disparities in Access to Effective Treatment for Infertility in the United States: An Ethics Committee Opinion*, 116 FERTILITY & STERILITY 54, 56 (2021).

92 Warnock, *supra* note 86.

93 *See supra* note 3–8 (and accompanying text).

94 McMahan & Savulesu, *supra* note 89, at 1, 5.

95 George Q. Daley et al., *After the Storm—A Responsible Path for Genome Editing*, 380 N. ENG. J. MED. 897, 899 (2019).

96 Ronald T. K. Pang & P. C. Ho, *Designer Babies*, 26 OBSTETRICS, GYNAECOLOGY & REPROD. MED. 59, 59 (2016); *see also* Jay Bennett, *Genetic Engineering Now Allows Parents to Select the Gender and Eye Color of Their Children*, POPULAR MECHS. (Feb. 5, 2016), www.popularmechanics.com.

97 *Cytoplasm*, NAT'L HUM. GENOME RSCH. INSTITUTE (July 11, 2024), www.genome.gov/genetics-glossary/Cytoplasm.

98 *Nucleus*, NAT'L HUM. GENOME RSCH. INSTITUTE (July 11, 2024), www.genome.gov/genetics-glossary/Nucleus; Nuffield Council on Bioethics, NOVEL TECHNIQUES FOR THE PREVENTION OF MITOCHONDRIAL DNA DISORDERS: AN ETHICAL REVIEW 18 (2012), www.nuffieldbioethics.org.

99 *Cytoplasm*, *supra* note 97.

100 *Mitochondria Is the Powerhouse of the Cell*, KNOW YOUR MEME (2021), https://knowyourmeme.com.

101 Nuffield Council on Bioethics, *supra* note 98 at 18–19; *see generally* Nuo Sun et al., *The Mitochondrial Basis of Aging*, 61 MOLECULAR CELL 654 (2016).

102 *Mitochondrial Replacement Techniques*, *supra* note 85 at 20–23 (2016).

103 *Baby Emma Conceived in Laboratory Through Cytoplasmic Transfer*, CBS EVENING NEWS (July 17, 1997), CBS Evening News Transcripts.

104 *See id.*
105 Carol Ann Campbell, *N.J. Doctors Pioneer a Fertility Procedure*, The Record (July 18, 1997).
106 *See Baby Emma Conceived*, *supra* note 103; Kathleen Kerr, *Baby Born from Mom's Repaired Egg*, Newsday (July 19, 1997).
107 *Dr. Richard Scott, Saint Barnabas Medical Center, & Pamela Madson, Resolve, Discuss the New Procedure of Cytoplasmic Transfer and The Hope It Gives to Infertile Couples*, CBS This Morning (July 18, 1997).
108 *See Baby Emma Conceived*, *supra* note 103; Jacques Cohen et al., *Birth of Infant After Transfer of Anucleate Donor Oocyte Cytoplasm into Recipient Eggs*, 350 Lancet 186 (July 19, 1997).
109 *See Baby Emma Conceived*, *supra* note 103.
110 *Dr. Richard Scott, Saint Barnabas Medical Center, & Pamela Madson, Resolve, Discuss the New Procedure of Cytoplasmic Transfer and The Hope It Gives to Infertile Couples*, *supra* note 107.
111 Marie Joyce, *Technique by Researchers May Help Infertile Women; Injection May Give Defective Cell a Boost*, Virginian-Pilot (July 18, 1997).
112 *Id.*
113 Lois Rogers, *Fertility Doctors Create Babies with Two Mothers*, Sunday Times (London) (May 16, 1999).
114 Transcript of Center for Biologics Evaluation and Research, Food and Drug Administration, Biological Response Modifiers Advisory Committee Open Session Meeting #32, 46 (May 9, 2002, 8:00 AM), www.fda.gov [https://wayback.archive.org].
115 Charlotte Pritchard, *The Girl with Three Biological Parents*, BBC (Sept. 1, 2014), www.bbc.com.
116 *See* discussion *infra* Chapter 7.
117 *See* Emily Mullin, *Patient Advocates and Scientists Launch Push to Lift Ban on "Three-Parent IVF*," Stat News (Apr. 16, 2019), www.statnews.com.
118 *Id.*
119 Jill Neimark, *A Baby with 3 Genetic Parents Seems Healthy, but Questions Remain*, NPR (Apr. 8, 2017, 5:00 AM), www.npr.org.
120 John Zhang et al., *Live Birth Derived from Oocyte Spindle Transfer to Prevent Mitochondrial Disease*, 34 Reprod. Biomedicine Online 361, 362 (2017), www.rbmojournal.com.
121 *See id.* at 363.
122 *Id.*
123 *Id.* at 364.
124 Jessica Hamzelou, *Exclusive: World's First Baby Born with New "3 Parent" Technique*, New Scientist (Sept. 27, 2016), www.newscientist.com/article/2107219-exclusive-worlds-first-baby-born-with-new-3-parent-technique/.
125 *See* Zhang et al., *supra* note 120, at 365.
126 *Id.*

127 *Id.*
128 *Id.* at 363.
129 *Id.* at 367.
130 *Id.*
131 *Id.*
132 *Id.*
133 *Form S-1 Registration Statement Under the Securities Act of 1933*, SEC (Aug. 28, 2012), www.sec.gov/Archives/edgar/data/1544227/000104746912008575/a2210793zs-1.htm.
134 *Id.* at 10.
135 *Id.* at 9 ("The United States does not have a fertility regulatory body separate and apart from the FDA. In September 2013, we received an 'untitled' letter from the FDA advising us to file an IND application for the AUGMENT treatment. Following the receipt of the FDA letter, we chose to suspend the availability of the AUGMENT treatment in the United States"); *see also* Karen Weintraub, *Turmoil at Troubled Fertility Company OvaScience*, MIT Techn. Rev. (Dec. 29, 2016), www.technologyreview.com.
136 *See* Alice Park, *Exclusive: Meet the World's First Baby Born with an Assist from Stem Cells*, Time (May 7, 2015, 5:00 AM), https://time.com.
137 *OvaScience Reports First Quarter 2018 Financial Results and Provides Business Update*, BioSpace (May 3, 2018), www.biospace.com.
138 *See* Katarina Lee, *An Ethical and Legal Analysis of OvaScience—a Publicly Traded Fertility Company and Its Lead Product AUGMENT*, 44 Am. J. L., Med. & Ethics 508, 511, 526–27 (2018).
139 *OvaScience and Millendo Therapeutics Announce Merger to Create Leading Rare Endocrine Disease Company*, BusinessWire (Aug. 9, 2018, 7:00 AM), www.businesswire.com.
140 *Tempest Closes Merger with Millendo and Completes PIPE Financing*, Tempest Therapeutics (June 28, 2021), https://ir.tempesttx.com.
141 *See* Dahhan v. OvaScience, Inc., F. Supp. 3d, 247, 247 (D. Mass. 2018); *SEC Charges Former Biotechnology Company CEO for Misleading Investors*, SEC (June 20, 2020), www.sec.gov; *see also* Order Instituting Cease-and-Desist Proceedings, SEC (2020), www.sec.gov; *OvaScience Securities Litigation*, Gilardi & Co. LLC, www.ovasciencesecuritieslitigation.com; Ivan Moreno, *OvaScience, VC Fund Settle Investor Class Action for $15M*, Law360 (Mar. 7, 2022, 5:30 PM), www.law360.com; Complaint at 2, Ratner v. OvaScience, No. 13-cv-12286 (D. Mass. Sept. 16, 2013).
142 James Gallagher, *Baby Born from Three People's DNA in UK First*, BBC News (May 9, 2023), www.bbc.com.
143 The UK's experience in the legalization of mitochondrial transfer impacted the Australian experience. *See generally* Myrisha S. Lewis, *Segmented Innovation in the Legalization of Mitochondrial Transfer: Lessons from Australia and the United Kingdom*, 22 Hous. J. Health L. & Pol'y 227 (2022).

144 Ian Sample, *First UK Baby with DNA from Three People Born After New IVF Procedure*, The Guardian (May 9, 2023), www.theguardian.com.

145 *Id.*

146 *Id.*

147 Paolo Rinaudo & Christos Coutifaris, *Meiotic Spindle Transfer for Infertility: Where Should We Go Next?*, 119 Fertility & Sterility 974, 974 (2023); Institute of Life, *Sixth Baby Born Using the Maternal Spindle Transfer Method, Developed by the Institute of Life—IASO and Embryotools Scientific Team in Greece*, PR Newswire (June 8, 2021, 11:41 AM), www.prnewswire.com.

148 *See* Mullin, *supra* note 117.

149 *MST Research*, Institute of Life, www.iolife.eu; *You*, Institute of Life, www.iolife.eu.

150 Susan Scutti, *Controversial IVF Technique Produces a Baby Girl—and for Some, That's a Problem*, CNN (Jan. 18, 2017, 4:08 PM), www.cnn.com; Rob Stein, *Clinic Claims Success in Making Babies with 3 Parents' DNA*, NPR (June 6, 2018, 5:11 AM), www.npr.org; Dorothy Walas, *3 Parent Baby—Groundbreaking Pronucleus Transfer—Interview with Nadiya Clinic*, EggDonationFriends, www.eggdonationfriends.com ("confirm[ing] that 7 babies have already been born thanks to nuclear transfer in Nadiya Clinic").

151 For an overview of the ethical issues accompanying mitochondrial transfer, *see Mitochondrial Replacement Techniques*, *supra* note 85.

152 *Mitochondrial Replacement Techniques*, *supra* note 85 at 79–80.

153 *See* Jaime King, *Predicting Probability: Regulating the Future of Preimplantation Genetic Screening*, 8 Yale J. Health Pol'y & Ethics 283, 288 at n.20 (2008).

CHAPTER 3. THE EVOLVING LAW OF ASSISTED REPRODUCTION

1 *Celebrity IVF Clinic to Be Sued over "Lost" Embryos . . . Kim K, Paris, Chrissy All Former Patients!!!*, TMZ (Sept. 13, 2024, 12:30 PM), www.tmz.com.

2 LePage v. Ctr. for Reprod. Med., P.C., No. SC-2022-0515, 2024 WL 656591(Ala., Feb. 16, 2024).

3 *See also* Nick Loeb, *Sofía Vergara's Ex-Fiancé: Our Frozen Embryos Have a Right to Live*, N.Y. Times (Apr. 29, 2015), www.nytimes.com.

4 Ally Mauch, *Sofia Vergara Wins Court Battle: Judge Rules That Ex Nick Loeb Can't Use Embryos Without Consent*, People (Mar. 3, 2021, 1:59 PM), https://people.com; Loeb v. Vergara, 313 So. 346, 387–91, 395 (La. Ct. App. 2021).

5 Jenny Johnston, *"They're Not Frozen Embryos, They're My Daughters Emma and Isabella!": When Sofia Vergara Was with Her Millionaire Ex-Fiancé, They Tried to Start an IVF Family. Years After They Split—Despite Her Vehement Objection—He Wants Them to Be Born*, DailyMail (Feb. 23, 2024, 3:05 PM), www.dailymail.co.uk; *see also* Loeb, *supra* note 3.

6 *See* Clare Huntington, *Postmarital Family Law: A Legal Structure for Nonmarital Families*, 67 Stan. L. Rev. 167, 171 (2015).

7 *Id.* at 178 ("Most states have some version of the marital presumption, which provides that any child born to the wife of a married man is presumed to be the child of the husband as well as the wife; thus, the father does not need to take an additional step to establish parental rights over his child").

8 June Carbone & Naomi Cahn, *Which Ties Bind? Redefining the Parent-Child Relationship in an Age of Genetic Certainty*, 11 WM. & MARY BILL RTS. J. 1011, 1018 (2003) (discussing the stigma related to nonmarital sex). *See generally* Solangel Maldonado, *Illegitimate Harm: Law, Stigma, and Discrimination Against Nonmarital Children*, 63 FLA. L. REV. 345 (2011) (discussing historical and modern stigma and discrimination that accompany children born to unmarried parents).

9 *See* Huntington, *supra* note 6, at 170.

10 *See* Dara E. Purvis, *The Origin of Parental Rights: Labor, Intent, and Fathers*, 41 FLA. STATE U. L. REV. 645, 646 (2014) (citing James G. Dwyer, *A Taxonomy of Children's Existing Rights in State Decision Making About Their Relationships*, 11 WM. & MARY BILL RTS. J. 845, 859–60, 865–81 (2003)).

11 Erica Pandey, *America the Single*, AXIOS (Feb. 25, 2023), www.axios.com; Richard Fry, *A Record-High Share of 40-Year-Olds in the U.S. Have Never Been Married*, PEW RSCH. CTR. (June 28, 2023), www.pewresearch.org.

12 *See, e.g.*, Purvis, *supra* note 10 at 664–65. *See generally* Douglas NeJaime, *Who Is a Parent?*, 43 FAM. ADVOC. 6 (2021).

13 *See* Purvis, *supra* note 10 at 694–95; *The Rights of Presumed (Putative) Fathers: Summary of State Laws*, CHILD WELFARE INFO. GATEWAY 2–3 (2007), https://irp-cdn.multiscreensite.com/fde8edc8/files/uploaded/putativeall.pdf.

14 *See, e.g.*, Clark v. Jeter, 486 U.S. 456, 456–57 (1988).

15 Jamie D. Pedersen, *The New Uniform Parentage Act of 2017*, AM. BAR ASS'N (Apr. 1, 2018), www.americanbar.org.

16 *See, e.g.*, National Conference of Commissioners on Uniform State Laws, *Uniform Parentage Act (2017)*, UNIFORM LAW COMMISSION (Jan. 25, 2024), www.uniformlaws.org.

17 *Id.*

18 *Id. See also Parentage Act*, UNIFORM LAW COMMISSION (last accessed June 8, 2025), https://www.uniformlaws.org.

19 *See generally* Courtney G. Joslin & Douglas NeJaime, *How Parenthood Functions*, 123 COLUM. L. REV. 319 (2023).

20 Elizabeth Yuko, *The First Artificial Insemination Was an Ethical Nightmare*, THE ATLANTIC (Jan. 8, 2016), www.theatlantic.com.

21 *Id.*

22 A. D. Hard, *Artificial Impregnation*, 27 MED. WORLD 163, 163 (1909).

23 *Id.*

24 *Id.*

25 *Id.*

26 Yuko, *supra* note 20 (citing to Hard, *supra* note 22 at 163).

27 Hard, *supra* note 22 at 163.
28 *Id.*
29 *See* Aaron D. Twerski, *Domestic Relations: The Present Law on Artificial Insemination*, 47 MARQ. L. REV. 585, 586–88 (1964) (comparing Illinois and New York state divorce cases with different views on whether artificial insemination constituted adultery); Dan M. Cain, *Artificial Insemination: A New Scientific Achievement Gives Rise to a Need for New Legislation in Texas*, 23 SW. L.J. 575, 576–77 (1969) (discussing early cases related to artificial insemination, including two Illinois cases defining artificial insemination as adultery).
30 *See, e.g.*, Judith Areen et al., FAMILY LAW: CASES AND MATERIALS, 717 n.1 (7th ed., West Academic 2019).
31 *See, e.g.*, *In re* K.M.H., 169 P.3d 1025, 1034 (Kan. 2007).
32 *Id.* at 1033.
33 *In re* K.M.H., *supra* note 31 at 1038; Naomi Cahn, *Do Tell! The Rights of Donor-Conceived Offspring*, 42 HOFSTRA L. REV. 1077, 1107–8 (2014); Naomi Cahn, *The Uncertain Legal Basis for the New Kinship*, 36 J. FAM. ISSUES 501, 505 (2014).
34 Steve Almasy, *Mother Loses Appeal in Turkey Baster Pregnancy Case*, CNN (Apr. 22, 2015, 2:22 AM), www.cnn.com.
35 *Id.*
36 *See* Carbone & Cahn, *supra* note 8 at 1020 ("Modern family law proceeds from the dismantling of the system designed to ensure that children would be raised by their genetic parents").
37 *Consumer Protection Issues Involving In Vitro Fertilization Clinics*, Hearing Before the Subcommittee on Regulation, Business Opportunities, and Energy of the Committee on Small Business, House of Representatives, 101st Cong. 1 (1989); *id.* at 169 (providing the testimony of William Macleod, Director of Consumer Protection, Federal Trade Commission, citing to the Office of Technology Assessment for the $1 billion figure).
38 *The Fertility Market Overview*, HARRIS WILLIAMS 1 (2023), www.harriswilliams.com; Cyrus Abbassi, *The State of the Fertility Industry*, HEALTH CARE L. BRIEF (Aug. 18, 2021), www.healthcarelawbrief.com/2021/08/the-state-of-the-fertility-industry/.
39 21 C.F.R. § 1271.85 (2004).
40 *See* Dov Fox, *Racial Classification in Assisted Reproduction*, 118 YALE L.J. 1844, 1846 (2009); Sonia F. Epstein & Polina N. Whitehouse, *Inheriting the Ivy League: The Market for Educated Egg and Sperm Donors*, HARV. CRIMSON (Apr. 30, 2020), www.thecrimson.com.
41 Tamar Lewin, *10 Things to Know About Being a Sperm Donor*, N.Y. TIMES (Nov. 3, 2016), www.nytimes.com; Luke Winkie, *Odd Job: Can a Man Earn a Living on Sperm Donation Alone? This Guy Did*, Vox (May 21, 2019, 2:30 PM), www.vox.com. *See generally* Hailey Eber, *This L.A. Sperm Bank Is More Exclusive than an Ivy League College*, LOS ANGELES MAG. (Apr. 2, 2019), https://lamag.com.
42 Epstein & Whitehouse, *supra* note 40; Kimberly D. Krawiec, *Sunny Samaritans and Egomaniacs: Price-Fixing in the Gamete Market*, 72 L. & CONTEMP. PROBS. 59,

66, 66 n.31 (2009); see also Diane Tober, *Compensating Egg Donors: United States vs. Spain*, IMPACT ETHICS (Feb. 4, 2019), https://impactethics.ca.

43 Tober, *supra* note 42.

44 Caitlin Tilley, *Maryland Couple Reveal How They Found Strangers on Facebook to Be Their Surrogates After Spate of Failed Pregnancies*, DAILY MAIL (Mar. 10, 2024), www.dailymail.co.uk; Rachel P. Kovner, *Egg-Seeking Ad Draws Nearly 30 Harvard Applicants*, HARV. CRIMSON (July 2, 1999), www.thecrimson.com; Paris Martineau, *Inside the Quietly Lucrative Business of Donating Human Eggs*, WIRED (Apr. 23, 2019, 7:00 AM), www.wired.com; Sonia F. Epstein & Polina N. Whitehouse, *Inheriting the Ivy League: The Market for Educated Egg and Sperm Donors*, THE HARVARD CRIMSON (April 30, 2020), https://www.thecrimson.com/article/2020/4/30/inheriting-the-ivy-league/.

45 Kimberly D. Krawiec, *Markets, Morals, and Limits in the Exchange of Human Eggs*, 13 GEO. J.L. & PUB. POL'Y 349, 354 n.22 (2015).

46 Hillary L. Berk, *Savvy Surrogates and Rock Star Parents: Compensation Provisions, Contracting Practices, and the Value of Womb Work*, 45 L. & SOC. INQUIRY 398, 409–11 (2020).

47 *See, e.g.*, Alexander M. Capron & Margaret Jane Radin, *Choosing Family Law over Contract Law as a Paradigm for Surrogate Motherhood*, 16 L. MED. & HEALTH CARE 34, 37 (1988).

48 *See, e.g.*, Johnson v. Superior Ct., 95 Cal. Rptr. 2d 864, 867 (Cal. App. Dep't Super. Ct. 2000); Norman v. Xytex Corp., 848 S.E.2d 835, 837–38 (Ga. 2020).

49 *The Donor Reserve Program*, CAL. CRYOBANK: BY COOPERSURGICAL, www.cryobank.com; *Pricing*, CAL. CRYOBANK: BY COOPERSURGICAL, www.cryobank.com/pricing.

50 *The Donor Reserve Program*, *id.*; *Pricing*, *id.*

51 Nellie Bowles, *The Sperm Kings Have a Problem: Too Much Demand*, N.Y. TIMES (June 25, 2023), www.nytimes.com.

52 *FDA Cracks Down on Fremont Man's Sperm Donations*, CBS NEWS (Dec. 7, 2011, 12:22 AM), www.cbsnews.com.

53 Anya Kamenetz, *Why Would Anyone Look for a Sperm Donor on Facebook?*, CUT (May 14, 2024), www.thecut.com.

54 Whitney Danhauer, *90 Day Fiance's Kyle Gordy Is a Sperm Donor: Details About the Reality Star's Unusual Hobby*, INTOUCH WKLY. (Apr. 23, 2024, 1:48 PM), www.intouchweekly.com.

55 Naomi Cahn & Sonia Suter, *Generations Later, the Rights of Donor-Conceived People Are Becoming Law*, THE HILL (Apr. 23, 2022, 4:00 PM), https://thehill.com.

56 *Id. See, e.g.*, Allie Jennerjahn, *New Colorado Law Takes Away Anonymity of Sperm and Egg Donors Starting in 2025*, DENVER 7: STATE NEWS (Jan. 1, 2025, at 10:17 A.M.), https://www.denver7.com.

57 *In re* Baby M, 537 A.2d 1227, 1235 (N.J. 1988).

58 *Id.* The "Surrogacy Parenting Agreement," signed by William Stern, Mary Beth Whitehead, and Richard Whitehead, and the agreement between William Stern

and the Infertility Center of New York are appendices included with the decision. *In re* Baby M, *supra* note 57, at 1265–73.

59 *In re* Baby M, *supra* note 57 at 1235.

60 *See, e.g.*, Carol Sanger, *(Baby) M Is for the Many Things: Why I Start with Baby M*, 44 St. Louis U. L.J. 1443, 1452 (2000).

61 *In re* Baby M, *supra* note 57 at 1235.

62 *Id.* at 1236.

63 *Id.*

64 *Id.*

65 *Id.* at 1236–37.

66 *Id.* at 1237.

67 *Id.*

68 *Id.*

69 *Id.* at 1237–38.

70 *Id.* at 1238.

71 *Id.* at 1240–50.

72 *Id.* at 1264.

73 *See* I. Glenn Cohen & Daniel L. Chen, *Trading-Off Reproductive Technology and Adoption: Does Subsidizing IVF Decrease Adoption Rates and Should It Matter?*, 95 Minn. L. Rev. 485, 487 (2010); *see also* Solangel Maldonado, *The Story of the Holyfield Twins: Mississippi Band of Choctaw Indians v. Holyfield*, in Family Law Stories 113 (Carol Sanger, ed.) (West Academic 2008) (observing that Mrs. Holyfield and her husband had difficulty succeeding in adoption processes due to the couple's age and Mr. Holyfield's heart condition).

74 *In re* Baby M, *supra* note 57 at 1236.

75 *Consent to Adoption*, Child Welfare Info. Gateway 3 (2021), https://cwig-prod-prod-drupal-s3fs-us-east-1.s3.amazonaws.com.

76 *In re* Baby M, *supra* note 57 at 1242.

77 *Id.* at 1246; *see also* N.J. Rev. Stat § 9:3–41 (1994); *Consent to Adoption, supra* note 75.

78 *See generally* Myrisha S. Lewis, *Is Germline Gene Editing Exceptional?*, 51 Seton Hall L. Rev. 735 (2021).

79 *In re* Baby M, *supra* note 57 at 1235.

80 *Id.*

81 *Id.* at 1241, 1248 ("They know little about the natural mother, her genetic makeup, and her psychological and medical history. Moreover, not even a superficial attempt is made to determine their awareness of their responsibilities as parents").

82 *Id.* at 1249.

83 *See Surrogacy Laws by State*, Legal Pro. Grps.: Am. Soc'y for Reprod. Med. (July 2024), https://connect.asrm.org.

84 *Gestational Carrier (Surrogate)*, Am. Soc'y for Reprod. Med. (2023), www.reproductivefacts.org.

85 *Surrogacy Laws by State*, *supra* note 83. For a discussion of surrogacy statutes, see Courtney G. Joslin, *Nurturing Parenthood Through the UPA (2017)*, YALE L.J. FORUM 589, 609–10 (Jan. 7, 2018), www.yalelawjournal.org.

86 *Surrogacy Laws by State*, *supra* note 83. New York passed the Child-Parent Security Act, functionally repealing N.Y. Code § 122. *See The Child-Parent Security Act: Gestational Surrogacy*, N.Y. STATE DEP'T OF HEALTH, www.health.ny.gov; *The Child-Parent Security Act: Gestational Surrogacy Agreements, Acknowledgment of Parentage and Orders of Parentage*, N.Y. STATE DEP'T OF HEALTH, www.health.ny.gov; N.Y. Dom. Rel. Law § 122 (2021).

87 Roe v. Wade, 410 U.S. 113, 158 (1973), *overruled by* Dobbs v. Jackson Women's Health Org., 597 U.S. 215 (2022) (overruling Planned Parenthood of Se. Pennsylvania v. Casey, 505 U.S. 833 (1992)).

88 Davis v. Davis, 842 S.W.2d 588, 597 (Tenn. 1992).

89 *Id.* at 604–5.

90 *See, e.g.*, *In re* the Marriage of Witten, 672 N.W.2d 768, 781 (Iowa 2003).

91 Szafranski v. Dunston, 34 N.E.3d 1132, 1136–37 (Ill. App. Ct. 2015).

92 *See RENEW Biobank*, STANFORD MEDICAL (2024), www.med.stanford.edu; *see also* Kirsten R. W. Matthews & Daniel Morali, *Can We Do That Here? An Analysis of U.S. Federal and State Policies Guiding Human Embryo and Embryoid Research*, 9 J.L. & BIOSCIENCES 1, 10–18 (2022) (describing state legislative bans, limitations, and permissiveness on human embryo research).

93 Holly Yan, *A Cleveland Fertility Clinic That Lost 4,000 Eggs and Embryos Just Got Hit with 2 More Lawsuits*, CNN (Feb. 5, 2020), www.cnn.com.

94 Edward Helmore, *Five Fertility Clinic Patients Awarded $15m After Failure of Freezing Tank*, THE GUARDIAN (June 12, 2021, 2:43 PM), www.theguardian.com.

95 Kathianne Boniello, *Couple Says Fertility Doc Mixed Up Embryos Again*, N.Y. POST (Apr. 2, 2022, 10:15 AM), https://nypost.com; Andrea Salcedo, *Couple Sues Fertility Clinic, Saying They Had to Abort Stranger's Baby*, WASH. POST (Apr. 6, 2022, 6:14 AM), www.washingtonpost.com; Christopher Weber, *California Parents Gave Birth to Each Other's Babies After Fertility Clinic Mix-Up, Lawsuit Says*, USA TODAY (Nov. 8, 2021, 7:29 PM), www.usatoday.com; Dov Fox, *Reproductive Negligence*, 117 COLUM. L. REV. 149, 152 (2017). *See generally* Perry-Rogers v. Fasano, 715 N.Y.S.2d 19 (N.Y. App. Div. 2000).

96 42 U.S.C. § 263a-1–7 (1992).

97 Michele Goodwin, *Prosecuting the Womb*, 76 GEO. WASH. L. REV. 1657, 1693 (2008); Marsha Garrison, *Regulating Reproduction*, 76 GEO. WASH. L. REV. 1623, 1655 (2008) (noting that "donor screening, donation limits, recordkeeping, and confidentiality [are] all . . . now largely unregulated"); Naomi R. Chan & Jennifer M. Collins, *Eight Is Enough*, 103 NW. U. L. REV. COLLOQUY 501, 507 (2009) (referring to "limited" regulation); Judith F. Daar, *Regulating Reproductive Technologies: Panacea or Paper Tiger?*, 34 HOUS. L. REV. 609, 615 (1997) (referring to "little formal regulation"); Steve P. Calandrillo & Chryssa V. Deliganis, *In*

Vitro Fertilization and the Law: How Legal and Regulatory Neglect Compromised a Medical Breakthrough, 57 ARIZ. L. REV. 311, 311–12 (2015).

98 *State-Specific Assisted Reproductive Technology Surveillance*, CTRS. FOR DISEASE CONTROL & PREVENTION, https://archive.cdc.gov.

99 *Id.*

100 *Id.*

101 Eli Y. Adashi et al., *Infertility Therapy-Associated Multiple Pregnancies (Births): An Ongoing Epidemic*, 7 REPROD. BIOMEDICINE ONLINE 515, 515–57 (2003) (providing an overview and summary of a presentation authored by Meredith Reynolds and Laura Schieve, *Incidence of Multiple Gestation Following IVF, Ovulation Induction and Ovulation Enhancement*, at a Bertarelli Foundation–sponsored meeting on reproductive medicine held at Weill Medical College, Cornell University, New York, on April 12–13, 2003).

102 *2021 National ART Summary*, CTRS. FOR DISEASE CONTROL & PREVENTION (Dec. 10, 2024), www.cdc.gov/art/php/national-summary/index.html.

103 *See, e.g.*, Johnson v. Calvert, 851 P.2d 776, 777 (Cal. 1993); *State-Specific Assisted Reproductive Technology Surveillance*, *supra* note 98.

104 *State-Specific Assisted Reproductive Technology Surveillance*, *supra* note 98.

105 *Id.*; *ART Success Rates*, CTRS. FOR DISEASE CONTROL & PREVENTION (Jan. 8, 2024), www.cdc.gov/art/success-rate/index.html; *IVF Success Indicator*, CTRS. FOR DISEASE CONTROL & PREVENTION (Sept. 13, 2019), www.cdc.gov.

106 *See also CLIA Law & Regulations*, CTRS. FOR DISEASE CONTROL & PREVENTION (Nov. 14, 2022), www.cdc.gov (providing links to the Clinical Laboratory Improvement Amendments, interpreting regulations, and interpretive guidelines).

107 *See JoBeth Williams*, IMDB, www.imdb.com/name/nm0001851/.

108 *Baby M: Awards and Nominations*, EMMYS, www.emmys.com.

109 *Awards Nominees and Winners: 1988—40th Emmy Awards*, EMMYS, www.emmys.com.

110 *Consumer Protection Issues*, *supra* note 37 at 3, 121–23.

111 *Id.* at 123.

112 *Id.*

113 *Id.* at 184.

114 *See generally* Eduardo Hariton et al., *Meeting the Demand for Fertility Services: The Present and Future of Reproductive Endocrinology and Infertility in the United States*, 120 FERTILITY & STERILITY 755 (2023).

115 Warning Letter from U.S. Food and Drug Administration and Federal Trade Commission to Fertility Nutraceuticals LLC and Norbert Gleicher, FTC (May 20, 2021), www.ftc.gov/system/files/warning-letters/fda-fertility-nutraceuticals.pdf (alteration in original); *see also Norbert Gleicher, MD, FACOB, FACS*, CTR. FOR HUM. REPROD. (2025), www.centerforhumanreprod.com.

116 *See* Anna C. Mastroianni, *Liability, Regulation and Policy in Surgical Innovation: The Cutting Edge of Research and Therapy*, 16 HEALTH MATRIX 351, 353–54 (2006).

117 Joseph S. Kass & Rachel V. Rose, *Medical Malpractice Reform: Historical Approaches, Alternative Models, and Communication and Resolution Programs*, 18 Am. Med. Ass'n J. Ethics 299, 299 (2016), doi:10.1001/journalofethics.2016.18.3.pfor6-1603; *see, e.g.*, Barry Furrow et al., Health Law Cases, Materials and Problems 208–18 (8th ed., West Academic 2018) (citing Hall v. Hilbun, 466 So.2d 856 (Miss. 1985); Brian K. Cooke et al., *The Elusive Standard of Care*, 45 J. of Am. Acad. Psychiatry & L. 358, 358 (2017).

118 Julia Belluz, *Thousands of Heart Patients Get Stents That May Do More Harm Than Good*, Vox (Nov. 6, 2017, 9:01 AM), www.vox.com; Paula Byrne et al., *Evaluating the Association Between Low-Density Lipoprotein Cholesterol Reduction and Relative and Absolute Effects of Statin Treatment: A Systematic Review and Meta-Analysis*, 182 J. of Amer. Med. Assoc. Intern Med. 474, 474 (2022); Maya Geradi, *Common Breast Cancer Treatment Ineffective, Yale Study Finds*, Yale Daily News (Dec. 3, 2019, 1:00 AM), https://yaledailynews.com.

119 *See* Camille Workman, *The 2017 Uniform Parentage Act: A Response to the Changing Definition of Family?*, 32 J. Am. Acad. Matrimonial Laws. 233, 235, 237 (2019).

120 Kara W. Swanson, *Adultery by Doctor: Artificial Insemination, 1890–1945*, 87 Chi.-Kent L. Rev. 591, 593 (2012).

121 Sonia Fader, *Sperm Banking History*, Cal. Cryobank: By CooperSurgical, www.cryobank.com; Robert Evans Wilson Jr., *I Was Conceived by Donor Insemination When It Was Illegal*, Psych. Today (May 3, 2023), www.psychologytoday.com ("Legally I was considered a bastard, which remained true until I was seven years old when, in 1964, my home state of Georgia became the first state in the union to recognize donor-conceived children as legitimate"); *see also* Norman, 848 S.E.2d, *supra* note 48 at 835.

122 *In-Vitro Fertilization—Oversight*, Hearing Before the Subcommittee on Health and the Environment of the Committee on Interstate and Foreign Commerce House of Representatives, 95th Cong., 107 (1978).

123 *Human Embryo Transfer*, Hearing Before the Subcommittee on Investigations and Oversight of the Committee on Science and Technology House of Representatives, 98th Cong., 163–66 (1984) (citing Lori Andrews); *id.* at 131–35 (citing Alexander Capron).

124 *Id.* at 109 (citing Alexander Capron).

125 *Id.* at 316 (providing the written testimony of Richard A. McCormick, SJ, and Rose F. Kennedy, professor of Christian ethics: "[the] rule is: procreation of children should be restricted to marriage").

126 *See Know Your Rights: Reproductive Health Care*, U.S. Dep't of Health & Hum. Servs. (June 25, 2022), www.hhs.gov; D. C. Wertz, *Embryo and Stem Cell Research in the United States: History and Politics*, 9 Gene Therapy 674, 674 (2002). *See also* Chapter 4 *infra*.

127 *See* Our Father (Blumhouse Productions 2022).

128 *See* Baby God (HBO Documentary Films 2020).

CHAPTER 4. LIFE, EMBRYOS, AND ABORTION

1 *See, e.g.*, Brian X. McCrone, *Pa. Lawmaker Leading Push to Ban Abortions: "I See It As Morally Wrong,"* NBC PHILA. (June 24, 2022, 3:19 PM), www.nbcphiladelphia.com; Molly Hennessy-Fiske, *Alabama Lawmakers Pass Legislation to Protect IVF Treatment*, WASH. POST (Feb. 29, 2024, 6:34 PM), www.washingtonpost.com; *see also* Anthony Adragna, *Rosendale Pushes Spending Amendment That Declares IVF "Morally Wrong,"* POLITICO (June 25, 2024, 4:44 PM), www.politico.com; David S. Cohen, Greer Donley & Rachel Rebouché, *The New Abortion Battleground*, 123 COLUM. L. REV. 1 (2023); Myrisha S. Lewis, *Personhood, Politics, Assisted Reproduction, and the Law Post-Dobbs*, 45 PACE L. REV. 83 (2024); Emily Bazelon, *Why "Fetal Personhood" Is Roiling the Right*, N.Y. TIMES (Mar. 3, 2024), www.nytimes.com.

2 *Medical and Social Choices for Infertile Couples and the Federal Role in Prevention and Treatment*, Hearing Before a Subcommittee on the Committee on Government Operations, 100th Cong. 27 (1988).

3 Ezekiel J. Emanuel, REINVENTING AMERICAN HEALTHCARE: HOW THE AFFORDABLE CARE ACT WILL IMPROVE OUR TERRIBLY COMPLEX, BLATANTLY UNJUST, OUTRAGEOUSLY EXPENSIVE, GROSSLY INEFFICIENT, ERROR PRONE SYSTEM 17–18 (Cambridge University Press 2014).

4 *See The U.S. Public Health Service Untreated Syphilis Study at Tuskegee: Effects on Research*, U.S. CTRS. FOR DISEASE CONTROL & PREVENTION, www.cdc.gov/tuskegee/about/effects-research.html.

5 *See Medical and Social Choices*, *supra* note 2 at 12.

6 *See id.* at 7.

7 *See id.* at 17 (noting that the Vanderbilt researcher's application was referred back to the NIH "for further review in light of . . . the Board's report").

8 *See id.* at 13.

9 *See id.* at 8.

10 *See id.* at 8–9.

11 *See id.* at 9.

12 *See id.* at 9–10 (statement of Robert E. Windom, MD, assistant secretary for health).

13 *See In-Vitro Fertilization—Oversight*, Hearing Before the Subcommittee on Health and the Environment of the Committee on Interstate and Foreign Commerce, 95th Cong., 114–15 (1978) (describing research regarding the process of combining egg and sperm in a culture dish and, following fertilization, transferring the embryo into the uterine cavity).

14 *See id.* at 115.

15 *See id.* at 115–16.

16 *Louise Brown: World's First IVF Baby's Family Archive Unveiled*, BBC NEWS (July 24, 2018), www.bbc.com.

17 *See, e.g.*, Clyde Haberman, *Scientists Can Design "Better" Babies. Should They?*, N.Y. TIMES (June 10, 2018), www.nytimes.com.

18 Victor Cohn, *First U.S. Test-Tube Baby Is Born: Norfolk Test-Tube Baby First in United States*, WASH. POST (Dec. 29, 1981, 12:00 AM), www.washingtonpost.com.
19 *See Human Embryo Transfer*, Hearing Before the Subcommittee on Investigations and Oversight of the Committee on Science and Technology House of Representatives, 98th Cong. 1 (1984).
20 *See id.* at 2.
21 *See id.* at 2, 34.
22 *See id.* at 72.
23 *See id.* at 26.
24 *See id.* at 109; *id.* at 174–75. *See generally* Kara W. Swanson, *Adultery by Doctor: Artificial Insemination, 1890–1945*, 87 CHI.-KENT L. REV. 591 (2012).
25 *See Human Embryo Transfer*, *supra* note 19 at 175.
26 *See id.* at 170.
27 *See Medical and Social Choices*, *supra* note 2 at 45; *see also Human Embryo Transfer*, *supra* note 19 at 297–98.
28 *See Medical and Social Choices*, *supra* note 2 at 45–46.
29 *See id.* at 58–59, 62 (statement of John Bollinger of the Paralyzed Veterans of America) (citing Marriage of Carney, 24 Cal. 3d 728 (1979)).
30 *See Medical and Social Choices*, *supra* note 2 at 46.
31 *See* I. Glenn Cohen & Daniel L. Chen, *Trading-Off Reproductive Technology and Adoption: Does Subsidizing IVF Decrease Adoption Rates and Should It Matter?*, 95 MINN. L. REV. 485, 487, 510, 551 (2010).
32 *See Human Embryo Transfer*, *supra* note 19 at 233 (quoting Professor Capron, who noted that the Warnock Report was "unenforceable"); Human Fertilisation and Embryology Act 1990, c. 37 (UK), www.legislation.gov.uk.
33 *See Human Embryo Transfer*, *supra* note 19 at 259.
34 *See id.* at 27.
35 *President Discusses Stem Cell Research*, WHITE HOUSE (Aug. 9, 2001, 8:01 PM), https://georgewbush-whitehouse.archives.gov.
36 *Id.*
37 *Id.*
38 June Carbone & Naomi Cahn, *Embryo Fundamentalism*, 18 WM. & MARY BILL RTS. J. 1015, 1025 (2010); *President Discusses Embryo Adoption and Ethical Stem Cell Research*, WHITE HOUSE (May 24, 2005, 2:07 PM), https://georgewbush-whitehouse.archives.gov.
39 *Current Embryo Adoption Awareness and Services Grant Recipients*, OFFICE OF POPULATION AFFS., www.opa.hhs.gov.
40 Alex Vass, *US Scientists Clone First Human Embryo*, 323 BRIT. MED. J. 1267, 1267 (2001).
41 *Stem Cell Program: Pluripotent Stem Cell Research*, BOS. CHILD.'S HOSP., www.childrenshospital.org.
42 *See generally* Gene Outka, *The Ethics of Embryonic Stem Cell Research and the Principle of "Nothing Is Lost,"* 9 YALE J. HEALTH POL'Y, L., & ETHICS 585 (2009).

43 *Stem Cell Program*, *supra* note 41.

44 Eli Y. Adashi & I. Glenn Cohen, *Selective Regrets: The "Dickey Amendments" 20 Years Later*, J. OF AMER. MED. ASSOC. NETWORK (Nov. 5, 2015), https://jamanetwork.com (alteration in original); Sherley v. Sebelius, 689 F.3d 776, 779 (D.C. Cir. 2012) (quoting Pub. L. No. 112-74, § 508).

45 Harris v. McRae, 448 U.S. 297, 318 (1980); 22 U.S.C. § 2151b ("(1) None of the funds made available to carry out subchapter I of this chapter may be used to pay for the performance of abortions as a method of family planning or to motivate or coerce any person to practice abortions"); Cynthia Soohoo, *Hyde-Care for All: The Expansion of Abortion-Funding Restrictions Under Health Care Reform*, 15 CUNY L. REV. 391, 392 (2012); *Statement on NIH Funding of Research Using Gene-Editing Technologies in Human Embryos*, NAT'L INSTS. OF HEALTH (Apr. 28, 2015), www.nih.gov.

46 *See Human Embryo Transfer*, *supra* note 19 at 31.

47 *See id.* at 52; The Department of Health, Education, and Welfare became the Department of Health and Human Services on May 4, 1980. *HHS Historical Highlights*, U.S. DEP'T OF HEALTH & HUM. SERVS. (Mar. 14, 2023), www.hhs.gov.

48 *See Human Embryo Transfer*, *supra* note 19 at 60.

49 *See id.* at 63.

50 *See id.* at 39.

51 *See id.* at 52, 63.

52 *See, e.g.*, Aziza Ahmed, *Race and Assisted Reproduction: Implications for Population Health*, 86 FORDHAM L. REV. 2801, 2806–8 (2018).

53 *See Human Embryo Transfer*, *supra* note 19 at 52.

54 *See id.*

55 *See Alternative Reproductive Technologies: Implications for Children and Families*, Hearing Before the Select Committee on Children, Youth, and Families, 100th Cong. 18 (1987).

56 *See Consumer Protection Issues Involving In Vitro Fertilization Clinics*, Hearing Before the Subcommittee on Regulation, Business Opportunities, and Energy of the Committee on Small Business, 101st Cong., 15 (June 1, 1988); *id.* at 159 (testimony of Gary Ellis from the Office of Technology Assessment) (noting that the "prolonged absence of an Ethics Advisory Board has essentially halted research in human in vitro fertilization").

57 *See Medical and Social Choices*, *supra* note 2 at 178.

58 *See id.* at 180–81.

59 *Consumer Protection Issues*, *supra* note 56 at 159 (statement of Gary Ellis in the Office of Technology Assessment); *see also Medical and Social Choices*, *supra* note 2 at 27 (noting that the regulation had been "ignored for 8 years of this administration").

60 *Id.* at 159–60.

61 *Medical Science and Bioethics: Attack of the Clones?*, Hearing Before the Subcommittee on Criminal Justice, Drug Policy and Human Resources of the

Committee on Government Reform, House of Representatives, 107th Cong., 16–17 (2002).

62 U.S. Const. amend. I.

63 *See, e.g.*, James Toomey, *"Religion," Before Darwin*, 101 WASH. U. L. REV. 661, 662–63 (2024); Nina Totenberg, *The Supreme Court Is the Most Conservative in 90 Years*, NPR (July 5, 2022, 7:04 AM), www.npr.org.

64 Nat'l Inst. of Family & Life Advocates v. Becerra, 138 S. Ct. 2361 (2018). Overt religious references were the subject of a settlement agreement after the case, but even if overt religious references are removed, abstinence-only education comports with conservative Christian religious views. *See, e.g.*, Bowen v. Kendrick, 487 U.S. 589, 108 S. Ct. 2562 (1988); Rebekah Saul, *Whatever Happened to the Adolescent Family Life Act?*, THE GUTTMACHER REPORT ON PUBLIC POLICY, ISSUES AND IMPLICATIONS (Apr. 1998), www.guttmacher.org.

65 *Alternative Reproductive Technologies*, *supra* note 55 at 1.

66 *Id.*

67 *Id.* at 2.

68 *Id.* at 63, 67, 121.

69 *Id.* at 4.

70 *See generally* Christopher E. Smith, *What If? Human Experience and Supreme Court Decision Making on Criminal Justice*, 99 MARQ. L. REV. 813 (2016). *See also* Michele Goodwin, *Complicit Bias and the Supreme Court*, 136 HARV. L. REV. F. 119, 136–39 (2022); Barry J. McMillion, *Supreme Court Appointment Process: Consideration by the Senate Judiciary Committee*, CONG. RSCH. SERV. 14–16 (2021), https://crsreports.congress.gov.

71 M. Best et al., *Protestant Christian Attitudes to ART*, HUM. REPROD. OPEN 1, 1 (2019).

72 Merril Pauls & Roger C. Hutchinson, *Bioethics for Clinicians: 28. Protestant Bioethics*, 166 CANADIAN MED. ASS'N J. 339, 339 (2002). *See generally* Cynthia B. Cohen, *Protestant Perspectives on the Uses of the New Reproductive Technologies*, 30 FORDHAM URBAN L.J. 135 (2002).

73 Megan Messerly, *Why the Southern Baptists' Vote Opposing IVF Could Change National Politics*, POLITICO (June 12, 2024, 4:41 PM), www.politico.com.

74 *See, e.g.*, *5 Facts About the History of the SBC and the Pro-Life Cause*, ETHICS & RELIGIOUS LIBERTY COMMISSION (Jan. 17, 2020), https://erlc.com; *Transcript: Pro-Life—and in Favor of Keeping Abortion Legal*, NPR (Dec. 9, 2008, 9:52 AM), www.npr.org; *see also* Brad Brooks, *US Southern Baptists Condemn IVF Procedure*, REUTERS (June 13, 2024, 11:03 AM), www.reuters.com.

75 *See Protestant Christian Attitudes to ART*, *supra* note 71 at 141 (2002).

76 Charles S. Bullock et al., *The Rise of the Christian Right in the South and Its Impact on National Politics*, in THE SOUTH AND THE TRANSFORMATION OF U.S. POLITICS 113 (Oxford Academic 2019).

77 LePage v. Ctr. for Reprod. Med., P.C., Nos. SC-2022-0515, SC-2022-0579, 2024 WL 656591, at *13 (Ala. Feb. 16, 2024).

78 Ruth Graham, *Southern Baptists Vote to Oppose Use of I.V.F.*, N.Y. TIMES (June 12, 2024), www.nytimes.com.

79 Roe v. Wade, 410 U.S. 113, 159 (1973).

80 *Id.* at 160–61.

81 *Id.* at 117–18, 164–65; Planned Parenthood of Southeastern Pennsylvania v. Casey, 505 U.S. 833, 872–73 (1992); *see also* Whole Woman's Health v. Hellerstedt, 136 S. Ct. 2292, 2300, 2320 (2016). *See generally* Mary Ziegler, ABORTION AND THE LAW IN AMERICA: ROE V. WADE TO THE PRESENT (Cambridge Univ. Press 2020).

82 Melissa Murray & Kristin Luker, CASES ON REPRODUCTIVE RIGHTS AND JUSTICE 789 (1st ed., West Academic 2014).

83 *See id. See also State Bans on Abortion Throughout Pregnancy*, GUTTMACHER (July 29, 2024), www.guttmacher.org; *see also* Grace Arnold, *The Impact of Targeted Regulation of Abortion Providers Laws on Abortions and Births*, 35 J. POPULATION ECON. 1443, 1443 (2022); Jasmine Wang et al., *Impacts of Targeted Regulation of Abortion Providers*, REGUL. REV. (Jan. 16, 2021), www.theregreview.org; Sarah Friedmann, *11 TRAP Laws That Prevent Abortion Across America*, BUSTLE (Jan. 22, 2018), www.bustle.com; Bonnie S. Jones et al., *State Law Approaches to Facility Regulation of Abortion and Other Office Interventions*, 108 AM. J. PUB. HEALTH 486, 486–87 (2018).

84 *Targeted Regulation of Abortion Providers*, GUTTMACHER (Aug. 31, 2023), www.guttmacher.org; *see also* Whole Woman's Health v. Hellerstedt, 136 S. Ct. 2292, 2303, 2312 (2016); *id.* at 2314–15 (citing Tex. Health & Safety Code Ann. § 245.010(a)); *id.* at 2300 (citing Tex. Health & Safety Code Ann. § 171.0031(a)); *id.* at 2318 (concluding that the surgical center requirement would "provide few, if any, health benefits for women, pose a substantial obstacle to women seeking abortions, and constitute an 'undue burden' on their constitutional right to do so"); Marcia Coyle, *Whole Woman's Health v. Hellerstedt: What the Supreme Court Is Deciding in the Most Important Abortion Ruling in Decades (Updated 2022)*, PBS (Jun. 9, 2016), www.pbs.org.

85 For more on the role of advocacy groups in promoting model legislation to undermine access to abortion in the United States (as well as efforts to ban it completely), *see* Ziegler, *supra* note 81 at 97, 106–12, 158, 165, 188–90, 196; Mary Ziegler & Robert L. Tsai, *How the Anti-Abortion Movement Used the Progressive Playbook to Chip Away at Roe v. Wade*, POLITICO (June 13, 2021, 7:00 AM), www.politico.com.

86 Nancy Scola, *Exposing ALEC: How Conservative-Backed State Laws Are All Connected*, THE ATLANTIC (Apr. 14, 2012), www.theatlantic.com; Jim Sergent et al., *Copy, Paste, Legislate: They Copied Bills from Corporations. These Lawmakers Say That's OK*, USA TODAY (Dec. 17, 2019, 5:55 AM), www.usatoday.com.

87 Dobbs v. Jackson Women's Health Org., 597 U.S. 215, 232 (2022); *see also* Memorandum of Law in Support of Plaintiffs' Motion for Preliminary Injunction, at 1–2, Jackson Women's Health Organization v. Dobbs, No. 3:18-cv-171-CWR-FKB, 2019 WL 1769540 (S.D. Miss. Mar. 28, 2019); Jackson Women's Health Org. v. Currier, 349 F. Supp. 3d. 536 (S.D. Miss. 2018), aff'd sub nom. Jackson Women's

Health Org. v. Dobbs, 945 F.3d. 265 (5th Cir. 2019), rev'd and remanded, 597 U.S. 215 (2022) (addressing Mississippi's 15-week abortion ban).

88 Miss. Code. Ann. § 41-41-191(4)(b) (West 2018).

89 Under the statute, "gestation" means the "time that has elapsed since the first day of the woman's last menstrual period." Miss. Code. Ann. § 41-41-191 (West 2018).

90 Dobbs, *supra* note 87 at 302.

91 *See Read Justice Alito's Initial Draft Abortion Opinion Which Would Overturn Roe v. Wade*, POLITICO (May 2, 2022, 9:20 PM), www.politico.com; Dobbs, *supra* note 87 at 263.

92 *See* Isabela Rosales et al., *This Couple Has to Leave Alabama or Risk Losing Their Eggs After State Ruling Forces Providers to Pause IVF Treatment*, CNN (Feb. 22, 2024, 7:08 AM), www.cnn.com/2024/02/22/us/alabama-embryos-ruling-ivf-treatment-leaving-state/index.html. *See generally* Lewis, *supra* note 1 (discussing personhood in the context of IVF and Alabama's pre-*Dobbs* and post-*Dobbs* rulings in relation to personhood and "wrongful death"); LePage, 2024 WL 656591, *supra* note 78 at *1.

93 *See, e.g.*, Gerard Letterie & Dov Fox, *Legal Personhood and Frozen Embryos: Implications for Fertility Patients and Providers in Post-Roe America*, J. OF L. & BIOSCIENCES, 1, 3–4 (explaining how *Dobbs* changed the "personhood" of embryos by overruling *Roe*); Joshua Sharfstein, *The Alabama Supreme Court's Ruling on Frozen Embryos*, JOHN HOPKINS: BLOOMBERG SCH. OF PUB. HEALTH (Feb. 27, 2024), https://publichealth.jhu.edu/2024/the-alabama-supreme-courts-ruling-on-frozen-embryos (discussing a recent Alabama Supreme Court case in which the court held that frozen embryos have "personhood" and "are children"); *See* Bazelon, *supra* note 1.

94 Roe, *supra* note 79 at 158 (1973), *overruled by* Dobbs v. Jackson Women's Health Org., 142 S. Ct. 2228 (2022), *abrogated by* Planned Parenthood of Southeastern Pennsylvania v. Casey, 505 U.S. 833 (1992).

95 *Self-Described Religious Identification of the Adult Population in the United States in 2022*, STATISTA (July 5, 2024), www.statista.com/statistics/183817/religious-identification-of-adult-population/; *2022 PRRI Census of American Religion: Religious Affiliation Updates and Trends*, PUBLIC RELIGION RESEARCH INSTITUTE (Feb. 24, 2023), www.prri.org.

96 Jonathan Evans, *U.S. Adults Are More Religious than Western Europeans*, PEW RSCH. CTR. (Sept. 5, 2018), www.pewresearch.org.

97 *An Examination of the 2016 Electorate, Based on Validated Voters*, PEW RSCH. CTR. (Aug. 9, 2018), www.pewresearch.org.

98 *Id.*

99 *Id.*

100 Perry Bacon Jr., *Why Religion Is Becoming an Even Stronger Force Within the Republican Party*, WASH. POST (Apr. 16, 2024, 7:30 AM), www.washingtonpost.com (citing Ryan Burge, *The Religious Composition of Political Parties over the Last 50 Years*, RELIGION UNPLUGGED (Nov. 7, 2023), https://religionunplugged.com).

101 Joseph G. Schenker, *Assisted Reproductive Practice: Religious Perspectives*, 10 Reprod. BioMedicine Online 310, 314–15 (2005); Mohammed Ali Al-Bar & Hassan Chamsi-Pasha, Contemporary Bioethics: Islamic Perspective 173, 174–80 (Springer 2015) (noting differences in perspectives of Sunni and Shia Muslims); Ariana Eunjung Cha, *Gifts from God: How Religion Is Coming to Terms with Modern Fertility Methods*, Wash. Post (Apr. 27, 2018), www.washingtonpost .com. *See generally* Ian H. Kerridge et al., *Religious Perspectives on Embryo Donation and Research*, 5 Clinical Ethics 35 (2010); Mansooreh Saniei & Mehdi Kargar, *Modern Assisted Reproductive Technologies and Bioethics in the Islamic Context*, 19 Theology & Sci. 146 (2021).

102 Daphna Birenbaum-Carmeli, *Thirty-Five Years of Assisted Reproductive Technologies in Israel*, 2 Reprod. biomedicine & soc'y online 16, 16 (2016).

103 *Abortion Funding Restriction Act*, Hearing Before the Subcommittee on the Constitution of the Committee on the Judiciary United States Senate, 99th Cong. 160 (1985).

104 *See generally* Myrisha S. Lewis, *Reproductive Innovation and Reproductive Exceptionalism: How Private Health Insurance Coverage of Fertility Treatment Complements Hostile Governmental Action and Expands Access to Assisted Reproduction in the United States*, in Health Law as Private Law (I. Glenn Cohen, Wendy Netter Epstein, Christopher Robertson, Carmel Shachar & Susannah Baruch eds.) (Cambridge University Press 2025) 144 at n.58.

105 *See Medical and Social Choices*, *supra* note 2 at 24 (citing a January 22 memorandum from the director of the NIH, Dr. Wyngaarden to Robert E. Windom, MD, assistant secretary for health).

106 *See, e.g.*, Eli Y. Adashi, *What the Great Divide over IVF Coverage Can Tell Us About the Future of Other High-Tech Interventions*, Health Affs. (Jan. 24, 2018), www.healthaffairs.org; *Federal Employee Family-Building Act of 1987*, Hearing Before the Subcommittee on Civil Service of the Committee on Post Office and Civil Service, 100th Cong. 10 (1988) at 1; *Frequently Questioned Services*, U.S. Off. of Pers. Mgmt., 1–2, www.opm.gov/retirement-services/publications -forms/benefits-administration-letters/2012/12-401attachment3.pdf (last visited Aug. 10, 2024).

107 *See generally* Lewis, *supra* note 104 at n.58.

108 Brittany Galla, *This Woman Worked at Starbucks to Get IVF Insurance Coverage—Here's Her Story*, Parade (Feb. 27, 2020), https://parade.com; Leticia Miranda & Louise Matsakis, *Some Starbucks Workers Forgo Paychecks to Access IVF Treatments*, NBC News (Mar. 28, 2022, 6:26 AM) www.nbcnews.com; Angelina Chapin, *Would You Work in an Amazon Warehouse Just to Get Pregnant? Women Are Pulling Graveyard Shifts in Backbreaking Jobs to Pay for IVF*, Cut (Aug. 5, 2022), www.thecut.com; Vanessa Grigoriadis, *I.V.F. Coverage Is the Benefit Everyone Wants*, N.Y. Times (Jan. 30, 2019), www.nytimes.com.

109 *Abortion Funding Restriction Act*, *supra* note 103 at 116.

110 *Federal Employee Family-Building Act of 1987*, *supra* note 106.

111 *Id.* at 20 (statement of Representative Patricia Schroeder) ("I am concerned, because as we heard from Federal employees here, their option was to leave the Federal Government. I don't think we want any more incentives to leave the Federal Government").
112 *Id.* at 35.
113 *Consumer Protection Issues*, *supra* note 56 at 18 ("Yet, in practice some 70 percent of infertility expenditures are reportedly reimbursed. Some individual procedures are covered, particularly if they are not identified as part of an overall treatment for infertility. In other instances, some physicians find disingenuous ways to invoice for infertility services, so as to obtain reimbursement from insurers for their patients").
114 *See Medical and Social Choices*, *supra* note 2 at 55–57 (comments from Resolve members about their insurance experiences).
115 *See generally* Lewis, *supra* note 104 at n.58.
116 *See generally id.*
117 *Federal Employee Family-Building Act of 1987*, *supra* note 106 at 28; *id.* at 59 ("Congress generally does not regulate medical practice, with the exception of drawing broad criteria for care delivered at Veterans' Administration hospitals or reimbursed by Federal insurance programs").
118 *Federal Employee Family-Building Act of 1987*, *supra* note 106 at 35; Lewis, *supra* note 104 at n.58.
119 *Covered Services: Assisted Reproductive Services*, TRICARE, www.tricare.mil (July 25, 2024); *Fertility Counseling and Treatment for Certain Veterans and Spouses*, GovInfo (Jan. 19, 2017), www.govinfo.gov.
120 *Veteran Access to Fertility Services: Appropriations*, Hearing Before House Subcommittee on Military Construction, Veterans' Affairs and Related Agencies, Committee on Appropriations 117th Cong. (2021).
121 *See generally* Lewis, *supra* note 104 at n.58.
122 *See generally id.*
123 *Human Cloning: Must We Sacrifice Medical Research in the Name of a Total Ban?*, Hearing Before U.S. Senate Committee on the Judiciary, 107th Cong. 31 (2002) (statement of R. Alta Charo).
124 For a discussion of the lead-up to and aftermath of Alabama's *Le Page* decision, including its connection to the 2024 presidential campaigns and discussions of personhood before and after the US Supreme Court's decision in *Dobbs v. Jackson Women's Health Organization*, *see generally* Lewis, *supra* note 1 at 83.
125 *See* Liz Baker, Debbie Elliott & Susanna Capelouto, *Alabama Governor Signs IVF Bill Giving Immunity to Patients and Providers*, NPR (updated Mar. 6, 2024, 10:56 PM), www.npr.org. *See also* Ala. Code 1975 § 6-5-810, Liability for damage to or death of an embryo when providing or receiving services related to in vitro fertilization; Ala. Code 1975 § 6-5-811, Compensatory damages; criminal immunity relating to in vitro fertilization.

CHAPTER 5. THE GENETIC REVOLUTION

1 Lynn B. Jorde & Michael J. Bamshad, *Genetic Ancestry Testing: What Is It and Why Is It Important?*, 323 J. of Amer. Med. Assoc. 1089, 1090 (2020); Ray A. Wickenheiser, *Forensic Genealogy, Bioethics and the Golden State Killer Case*, 1 Forensic Sci. Int'l: Synergy 114, 115 (2019).

2 Katherine J. Wu, Carl Zimmer & Elian Peltier, *Nobel Prize in Chemistry Awarded to 2 Scientists for Work on Genome Editing*, N.Y. Times (Oct. 6, 2021), www.nytimes.com.

3 Henry T. Greely, *CRISPR'd Babies: Human Germline Genome Editing in the "He Jiankui Affair,"* 6 J.L. & BioSci. 111 (2019).

4 *See Human Embryo Transfer*, Hearing Before the Subcommittee on Investigations and Oversight of the Committee on Science and Technology House of Representatives, 98th Cong. 3 (1984).

5 *See id.* at 3.

6 *See id.* at 21.

7 *See id.* at 76.

8 *See id.*

9 Asude Alpman Durmaz et al., *Evolution of Genetic Techniques: Past, Present, and Beyond*, 2015 BioMed Rsch. Int'l, 1, 2 (2015).

10 Khiara M. Bridges, *The Dysgenic State: Environmental Injustice and Disability-Selective Abortion Bans*, 110 Cal. L. Rev. 297, 340 (2022).

11 *Pregnancy and Family Planning*, Nat'l Soc'y of Genetic Counselors, www.aboutgeneticcounselors.com.

12 Theodore Friedmann, *A Brief History of Gene Therapy*, 2 Natural Genetics 93, 94 (1992).

13 Agisha Raaje, *Role of Recombinant DNA Technology in Medicine*, 6 Int. J. Sci. & Res. 792–93 (2017); Suliman Kahn et al., *Role of Recombinant DNA Technology to Improve Life*, Int. J. Genomics 1, 2 (2016).

14 Raaje, *supra* note 13 at 792; I. P. Nascimento & L. C. C. Leite, *Recombinant Vaccines and the Development of New Vaccine Strategies*, 45 Brazilian J. Med. & Bio. Res. 1102, 1104–5 (2012).

15 Friedmann, *supra* note 12 at 95.

16 Paul Berg et al., *Summary Statement of the Asilomar Conference on Recombinant DNA Molecules*, 72 Proceedings of the Nat'l Acad. of Scis. 1981 (1975).

17 *1972: First Recombinant DNA*, Nat'l Human Genome Research Inst. (April 26, 2013), www.genome.gov.

18 *The Nobel Prize in Chemistry 1980*, The Nobel Prize (1980), www.nobelprize.org/prizes/chemistry/1980/summary/.

19 Stanley N. Cohen & Herbert W. Boyer, *Process for Producing Biologically Functional Molecular Chimeras*, U. S. Patent 4,237,224, initially filed November 4, 1974, issued December 2, 1980. *See generally* Diamond v. Chakrabarty, 447 U.S. 303, 318 (1980).

20 Paul Berg & Janet E. Mertz, *Personal Reflections on the Origins and Emergence of Recombinant DNA Technology*, 184 Genetics 9, 16 (2010).

21 *About Our Founders*, GENENTECH (2025), www.gene.com/about-us/leadership/our-founders.

22 *1972: First Recombinant DNA*, *supra* note 17; Cohen & Boyer, *supra* note 19.

23 Rajendra K. Bera, *The Story of the Cohen–Boyer Patents*, 96 CURRENT SCIENCE 760, 761 (2009).

24 Stanford University, *Office of Technology Licensing, Life of a Stanford Invention*, www.stanford.edu.

25 *Id.*

26 Darius Kharabi, *A Real Options Analysis of Pharmaceutical-Biotechnology Licensing*, 11 STAN. J.L. BUS. & FIN. 201, 203 (2006).

27 *Patent, Then Publish*, GENENTECH (July 21, 2016), www.gene.com/stories/patent-then-publish.

28 Andrew Pollack, *Roche Agrees to Buy Genentech for $46.8 Billion*, N.Y. TIMES (Mar. 12, 2009), www.nytimes.com/ [https://perma.cc/V846-YEPY].

29 Emily Moskal, *Nobel Prize Winner and Recombinant DNA Pioneer Paul Berg Dies*, Press Release, STANFORD MEDICINE (Feb. 17, 2023), https://med.stanford.edu.

30 Paul Berg, *Asilomar and Recombinant DNA*, THE NOBEL PRIZE (Aug. 26, 2004), www.nobelprize.org/prizes/chemistry/1980/berg/article/.

31 Maryann P. Feldman, Alessandra Colaianni, & Connie Kang Liu, *Lessons from the Commercialization of the Cohen-Boyer Patents: The Stanford University Licensing Program* in INTELLECTUAL PROPERTY MANAGEMENT IN HEALTH AND AGRICULTURAL INNOVATION: A HANDBOOK OF BEST PRACTICES 1797 (eds. Anatole Krattiger, Richard T. Mahoney, Lita Nelsen, et al.)(2007).

32 Suliman Khan et al., *Role of Recombinant DNA Technology to Improve Life*, 2016 INT'L J. OF GENOMICS 1, 3 (2016).

33 *See* Maxine Singer & Dieter Soll, *Guidelines for DNA Hybrid Molecules*, 181 SCIENCE 4105, Letters (Sept. 21, 1973).

34 *Id.*

35 *Id.*

36 *Id.*

37 *Id.*

38 *Id.*

39 Berg & Mertz, *supra* note 20 at 13.

40 Inst. of Med., BIOMEDICAL POLITICS 268 (National Academies Press 1991).

41 *See* Berg et al., *supra* note 16.

42 Paul Berg et al., *Potential Biohazards of Recombinant DNA Molecules*, 71 PROC. NAT'L ACAD. SCIS. 2593, 2593–94 (July 1974).

43 *Id.* at 2593–94.

44 *See, e.g.*, Barbara J. Evans, *Governance at the Institutional and National Level*, in INT'L SUMMIT ON HUMAN GENE EDITING COMMISSIONED PAPERS (National Academies Press, 2015), https://nap.nationalacademies.org.

45 *See* Berg et al., *supra* note 42 at 2593–94; *The Nobel Prize in Physiology or Medicine 1975*, THE NOBEL PRIZE, www.nobelprize.org; *The Nobel Prize in Chemistry 1980*,

supra note 18; Cohen & Boyer, *supra* note 19; *The Nobel Prize in Physiology or Medicine 1962*, THE NOBEL PRIZE, www.nobelprize.org.

46 *See* Berg et al., *supra* note 42 at 2593.

47 *Id.*

48 *Id.*

49 *Id.*

50 *See* Stephen P. Goff & Thomas Shenk, *Paul Berg: Recombinant DNA Trailblazer*, 120 PROC. NAT'L ACAD. SCIS. e3318196120 at 2.

51 *Id.*

52 *Id.*

53 Lilla Botos, Erzsébet Szatmári & Gyula Richárd Nagy, *Prenatal and Postnatal Genetic Testing Toward Personalized Care: The Non-Invasive Perinatal Testing*, 72 MOLECULAR AND CELLULAR PROBES 1, 1 (Dec. 2023).

54 *See, e.g.*, Filipa Carvalho et al., *ESHRE PGT Consortium Good Practice Recommendations for the Organisation of PGT*, HUM. REPROD. OPEN 1, 2 (Feb. 2020).

55 *See PGD Q&A*, CTR. FOR ADVANCED REPRODUCTIVE SERV. (Sept. 14, 2020) https://uconnfertility.com; *see also Preimplantation Genetic Testing*, NYU LANGONE HEALTH (2025), https://nyulangone.org; Elkin Muñoz et al., *To Transfer or Not to Transfer: The Dilemma of Mosaic Embryos—A Narrative Review*, 48 REPRODUCTIVE BIOMEDICINE ONLINE 1, 1 (Nov. 2, 2023), www.rbmojournal.com.

56 *See* Botos, Szatmári & Nagy, *supra* note 53 at 1; Gareth M. Thomas et al., *Keeping the Backdoor to Eugenics Ajar? Disability and the Future of Prenatal Screening*, AMA J. OF ETHICS (Apr. 2016), https://journalofethics.ama-assn.org.

57 *See* Myrisha S. Lewis, *Is Germline Gene Editing Exceptional?*, 51 SETON HALL LAW REVIEW 735 (2021).

58 *Human Genome Editing: Sci., Ethics, and Governance*, NAT'L ACADS. SCIS., ENG'G & MED., 126 (2017) (citations omitted).

59 See George Q. Daley et al., *After the Storm—A Responsible Path for Genome Editing*, 380 NEW ENG. J. MED. 897, 897 (2019).

60 *Id.* at 899.

61 *See* Botos, Szatmári & Nagy, *supra* note 53 at 2–3; Sonia M. Suter, *Did You Give the Government Your Baby's DNA? Rethinking Consent in Newborn Screening*, 15 MINN. J. L. SCI. & TECH. 729 (2014).

62 *Cloning Fact Sheet*, NAT'L HUMAN GENOME RES. INST. (Aug. 15, 2020), www.genome.gov.

63 *See id.*

64 Sarah Kuta, *Scientists Record the First "Virgin Birth" in a Crocodile*, SMITHSONIAN MAGAZINE, Jun. 7, 2023, www.smithsonianmag.com/smart-news/scientists-record-the-first-virgin-birth-in-a-crocodile-180982318/.

65 *See Cloning Fact Sheet*, *supra* note 62.

66 *Id.*

67 *Id.*

68 *See id.*; Leslie A. Pray, *The Biotechnology Revolution: PCR and the Use of Reverse Transcriptase to Clone Expressed Genes*, NATURE EDUCATION (2008), www.nature.com.

69 Nat'l Library of Medicine, *What Are Genome Editing and CRISPR-Cas9?*, MEDLINE (Mar. 22, 2022), https://medlineplus.gov.

70 *Id.*

71 *See* Greely, *supra* note 3 at 115.

72 *Human Cloning: Must We Sacrifice Medical Research in the Name of a Total Ban?*, Hearing Before US Senate Committee on the Judiciary, 107th Cong. 31 (2002), at 42 (providing the statement of Andrew Kimball).

73 *See, e.g.*, Sheryl Gay Stolberg, *F.D.A. Officials Fault Penn Team in Gene Therapy Death*, N.Y. TIMES (Dec. 9, 1999), https://archive.nytimes.com/www.nytimes.com/library/national/science/health/120999hth-gene-therapy.html ("One reason the Penn study has generated so much controversy is that Jesse Gelsinger was not sick before he died"); Rick Weiss & Deborah Nelson, *Teen Dies Undergoing Experimental Gene Therapy*, WASH. POST (Sept. 29, 1999), www.washingtonpost.com/wp-srv/WPcap/1999-09/29/060r-092999-idx.html ("The method was controversial because the genetically altered virus, which often causes severe inflammation, risked exacerbating the disease in some patients when it was injected directly into their livers, while promising at best only a transient improvement").

74 Stolberg, *supra* note 73.

75 *Id.*

76 *FDA Approval Brings First Gene Therapy to the United States*, Press Release, FDA (Aug. 30, 2017), www.fda.gov/news-events/press-announcements/fda-approval-brings-first-gene-therapy-united-states.

77 *FDA Approves First Gene Therapies to Treat Patients with Sickle Cell Disease*, News Release, FDA (Dec. 8, 2023), www.fda.gov.

78 *Id.*

79 Megan Molteni, *UC Berkeley Loses CRISPR Patent Case, Invalidating Patent Rights It Granted Gene-Editing Companies Developing Human Therapies*, STAT NEWS (Feb. 28, 2022), www.statnews.com.

80 *See, e.g.*, Jason Mast, Allison DeAngelis & Megan Molteni, *CRISPR Patent Fight Redux? A New Battle Is Brewing Among Biotechs over Next-Gen Gene-Editing Tools*, Special Report, STAT NEWS (Mar. 1, 2023), www.statnews.com.

81 Nat'l Library of Medicine, *supra* note 69.

82 *Id.*

83 *The Nobel Prize in Chemistry 2020*, Press Release, THE NOBEL PRIZE (Oct. 7, 2020), www.nobelprize.org.

84 *See* Jason Mast, Allison DeAngelis & Megan Molteni, *supra* note 80.

85 National Academies of Sciences, Engineering, and Medicine, IN VITRO–DERIVED HUMAN GAMETES AS A REPRODUCTIVE TECHNOLOGY: SCIENTIFIC, ETHICAL,

AND REGULATORY IMPLICATIONS: PROCEEDINGS OF A WORKSHOP 93 (National Academies Press 2023).

86 *Jennifer Doudna: Jennifer Doudna Wins Nobel Prize in Chemistry*, LAWRENCE BERKELEY NAT'L LAB. (Oct. 7, 2020), www.lbl.gov.

87 *Id.*

88 Manas Mishra, *Nobel Laureate Doudna's Biotech Mammoth Hits over $1 Bln in Valuation*, REUTERS (Sept. 9, 2021, 6:02 AM), www.reuters.com.

89 *Id.*

90 Dieter Egli et al., *Inter-Homologue Repair in Fertilized Human Eggs?*, 560 NATURE E5 (2018).

91 Hong Ma et al., *Correction of a Pathogenic Gene Mutation in Human Embryos*, 548 NATURE 413, 416 (2017); Dan Liang et al., *Limitations of Gene Editing Assessments in Human Preimplantation Embryos*, 14 NATURE COMMUNICATIONS 1–2 (2023), https://doi.org/10.1038/s41467-023-36820-6.

92 Sharon Begley, *U.S. Scientists Edit Genome of Human Embryo, but Cast Doubt on Possibility of "Designer Babies,"* STAT NEWS, Aug. 2, 2017, www.statnews .com/; Hong Ma et al., *supra* note 91 at 416 (replying to Egli et al., *supra* note 90; Fatwa Adikusuma et al., *Large Deletions Induced by Cas9 Cleavage*, Brief Communications Arising, 560 NATURE E8 (2018) (arising from Hong Ma et al., *supra* note 91 at 416).

93 *See* Begley, *supra* note 92.

94 *Id.*

95 Sharon Begley, *Those CRISPR'd Human Embryos? We Got It Right, Scientists Insist, Rejecting Criticism*, STAT NEWS (Aug. 8, 2018), www.statnews.com.

96 Gina Kolata, Sui-Lee Wee & Pam Belluck, *Chinese Scientist Claims to Use CRISPR to Make First Genetically Edited Babies*, N.Y. TIMES (Nov. 26, 2018) www.nytimes.com.

97 Hannah Devlin, *Scientist Who Edited Babies' Genes Says He Acted "Too Quickly,"* THE GUARDIAN (Feb. 4, 2023, 4:00 AM), www.theguardian.com.

98 *See, e.g.*, Gina Kolata & Pam Belluck, *Why Are Scientists So Upset About the First CRISPR Babies?*, N.Y. TIMES (Dec. 5, 2018), www.nytimes.com; Greely, *supra* note 3 at 118.

99 *See* Greely, *supra* note 3 at 132.

100 *Id.* at 118.

101 Roy J. Britten, *Divergence Between Samples of Chimpanzee and Human DNA Sequences Is 5%, Counting Indels*, PROC. NAT'L ACAD. SCI. USA (Oct. 4, 2002), www.pnas.org. *See also* Maria V. Sintsova & Anton A. Buzdin, *Differences Between Human and Chimpanzee Genomes and Their Implications in Gene Expression, Protein Functions and Biochemical Properties of the Two Species*, 21 (Suppl. 7) BMC GENOMICS 535 (2020).

102 *See, e.g.*, *Preclinical Therapeutics Recharge Rates*, UCSF HELEN DILLER FAMILY COMPREHENSIVE CANCER CENTER (2025), https://cancer.ucsf.edu. *See also* Kaori Yoshida, *Lab Monkey Prices Soar in U.S. After China Cuts Off Exports*, NIKKEI

ASIA (May 16, 2023), https://asia.nikkei.com; David Masopust, Christine P. Sivula & Stephen C. Jameson, *Of Mice, Dirty Mice, and Men: Using Mice to Understand Human Immunology*, 199 J. OF IMMUNOLOGY 383, 384 (2017).

103 *Artificial Selection*, NAT'L GEOGRAPHIC SOC. (updated Oct. 19, 2023), https://education.nationalgeographic.org.

104 David Zucchino, *From Pot to Hot: How a Grower Produced World's Most Fiery Chile Pepper*, L.A. TIMES (Nov. 16, 2014), www.latimes.com.

105 Warren E. Leary, *F.D.A. Approves Altered Tomato That Will Remain Fresh Longer*, N.Y. TIMES (May 19th, 1994), www.nytimes.com; U.S. Food and Drug Admin., *Science and History of GMOs and Other Food Modification Processes* (Mar. 5, 2024), https://www.fda.gov.

106 Ben Tinker, *New Frontier in Apples: Red or Golden but Never Brown*, CNN (Feb. 16, 2015), www.cnn.com; *AquAdvantage Salmon Fact Sheet*, FDA (Mar. 7, 2023), www.fda.gov.

107 *See Cloning Fact Sheet*, *supra* note 55; *Animal Cloning: A Risk Assessment*, FDA (2008), www.fda.gov.

108 Lisa Baertlein, *U.S. Food Makers Sue to Stop Vermont's GMO Labeling Law*, REUTERS (June 12, 2014), www.reuters.com.

109 *See, e.g.*, Evans, *supra* note 36.

110 *See* Myrisha S. Lewis, *Segmented Innovation in the Legalization of Mitochondrial Transfer: Lessons from Australia and the United Kingdom*, 22 HOUS. J. HEALTH L. & POL'Y 317 (2022).

111 Karen Weintraub, *First He Pioneered a New Way of Making Life. Now He Wants to Try It in People*, STAT NEWS (July 8, 2016), www.statnews.com.

112 *Id.*

113 *Id.*

114 *Id.*

115 *Id.*

116 *Id.*

117 *See* Hong Ma et al., *Germline Transmission of Donor, Maternal and Paternal mtDNA in Primates*, 36 HUM. REPROD. 493, 493 (2021), https://doi.org/10.1093/humrep/deaa308.

118 *Id.* at 493, 494.

119 *Id.* at 493.

120 *Id.* at 502.

121 *Id.* at 493, 494–97, and 500.

122 *Id.* at 494.

123 *Id.* at 497.

124 *See* Weintraub, *supra* note 108.

125 42 U.S.C. § 2181—Inventions relating to atomic weapons, and filing of reports; 35 U.S. Code § 101—Inventions patentable.

CHAPTER 6. SELF-REGULATION, TECHNO-ANXIETY, AND THE GROWING ROLE OF THE FEDERAL GOVERNMENT IN THE REGULATION OF GENETIC INNOVATION AND EMBRYONIC RESEARCH

1 *In-Vitro Fertilization: Oversight*, Hearing before the Subcommittee on Health and the Environment, House of Representatives, 95th Congress (Aug. 4, 1978), at 110–11.

2 *See, e.g., Alternative Reproductive Technologies: Implications for Children and Families*, Hearing Before the Select Committee on Children, Youth, and Families, House of Representatives, 100th Congress (May 21, 1987), at 8, 20.

3 Rachel Roubein, Laurie McGinley & David Ovalle, *Abortion Pill Fight May Have Broader Implications for FDA Drug Approval*, WASH. POST (Mar. 15, 2023, 5:12 PM), www.washingtonpost.com; Daniel G. Aaron, *The Fall of FDA Review*, 22 YALE J. OF HEALTH POL'Y, LAW, AND ETHICS 95, 99–103 (2023).

4 Michael D. Frakes & Melissa F. Wasserman, *Does the U.S. Patent and Trademark Office Grant Too Many Bad Patents?: Evidence from a Quasiexperiment*, 67 STAN. L. REV. 613, 615 (2015) (citing James Bessen & Michael J. Meurer, PATENT FAILURE: HOW JUDGES, BUREAUCRATS, AND LAWYERS PUT INNOVATORS AT RISK (Princeton University Press 2008); Dan L. Burk & Mark A. Lemley, THE PATENT CRISIS AND HOW THE COURTS CAN SOLVE IT (Oxford Academic 2009); Adam B. Jaffe & Josh Lerner, INNOVATION AND ITS DISCONTENT: HOW OUR PATENT SYSTEM IS ENDANGERING INNOVATION AND PROGRESS, AND WHAT TO DO ABOUT IT (Princeton University Press 2004)).

5 *Medical Science and Bioethics: Attack of the Clones?*, Hearing before the House Subcommittee on Criminal Justice, Drug Policy, and Human Resources, 107th Congress (May 15, 2002), at 407 (citing Andrew Pollack, *Debate on Human Cloning Turns to Patents*, N.Y. TIMES (May 17, 2002)); *id.* at 407–13.

6 *Id.*

7 *See About the Center for Tobacco Products (CTP)*, U.S. FOOD AND DRUG ADMIN. (Dec. 18, 2023), www.fda.gov.

8 Historic Jamestowne, *Tobacco*, https://historicjamestowne.org/collections/artifacts/category/tobacco/. *See, e.g., Electronic Vaping Device*, US9282772B2, https://patents.google.com/patent/US9282772B2/en. *But see* Philip J. Hilts, *Method to Produce Safer Cigarette Was Found in 60's, but Company Shelved Idea*, N.Y. TIMES (May 13, 1994), www.nytimes.com; Warren E. Leary, *Cigarette Company Developed Tobacco with Stronger Nicotine; Head of F.D.A. Tells of Chemical Manipulation*, N.Y. TIMES (June 22, 1994), www.nytimes.com; *Historical Timeline of Vaping & Electronic Cigarettes*, CASAA (2025), https://casaa.org/education/vaping/historical-timeline-of-electronic-cigarettes/; *see also* Kim Lyons, *New Juul Patent Application Hints at AI-Powered Vape to Help Users Quit Nicotine*, THE VERGE (Feb. 25, 2020, 10:28 AM), www.theverge.com.

9 *Human Embryo Transfer*, Hearing before the Subcommittee on Investigations and Oversight of the Committee on Science and Technology, House of Representatives, 98th Congress (Aug. 8, 9, 1984), at 224 (providing the written testimony of George Annas).

10 *Human Embryo Transfer*, *supra* note 9 at 302–3; George Annas, *Surrogate Embryo Transfer: The Perils of Patenting*, 14 HASTINGS CENT. REP. 25, 25 (June 1984); Harris Brotman, *Human Embryo Transplants*, N.Y. TIMES (Jan. 8, 1984), www.nytimes.com.

11 *Human Embryo Transfer*, *supra* note 9 at 302–3.

12 Cristine Russell, *House Questions Ethics of Embryo Implant*, WASH. POST (Aug. 9, 1984, 8:00 PM), www.washingtonpost.com.

13 *Human Embryo Transfer*, *supra* note 9 at 301.

14 Annas, *supra* note 10 at 25–26.

15 Mark V. Sauer, *Revisiting the Early Days of Oocyte and Embryo Donation: Relevance to Contemporary Clinical Practice*, 110 FERTILITY AND STERILITY 981, 983 (2018); *id.* at 986 (discussing uterine lavage's potential reintroduction into reproductive medicine practice). *See also* Sam Najmabadi et al., *Human Uterine Lavage: First Live Births from In Vivo Conceived Genetically Screened Blastocysts*, 40 ADV. THER. 2534 (2023).

16 Paul Berg & Janet E. Mertz, *Personal Reflections on the Origins and Emergence of Recombinant DNA Technology*, 184 GENETICS 9, 15 (2010).

17 *Id.*

18 *Id. See also* Stanford University, *Office of Technology Licensing, Life of a Stanford Invention*, www.stanford.edu.

19 Berg & Mertz, *supra* note 16 at 14.

20 S. J. Liebowitz & Stephen E. Margolis, *Path Dependence, Lock-In, and History*, 11 J. OF L., ECON., AND ORG. 205, 205 (1995).

21 *See* Mark J. Roe, *Chaos and Evolution in Law and Economics*, 109 HARV. L. REV. 641, 643–44 (1996) (explaining path dependence).

22 Sharon Begley, *From Assisted Hatching to Embryo Glue, Most IVF "Add-Ons" Rest on Shaky Science, Studies Find*, STAT NEWS (Nov. 5, 2019), www.statnews.com/2019/11/05/ivf-add-ons-shaky-science-studies/; Isabella Cueto, *New Research Casts Fresh Doubt on a Common Procedure That Promises to Increase the Odds of IVF*, STAT NEWS (Nov. 26, 2021), www.statnews.com (citing Junhao Yan et al., *Live Birth With or Without Preimplantation Genetic Testing for Aneuploidy*, 395 NEW ENGLAND J. OF MED. 2047 (2021)).

23 Nat'l Acads. of Scis., Eng'g, and Med., IN VITRO–DERIVED HUMAN GAMETES AS A REPRODUCTIVE TECHNOLOGY: SCIENTIFIC, ETHICAL, AND REGULATORY IMPLICATIONS: PROCEEDINGS OF A WORKSHOP 98 (National Academies Press 2023) (discussing how the Dickey-Wicker Amendment will preclude NIH funding of human in vitro gametogenesis).

24 Rebecca S. Eisenberg, *The Role of the FDA in Innovation Policy*, 13 MICH. TELECOMM. & TECH. L. REV. 345, 348 (2007).

25 21 U.S.C. § 355.

26 *Drug Approval Process*, FDA, www.fda.gov; U.S. Food and Drug Admin., *Patents and Exclusivity*, FDA/CDER SBIA CHRONICLES (May 19, 2015), www.fda.gov.

27 *Patents and Exclusivity*, *supra* note 26.

28 *Human Cloning: Must We Sacrifice Medical Research in the Name of a Total Ban?*, Hearing Before the Senate Judiciary Committee, 107th Congress, 2d Session (Feb. 5, 2002), at 1.
29 *The Life of Dolly*, UNIV. EDINBURGH (Sept. 2, 2024), https://vet.ed.ac.uk.
30 *Id.*
31 *Human Embryo Transfer*, *supra* note 9 at 23, 241.
32 Meredith Wadman, *Dolly: A Decade On*, 445 NATURE 800, 800–801 (2007); Ewen Callaway, *Dolly at 20: The Inside Story on the World's Most Famous Sheep*, 534 NATURE 604 (2016).
33 *Review of the President's Commission's Recommendations on Cloning*, Hearing before the Committee on Science, Subcommittee on Technology, U.S. House of Representatives, 105th Congress (June 12, 1997), at 1.
34 *Id.* at 9; Nat'l Bioethics Advisory Comm., CLONING HUMAN BEINGS: REPORT AND RECOMMENDATIONS OF THE NATIONAL BIOETHICS ADVISORY COMMITTEE (1997).
35 *Scientific Discoveries in Cloning: Challenges for Public Policy*, Hearing Before the Senate Subcommittee on Public Health and Safety of the Committee on Labor and Human Resources (Mar. 12, 1997), at 1.
36 *Review of the President's Commission's Recommendations on Cloning*, *supra* note 33 at 1.
37 *See Human Cloning*, *supra* note 28 at 12, 14 (providing the statement of Representative James C. Greenwood discussing a hearing he held on March 28, 2001, "in the Energy and Commerce Oversight and Investigation Subcommittee that found that the science existed and that there were sufficiently funded fringe groups that sought to clone a human being").
38 Raja Mishra, *Woman Carries Human Clone, Group Says*, BOSTON GLOBE (July 25, 2002), Thursday, Third Edition, National/Foreign, p. A15 (cited in *Medical Science and Bioethics: Attack of the Clones?*, *supra* note 5 at 246)).
39 *Medical Science and Bioethics: Attack of the Clones?*, *supra* note 5 at 252–54 (citing *Human Embryo Created Through Cloning*, CNN.COM (Nov. 26, 2001)).
40 *Id.* at 250–51.
41 *Id.* at 246–47.
42 *Id.* at 260 (citing John Follain, *Second Scientists Set to Clone Humans: Project to Go Ahead Despite Concerns over Malformations*, THE SUNDAY TIMES (Apr. 14, 2002), A6).
43 *See Medical Science and Bioethics: Attack of the Clones?*, *supra* note 5.
44 *Id.* at 1–2.
45 *Id.* at 2.
46 *Id.* at 2.
47 *Id.* at 2.
48 *Id.* at 8.
49 *See, e.g.*, *The Threat of Human Cloning*, THE NEW ATLANTIS (Summer 2015), www.thenewatlantis.com (providing an appendix of state laws on cloning).

50 *Review of the President's Commission's Recommendations on Cloning*, *supra* note 33 at 2, 32.
51 Nat'l Bioethics Advisory Comm., *supra* note 34 at 3.
52 *Review of the President's Commission's Recommendations on Cloning*, *supra* note 33 at 2.
53 Nat'l Bioethics Advisory Comm., *supra* note 34 at iv.
54 *Review of the President's Commission's Recommendations on Cloning*, *supra* note 33 at 2.
55 *Review of the President's Commission's Recommendations on Cloning*, *supra* note 33 at 7.
56 Nat'l Bioethics Advisory Comm., *supra* note 34 at 43–58.
57 *Ethics and Theology: A Continuation of the National Discussion on Human Cloning*, Hearing Before the Subcommittee on Public Health and Safety of the Committee on Labor and Human Resources, U.S. Senate, 105th Cong. (June 17, 1997).
58 Nat'l Bioethics Advisory Comm., *supra* note 34 at 63–83.
59 Nat'l Bioethics Advisory Comm., *supra* note 34 at 87–127.
60 *Medical Science and Bioethics: Attack of the Clones?*, *supra* note 5 at 336 (providing Jeremy Manier, *Cloning Backers Bank on Science; New Research Is Timed to Sway Political Debate*, CHICAGO TRIBUNE (May 7, 2002)).
61 *Review of the President's Commission's Recommendations on Cloning*, *supra* note 33 at 214.
62 *Ethics and Theology*, *supra* note 57 at 35.
63 Nat'l Bioethics Advisory Comm., *supra* note 34 at 101.
64 *Id.* at 122.
65 *Human Cloning*, Senate Committee on Commerce, Science, and Transportation, 107th Congress (May 2, 2001); *Cloning, 2002*, Special Hearing Before the Senate Subcommittee on Labor, HHS, and Education Appropriations, 107th Congress, (Jan. 24, 2002).
66 *Medical Science and Bioethics: Attack of the Clones?*, *supra* note 5 at 342 (citing Associated Press, *Poll: Public Overwhelmingly Opposes Cloning; Fewer Support Federal Funding of Stem Cell Research* (Apr. 9, 2002)).
67 *Id.* at 342–48.
68 *The Promise of Human Embryonic Stem Cell Research*, Special Hearing Before the Subcommittee on Labor, HHS, Education, and Related Agencies, 111th Congress (Sept. 16, 2010), at 3.
69 *The Promise of Human Embryonic Stem Cell Research*, *supra* note 68 at 72.
70 *Medical Science and Bioethics: Attack of the Clones?*, *supra* note 5 at 56.
71 *See Human Cloning*, *supra* note 28 at 5.
72 *Medical Science and Bioethics: Attack of the Clones?*, *supra* note 5 at 95–96.
73 *Id.* at 5.
74 Tanya Ballard Brown, *Conservative Icon Phyllis Schlafly Dies at 92*, NPR, (Sept. 5, 2016, 9:20 PM), www.npr.org/sections/thetwo-way/2016/09/05/492748832/conservative-icon-phyllis-schlafly-dies-at-92.

75 *Medical Science and Bioethics: Attack of the Clones?*, *supra* note 5 at 491 (citing Phyllis Schlafly, *Ban Cloning, Without an Enron Loophole*, COPLEY NEWS SERVICE (Apr. 15, 2002)).
76 *See Human Cloning*, *supra* note 28 at 1.
77 *Id.* at 5; *id.* at 15 (providing the statement of Senator Harlen Specter, who noted, "In hearings which we had in the Appropriations Subcommittee for Health and Human Services, we called it a nuclear transplant, and I see that Senator Hatch today has called it DNA regenerative therapy").
78 *See Human Cloning*, *supra* note 28 at 5.
79 *Medical Science and Bioethics: Attack of the Clones?*, *supra* note 5 at 16.
80 *Id.*
81 *Id.* at 35.
82 *Id.*
83 *Id.*
84 *Id.* at 54.
85 *Id.* at 250 (citing Agence France Presse, *Cloning on Six Couples to Start This Year: British Press* (July 21, 2002).
86 *See Human Cloning*, *supra* note 28 at 8.
87 *Id.* at 8, 11.
88 *Id.* at 74.
89 The White House, President George W. Bush, *President Discusses Stem Cell Research* (Aug. 9, 2001), https://georgewbush-whitehouse.archives.gov/news/releases/2001/08/20010809-2.html.
90 *The Promise of Human Embryonic Stem Cell Research*, *supra* note 68 at 1.
91 *Id.*
92 *Id.* at 3.
93 *President Discusses Stem Cell Research*, *supra* note 89.
94 *Id.*
95 *Id.*
96 Andrew Glass, *Stem Cell Research Gets Federal OK*, POLITICO (Aug. 9, 2018), www.politico.com/story/2018/08/09/stem-cell-research-gets-federal-ok-aug-9-2001-764402.
97 Sheila Kaplan, *Nancy Reagan: A "True Champion" of Alzheimer's Disease and Stem-Cell Research*, STAT NEWS (Mar. 6, 2016), www.statnews.com.
98 *The Dangers of Cloning and the Promise of Regenerative Medicine*, Hearing of the Senate Committee on Health, Education, Labor, and Pensions, 107th Congress (Mar. 5, 2002).
99 *Id.* at 2.
100 *Id.* at 19, 29–43.
101 *The Promise of Human Embryonic Stem Cell Research*, *supra* note 68.
102 *Id.* at 6–23.
103 *Id.* at 24–26.

104 *Id.* at 44.
105 *Medical Science and Bioethics: Attack of the Clones?*, *supra* note 5 at 270–22 (citing Paul Jacobs, *University of California–San Francisco Acknowledges Tests on Human Cloning*, SAN JOSE MERCURY NEWS (May 25, 2002)).
106 *The Promise of Human Embryonic Stem Cell Research*, *supra* note 68 at 463.
107 *Id.* at 35.
108 *Id.* at 31.
109 *Id.*
110 Davis v. Davis, 842 S.W. 2d 588 (Tenn. 1992).
111 *See, e.g.*, LePage v. Ctr. for Reprod. Med., P.C., No. SC-2022-0515, 2024 WL 656591 (Ala., Feb. 16, 2024); Aria Bendix & Bracey Harris, *Two Alabama Fertility Clinics Say They Will Resume IVF Services After Bill to Protect Doctors Passes*, NBC NEWS (Updated Mar. 7, 2024, 12:51 PM), www.nbcnews.com.
112 *Human Cloning*, *supra* note 28 at 18 (providing the statement of Representative Weldon).
113 *In-Vitro Fertilization*, *supra* note 1 at 91.
114 *Human Cloning*, *supra* note 28 at 4.
115 *The Promise of Human Embryonic Stem Cell Research*, *supra* note 68 at 32.
116 *Id.* at 42.
117 *See* President Obama, Executive Order 13505, *Removing Barriers to Responsible Research Involving Human Stem Cells* (Mar. 9, 2009).
118 *The Promise of Human Embryonic Stem Cell Research*, *supra* note 68 at 42, 88.
119 *Id.*
120 *Id.* at 71.
121 Meredith Wadman, *Scientists Decry President Bush's Veto of Stem-Cell Bill*, NATURE (June 21, 2007), www.nature.com.
122 David Greene, *Bush Vetoes Bill to Expand Stem Cell Research*, NPR (July 19, 2006, 2:19 PM), www.npr.org.
123 *See* 5 U.S.C.A. § 1001 et seq. *See, e.g.*, 41 C.F.R. §§ 102–3.10.
124 *The Federal Advisory Committee Act Brochure*, U.S. GENERAL SVCS. ADMIN. (Aug. 21, 2024), www.gsa.gov.
125 *Id.*
126 Lee Fang, *Where Have All the Lobbyists Gone?*, THE NATION (Feb. 19, 2014), www.thenation.com/article/archive/shadow-lobbying-complex/.
127 Marta Sienkiewicz et al., *Navigating Interests in a Science for Policy Environment*, in SCIENCE FOR POLICY HANDBOOK, 112–13 (Science Direct 2020).
128 *Id.* at 112.
129 Citizens United v. Federal Election Commission, 558 U.S. 310 (2010).
130 Kavitha Surana, *"We Need to Defend This Law": "Inside an Anti-Abortion Meeting with Tennessee's GOP Lawmakers*, PROPUBLICA (Nov. 15, 2022, 12 PM), www.propublica.org.
131 *Id.*
132 *Id.*

133 14 C.F.R. § 1230.102—Definitions for purposes of this policy.

134 *Id.*

135 *Federal Policy for the Protection of Human Subjects*, 34 § 97.101–4 (1991), www.ecfr.gov/current/title-34/subtitle-A/part-97.

136 Nat'l Research Act of 1974 H.R.7724, 93rd Cong. 88 § 101 (1973), www.congress.gov.

137 *See* Barry Furrow et al., HEALTH LAW: CASES, MATERIALS AND PROBLEMS 1481 (8th ed., West Academic 2018); *see, e.g.*, *Institutional Review Boards Frequently Asked Questions: Guidance for Institutional Review Boards and Clinical Investigators*, U.S. FOOD & DRUG ADMIN. (Jan. 1998), www.fda.gov.

138 *Federal Policy for the Protection of Human Subjects ("Common Rule")*, U.S. DEPT. HEALTH & HUMAN SVCS. (updated Mar. 18, 2016), www.hhs.gov/ohrp/regulations-and-policy/regulations/common-rule/index.html.

139 *Research Implications*, CDC (Apr. 21, 2021), www.cdc.gov; 93 P.L. 348 (1974).

140 93 P.L. 348 (1974); *Institutional Review Boards (IRBs) and Protection of Human Subjects in Clinical Trials*, FDA (Sept. 11, 2019), www.fda.gov; Christine Grady, *Institutional Review Boards; Purposes and Challenges*, 148 CHEST 1148–55 (Nov. 2015).

141 *Guidance Regarding Federal Requirements for IRB Review of Grants*, NW. UNIV. (last visited Sept. 20, 2022), https://irb.northwestern.edu/resources-guidance/policies-guidance/guidance-regarding-federal-requirements-for-irb-review-of-grants.html; *IRBs*, HHS: OFF. RSCH. INTEGRITY, https://ori.hhs.gov/content/chapter-3-The-Protection-of-Human-Subjects-IRBs; *Serve on Boards to Review and Monitor Clinical Trials; Institutional Review Boards*, NATIONAL CENTER FOR ADVANCING TRANSLATIONAL SCIENCES, https://toolkit.ncats.nih.gov/module/clinical-trials-and-fda-review/serving-on-boards-to-review-and-monitor-clinical-trials/institutional-review-board/.

142 45 C.F.R. § 46.107 IRB membership.

143 Luis Bradley Fandino, Alexander F.C. Hulsbergen & Marike L.D. Broekman, *Oversight in Surgical Innovation: A Response to Ethical Challenges*, 42 WORLD. J. SURGERY 2773, 2773 (2018).

144 *See, e.g.*, Furrow et al., *supra* note 137 at 1492–94.

145 *After Asilomar* (editorial), 526 NATURE 293, 293 (2015).

146 Berg and Mertz, *supra* note 16 at 16 (citing Paul Berg et al., *Summary Statement of the Asilomar Conference on Recombinant DNA Molecules*, 72 PROC. NAT'L ACAD. SCI. 1981 (1975)).

147 Paul Berg et al., *Summary Statement of the Asilomar Conference on Recombinant DNA Molecules*, 72 PROC. NAT'L ACAD. SCI. 1981 (1975).

148 *Id.* at 1984 (1975).

149 Berg and Mertz, supra note 16 at 16 (citing NIH, *Guidelines for Research Involving Recombinant DNA*, 1976).

150 Alexander M. Capron, *Prologue: Why Recombinant DNA?*, 51 S. CAL. L. REV. 973, 975 (1978).

151 *See* Myrisha S. Lewis, *How Subterranean Regulation Hinders Innovation in Assisted Reproductive Technology*, 39 CARDOZO L. REV. 1239, 1243 (2018); *see, e.g.*, U.S. Dep't of Health and Human Svcs., *Federalwide Assurance Instructions* (July 31, 2017), www.hhs.gov.

152 *See* Stephen P. Goff and Thomas Shenk, *Paul Berg: Recombinant DNA Trailblazer*, 120 PROCEEDINGS NAT'L ACAD. SCIS. e3318196120 at 2 (2023).

153 *See, e.g., Points to Consider in the Design and Submission of Human Somatic-Cell Gene Therapy Protocols*, 50 FED. REG. 33,463, 33,464 (Aug. 19, 1985).

154 *See id.*

155 LeRoy Walters, Robert M. Cook-Deegan & Eli Y. Adashi, *Governing Heritable Human Genome Editing: A Textual History and a Proposal for the Future*, Perspective, 4 CRISPR J. 469, 470–72 (2021).

156 *Id.*

157 Francis S. Collins & Scott Gottlieb, *The Next Phase of Human Gene-Therapy Oversight*, 379 N ENGL. J. MED. 1393 (2018).

158 *See* Russell A. Spivak, I. Glenn Cohen & Eli Y. Adashi, *Germ-Line Gene Editing and Congressional Reaction in Context: Learning from Almost 50 Years of Congressional Reactions to Biomedical Breakthroughs*, 30 J.L. & HEALTH 20, 20, 22–23 (citing Consolidated Appropriations Act of 2016, Pub. L. No. 114-92, § 749, 129 Stat. 2242, 2283 (2015)).

159 Hannah Devlin, *Scientist Who Edited Babies' Genes Says He Acted "Too Quickly,"* THE GUARDIAN (Feb. 4, 2023, 4:00 AM), www.theguardian.com; Dennis Normile, *Chinese Scientist Who Produced Genetically Altered Babies Sentenced to 3 Years in Jail*, SCIENCE (Dec. 30, 2019), www.science.org/content/article/chinese-scientist-who-produced-genetically-altered-babies-sentenced-3-years-jail; Associated Press, *Hong Kong Pulls Visa for Man Behind Gene-Edited Babies Claim*, U.S. NEWS (Feb. 21, 2023 5:13 AM), www.usnews.com/news/health-news/articles/2023-02-21/scientist-behind-gene-edited-babies-eyes-work-in-hong-kong.

160 Devlin, *supra* note 159; Simone McCarthy, *Controversial Chinese Scientist He Jiankui Proposes New Gene Editing Research*, CNN (July 3, 2023), www.cnn.com/2023/07/03/china/he-jiankui-gene-editing-proposal-china-intl-hnk-scn/index.html.

161 Devlin, *supra* note 159.

162 *Statement on NIH Funding of Research Using Gene-Editing Technologies in Human Embryos*, NAT'L INSTS. HEALTH (Apr. 28, 2015), www.nih.gov.

163 Jane Qiu, *American Scientist Played More Active Role in "CRISPR Babies" Project than Previously Known*, STAT NEWS (Jan. 31, 2019), www.statnews.com.

164 *See, e.g.*, Eric S. Lander et al., *Adopt a Moratorium on Heritable Genome Editing*, 567 NATURE 165, 168 (2019); *Broad Scientists and Geneticists Discuss Issues Raised by Clinical Germline Genome Editing*, BROAD INST. (Nov. 26, 2018), www.broadinstitute.org; Bryan Cwik, *Revising, Correcting, and Transferring Genes*, AM. J. BIOETHICS (Aug. 6, 2020), at 7; Alice Park, *Experts Are Calling for a Ban on Gene Editing of Human Embryos. Here's Why They're Worried*, TIME (Mar. 13, 2019, 2:22 PM), https://time.com.

165 *Human Embryo Transfer*, *supra* note 9 at 20.

166 Steve Connor, *Three-Parent Baby Pioneer: "The Brits Will Be Ahead of the World"; Despite the Death of Prematurely Born Twins, the Doctor Behind a Revolutionary Fertility Technique Tells Steve Connor It Is Safe*, INDEPENDENT (Jan. 16, 2015). (Dr. Jamie Grifo noted, "What was threatening was they couldn't give me a sense of what the consequences would be . . . if I continued. They made it sound as if there would be recourse without saying it. I was very threatened.")

167 *See, e.g.*, Nat'l Right to Life, *Human Cloning Legislation in Congress: Misconceptions and Realities* (Sept. 13, 2005), www.nrlc.org.

168 *See, e.g.*, H. L. A. Hart, *Positivism and the Separation of Law and Morals*, 71 HARV. L. REV. 593, 598 (1958).

169 *Id.*

170 Lon L. Fuller, *Positivism and Fidelity to Law—A Reply to Professor Hart*, 71 HARV. L. REV. 630, 631 (1958).

171 *Id.* at 651.

172 *Id.*

CHAPTER 7. "LOST" FDA FILES, MORALITY, AND THE ABORTION DEBATE

1 FDA v. Alliance for Hippocratic Medicine, 602 U.S. 367 (2024). *See also* Andy Sullivan, *Explainer: How Abortion Became a Divisive Issue in U.S. Politics*, EDT (June 24, 2022, 11:49 PM), www.reuters.com; Amer. College of Obstetricians and Gynecologists, *ACOG Guide to Language and Abortion*, www.acog.org.

2 Alliance for Hippocratic Medicine, *supra* note 1.

3 *See* David S. Cohen, Greer Donley & Rachel Rebouché, *Abortion Pills*, 76 STANFORD L. REV. 317, 324 (2024).

4 *Medical Abortion*, CLEVELAND CLINIC (Jan. 16, 2024), https://my.clevelandclinic.org.

5 *See The Abortion Pill*, PLANNED PARENTHOOD, www.plannedparenthood.org/learn/abortion/the-abortion-pill.

6 Benten v. Kessler, 799 F. Supp. 281, 286 (E.D.N.Y. 1992).

7 *Id.* at 284.

8 *Id.* at 286.

9 *Id.* at 290.

10 Benten v. Kessler, 505 U.S. 1084, 1084 (1992).

11 *Hearing on the Effect of Federal Ban of RU 486 on Medical Research, New Drug Development, and Pharmaceutical Manufacturers*, 102nd Congress (July 28, 199), at 1–2.

12 *Id.* at 3–4.

13 *Id.* at 8, 12–13.

14 *Mifeprex (Mifepristone) Approval Letter*, FDA (Sept. 28, 2000), www.accessdata.fda.gov.

15 *Questions and Answers on Mifepristone for Medical Termination of Pregnancy Through Ten Weeks Gestation*, FDA (Sept. 1, 2023), www.fda.gov.

16 *See* Planned Parenthood, *supra* note 5.

17 Cohen, Donley & Rebouché, *supra* note 3 at 324.

18 Rachel K. Jones and Amy Friedrich-Karnik, *Medication Abortion Accounted for 63% of All US Abortions in 2023—An Increase from 53% in 2020*, Policy Analysis, GUTTMACHER (Mar. 2024), www.guttmacher.org.

19 Cohen, Donley & Rebouché, *supra* note 3 at 325–26.

20 *See, e.g.*, R. Alta Charo, *Review: Who Controls Birth Control?*, 9 THE WOMEN'S REV. OF BOOKS 18, 19 (1992) (reviewing Renate Klein, Janice Raymond & Lynette Dumble, RU 486: MISCONCEPTIONS, MYTHS, AND MORALS (Spinifex Press 2013); and Etienne-Emile Baulieu & Mort Rosenblum, THE "ABORTION" PILL (Simon & Schuster 1991)).

21 Lauren Collins, *The Complicated Life of the Abortion Pill: A French Doctor's Invention and Post-Roe America*, THE NEW YORKER, July 5, 2022, www.newyorker.com.

22 *Id.*

23 *Id.*

24 *See* Margaret Talbot, *The Little White Bombshell*, N.Y. TIMES (July 11, 1999), sec. 6, p. 39, www.nytimes.com.

25 *See* Collins, *supra* note 21.

26 R. Alta Charo, *supra* note 20 at 18–19; Talbot, *supra* note 24.

27 Institute of Medicine Committee to Study Decision Making, Division of Health Sciences Policy, A POLITICAL HISTORY OF RU-486 IN BIOMEDICAL POLITICS (Kathi E. Hanna ed.) (National Academies Press 1991), 66.

28 *See* R. Alta Charo, *supra* note 20 at 19.

29 *See* A POLITICAL HISTORY OF RU-486 IN BIOMEDICAL POLITICS, *supra* note 27 at 66.

30 *See* Collins, *supra* note 21.

31 *See* R. Alta Charo, *supra* note 20 at 19; A POLITICAL HISTORY OF RU-486 IN BIOMEDICAL POLITICS, *supra* note 27.

32 *See* R. Alta Charo, *supra* note 20 at 19.

33 *Id.*

34 *See* Talbot, *supra* note 24.

35 *See* Melody Peterson, *Abortion Pill Distributor Energized by New Mission*, N.Y. TIMES (Sept. 30, 2000), A10.

36 *Id.*

37 *See* Talbot, *supra* note 24.

38 *See id.*

39 *Questions and Answers on Mifepristone*, *supra* note 15.

40 *Human Cloning: Must We Sacrifice Medical Research in the Name of a Total Ban?*, Senate Judiciary Committee, 107th Congress, 2d Session (Feb. 5, 2002), HRG-2002-SJS-0045, at 62 (providing the statement of Andrew Kimbrell).

41 *Cloning: Legal, Medical, Ethical, and Social Issues*, Hearing Before the Subcommittee on Health and Environment, 105th Cong. (Feb. 12, 1998), at III; *The Prohibition of Federal Government Funding of Human Cloning Research*,

Hearing Before the House Committee on Science, 105th Cong. (July 22, 1997); *Human Cloning*, Hearing Before the Subcommittee on Crime of the Committee on the Judiciary, House of Rep., 107th Cong. (June 07, 2001); *Human Cloning Prohibition Act of 2001 and the Cloning Prohibition Act of 2001*, Hearing Before the Subcommittee on Health, 107th Cong. (June 20, 2001).

42 *See Human Cloning: Must We Sacrifice*, *supra* note 40 at 20–21 (providing the statement of Irving L. Weissman, MD, who appeared as "Chair of the National Academies' Panel on Scientific and Medical Aspects of Human Reproductive Cloning, which released its report on January 18 of this year").

43 *See also* City Council, Cambridge, Massachusetts, Ordinance for the Use of Recombinant DNA Molecule Technology in the City of Cambridge, Ordinance No. 874 (Jan. 27, 1977).

44 Jack Balkin, *The Cloning Conundrum*, N.Y. Times (Jan. 30, 2002).

45 *Medical Science and Bioethics: Attack of the Clones?*, Hearing Before the House Subcommittee on Criminal Justice, Drug Policy, and Human Resources (May 15, 2002), 126.

46 *Id.*

47 *Id.*

48 *Id.* at 127.

49 *Id.* at 128.

50 *Id.*

51 *Id.*

52 *Id.*

53 *Id.* at 129–30.

54 *Id.* at 287 (citing Associated Press, *Doctor Agrees Not to Try Human Cloning, for Now*, Washington Dateline (June 29, 2001)).

55 *Id.*

56 *Id.*

57 *Medical Science and Bioethics*, *supra* note 45 at 131–33.

58 *Id.* at 132–33.

59 *Id.* at 136.

60 *Id.* at 252–53.

61 *See Human Cloning: Must We Sacrifice*, *supra* note 40 at 49. Professor Henry T. Greely characterized the FDA's assertion of jurisdiction over cloning as "questionable"; Professor Alta Charo found it "unproblematic although certainly Congress could help by making it easier to understand." Outside of congressional testimony, others, including myself, have argued that human cloning is outside of the FDA's jurisdiction. After the hearing, in his response to questions posed by Senator Feinstein, Professor Greely cited two law review articles on the subject: Elizabeth C. Price, *Does the FDA Have Authority to Regulate Human Cloning?*, 11 Harv. J. L. & Tech. 619 (1998); and Gregory J. Rokosz, *Is the Reach of FDA Authority Too Far a Stretch?*, 30 Seton Hall L. Rev. 464 (2000)). *See Human Cloning: Must We Sacrifice*, *supra* note 40 at 70.

62 *See Human Cloning: Must We Sacrifice*, *supra* note 40 at 78 (providing the statement of Senator Maria Cantwell of the State of Washington).

63 *See, e.g.*, Paul Gowder, *Why Majority Religions Should Not Be Accommodated*, 108 Iowa L. Rev. 2153 (2023).

64 *See id.*; Ben Olinsky & Grace Oyenubi, *The Supreme Court's Extreme Majority Risks Turning Back the Clock on Decades of Progress and Undermining Our Democracy*, Ctr. for Amer. Progress (June 13, 2022), www.americanprogress.org/article/the-supreme-courts-extreme-majority-risks-turning-back-the-clock-on-decades-of-progress/.

65 *NIH Reauthorization*, April 15, 1991, Hearings Before the Subcommittee on Health and the Environment to Consider H.R. 1532, pp. 5–125, Committee on Energy and Commerce Serial No. 102-24.

66 *Id.*

67 *See id.* at 1-2, 126, 140–41.

68 *See id.* at 126.

69 *See id.* at 127.

70 *Id.*

71 *Id.* at 4.

72 *See* 42 U.S.C. §§ 263a-1 to -7 (2012) (codifying the Fertility Clinic Success Rate Act).

73 *Id.*

74 *See* Rokosz, *supra* note 61 at 464, 503 n.201 (citing Price, *supra* note 61 at 619, 631).

75 *See Human Cells, Tissues, and Cellular and Tissue-Based Products; Establishment Registration and Listing*, 66 Fed. Reg. 5447 (Jan. 19, 2001).

76 21 C.F.R. § 1271.3 (2016).

77 *See* 2001 HCT/P Rule, *supra* note 75.

78 *See* Cynthia Soohoo, *Hyde-Care for All: The Expansion of Abortion-Funding Restrictions Under Health Care Reform*, 15 CUNY L. Rev. 391, 391 (2012).

79 Harris v. McRae, 448 U.S. 297, 318 (1980).

80 *See* 22 U.S.C. § 2151b ("(1) None of the funds made available to carry out subchapter I of this chapter may be used to pay for the performance of abortions as a method of family planning or to motivate or coerce any person to practice abortions").

81 22 U.S.C.A. § 2151b (West).

82 *Abortion Funding Restriction Act*, Hearings Before the Subcommittee on the Constitution, 99th Congress (Apr. 2 and July 22, 1985) at 150 (providing the testimony of Dr. Byron Masterson, who represented both the American College of Obstetrics and Gynecology and the American Medical Association).

83 *Id.* at 150.

84 *Id.* at 151.

85 Navy Med. Female Force Readiness Clinical Committee, *What to Know: Accessing Plan B®*, Patient Guide, www.med.navy.mil/.

86 Katie Moisse and Mikaela Conley, *Plan B: HHS Prevents Morning After Pill from Hitting Drug Store Shelves*, ABC News (Dec. 7, 2011), https://abcnews.go.com.

87 Lisa Heinzerling, *The FDA's Plan B Fiasco: Lessons for Administrative Law*, 102 Georgetown L. J. 927, 947 (2014).

88 *Id.* at 955–56; *id.* at 961–62.

89 *See generally id.* Subsequent versions of Plan B and Plan B One-Step, and their generic versions, are now available on the market.

90 *See* Heinzerling, *supra* note 87 at 939.

91 Tummino v. Torti, 603 F. Supp. 2d 519, 535 (E.D.N.Y. 2009), amended sub nom. Tummino v. Hamburg, No. 05-CV-366 ERK VVP, 2013 WL 865851 (E.D.N.Y. Mar. 6, 2013). *See also* Heinzerling, *supra* note 87 at 944–45.

92 *See* Heinzerling, *supra* note 87 at 950.

93 *Food and Drug Administration: Decision Process to Deny Initial Application for Over-the-Counter Marketing of the Emergency Contraceptive Drug Plan B Was Unusual*, Govt. Acctg. Offc. (Nov. 2005), GAO-06-109, www.gao.gov.

94 Myrisha S. Lewis, *How Subterranean Regulation Hinders Innovation in Assisted Reproductive Technology*, 39 Cardozo Law Review 1239 (2018).

95 Stuart L. Nightingale, *Letter About Human Cloning*, U.S Food and Drug Admin. (Oct. 26, 1998), www.fda.gov/ScienceResearch/SpecialTopics/RunningClinicalTrials/ucm150508.htm.

96 *Id.*

97 *Id.*

98 Letter from Kathryn C. Zoon, PhD, Dir. Ctr. for Biologics Evaluation & Research, U.S. Food & Drug Admin., to Sponsors/Researchers (July 6, 2001). The letter is reproduced in Appendix A, *infra*.

99 *Id.*

100 *Id.*

101 *See* Lewis, *supra* note 94 at 1270–71.

102 *See, e.g.*, *The Dangers of Cloning and the Promise of Regenerative Medicine*, Hearing Before the Senate Committee on Health, Education, Labor, and Pensions (March 5, 2002) (referencing the bill to make human reproductive cloning illegal sponsored by Senators Feinstein and Kennedy).

103 *See* Lewis, *supra* note 94 at 1242 at n.6 (2018).

104 21 C.F.R. § 601.50.

105 *See* Transcript of Center for Biologics Evaluation and Research, Food and Drug Administration, Biological Response Modifiers Advisory Committee Open Session Meeting #32, 48–55 (May 9, 2002, 8:00 AM).

106 Steve Connor, *Three-Parent Baby Pioneer: "The Brits Will Be Ahead of the World"; Despite the Death of Prematurely Born Twins, the Doctor Behind a Revolutionary Fertility Technique Tells Steve Connor It Is Safe*, Independent (Jan. 17, 2015).

107 *Issuance of Untitled Letters*, FDA (Feb. 7, 2024), www.fda.gov/inspections-compliance-enforcement-and-criminal-investigations/compliance-actions-and-activities/issuance-untitled-letters.

108 *See* Letter from Mary A. Malarkey, Dir., Office of Compliance & Biologics Quality, U.S. Food & Drug Admin., to John Zhang, Chief Exec. Officer, Darwin Life, Inc.

& New Hope Fertility Ctr. (Aug. 4, 2017), www.fdanews.com/ext/resources/files/2017/08/08-07-17-CRL.pdf?1504514387.

109 *Id.*

110 Dori C. Woods & Jonathan L. Tilly, *The Next (Re)Generation of Ovarian Biology and Fertility In Women: Is Current Science Tomorrow's Practice?*, 98 FERTILITY AND STERILITY 3, 8 (2012).

111 OvaScience, Inc., *Annual Report (Form 10-K)*, at 15 (Mar. 16, 2015), www.sec.gov.

112 *Id.*

113 *See* FOIA Request 2016-4882 (on file with author).

114 *See* Complaint at 2, Ratner v. OvaScience, No. 13-cv-12286 (D. Mass. Sept. 16, 2013); Dahhan v. OvaScience, Inc., No. 1:17-CV-10511-IT, 2018 WL 3429901, at *1 (D. Mass.) (July 16, 2018).

115 OvaScience, Inc., *supra* note 111 at 15.

116 Karen Weintraub, *Turmoil at Troubled Fertility Company OvaScience*, MIT TECHNOLOGY REVIEW (Dec. 29, 2016), www.technologyreview.com/2016/12/29/106805/turmoil-at-troubled-fertility-company-ovascience/.

117 *OvaScience and Millendo Therapeutics Announce Merger to Create Leading Rare Endocrine Disease Company*, BUSINESS WIRE (Aug. 9, 2018), www.businesswire.com.

118 *SEC Charges Former Biotechnology Company CEO for Misleading Investors*, U.S. SEC (June 30, 2020), www.sec.gov.

119 *Id.*

120 *Tempest Closes Merger with Millendo and Completes PIPE Financing*, Tempest Therapeutics (June 28, 2021), https://ir.tempesttx.com. For more on the corporate actions of Millendo Therapeutics, *see, e.g.*, Brittany Meiling, *After Axing a Top Drug, Millendo Bags a PhII Replacement with Biotech Buyout*, ENDPOINTS NEWS (Dec. 20, 2017, 08:01 AM), https://endpts.com.

121 21 C.F.R. § 10.115.

122 Daniel J. Kenny & Catherine M. Sharkey, *FDA Leads, States Must Follow*, 102 WASH. U. L. REV. 155, 166 (2024) (citations omitted).

123 Nicholas R. Parrillo, *Federal Agency Guidance and the Power to Bind: An Empirical Study of Agencies and Industries*, 36 YALE J. ON REG. 165 (2016).

124 *Id.* at 184–85.

125 *See id.* at 186.

126 *See id.* at 187 (2016) (citation omitted).

127 *See id.* at 192 (2016) (citation omitted); *id.* at 198–99, 253.

128 *See* Parrillo, *supra* note 123 at 199.

129 *Id.* at 201–4.

130 *See id.* at 258, 261. *Id.* at 264 ("According to Thompson, counsel to device-maker trade associations, including that they 'often' had 'helped write' it, meaning they had a 'sense of ownership' of it").

131 *See* Parrillo, *supra* note 123 at 259.

132 *See id.* at 210.

133 Connor, *supra* note 106.

134 *See* Parrillo, *supra* note 123 at 212.

135 *See id.* at 256.

136 *See, e.g.*, Richard A. Merrill, *The Architecture of Government Regulation of Medical Products*, 82 VA. L. REV. 1753, 1864 (1996) ("The FD&C Act provides formal procedures for challenging agency decisions, but these administrative safeguards are almost never invoked. Nor are FDA's decisions—to grant, withhold, or delay approval—commonly challenged in court. Statutory directives do not materially affect the conduct or pace of agency review, nor do they control its evolving requirements for the data product sponsors must submit to gain marketing approval. The FDA product approval system is, in short, remarkably free from conventional legal constraint").

137 FDA v. Brown & Williamson Tobacco Corp., 529 U.S 120 (2000).

138 King v. Burwell, 576 U.S. 473, 486 (2015).

139 Pub. L. No. 111-31 (June 22, 2009).

140 *See* United States v. Regenerative Scis. LLC, 741 F.3d 1314, 1317 and 1321 (D.C. Cir. 2014); *see also* Myrisha S. Lewis, *Halted Innovation: The Expansion of Federal Jurisdiction over Medicine and the Human Body*, 2018 UTAH L. REV. 1073, 1098, 1105-08 (2018).

141 *See generally* Regenerative Scis., *supra* note 140; Lewis, *supra* note 140.

142 Rachel Sachs, W. Nicholson Price II & Patricia J. Zettler, *Rethinking Innovation at FDA*, 104 B.U. L. REV. 513, 546–47 (2023).

143 *Trust in CDC and FDA Is at a Low*, NPR (Sept. 25, 2020), www.npr.org; Selena Simmons-Duffin, *Poll Finds Public Health Has a Trust Problem*, NPR (May 13, 2021), www.npr.org (noting that "only 37% of Americans said they had a [great deal or] lot of trust in the National Institutes of Health or the Food and Drug Administration" and "52% of Americans have a great deal [or lot] of trust in CDC").

144 *See* Daniel G. Aaron, *The Fall of FDA Review*, 22 YALE J. OF HEALTH POL'Y, L., & ETHICS 95, 123 (2023).

145 *See id.* at 170–71; *id.* at 105 (2023) (citing Robert M. Califf et al., *Seven Former FDA Commissioners: The FDA Should Be an Independent Federal Agency*, 38 HEALTH AFFAIRS 84 (2019)).

146 Russell A. Spivak et al., *Germ-Line Gene Editing and Congressional Reaction in Context: Learning from Almost 50 Years of Congressional Reactions to Biomedical Breakthroughs*, 30 J. L. & HEALTH 20, 22 n.1 (citing Consolidated Appropriations Act of 2016, Pub. L. No. 114-92, § 749, 129 Stat. 2242, 2283 (2015)).

147 *See id.*

148 Jocelyn Kaiser, *Update: House Spending Panel Restores U.S. Ban on Gene-Edited Babies*, AM. ASS'N FOR THE ADVANCEMENT OF SCI. (June 4, 2019), www.science.org; Consolidated Appropriations Act of 2024, Pub. L. No. 118-42, § 737, 138 Stat. 25, 2283 (2015).

149 King v. Burwell, 576 U.S. 473, 491 (2015).

150 *See, e.g.*, Letter from FDA to Darwin Life, *supra* note 108.

151 *See* Heinzerling, *supra* note 87 at 952 (describing judicial actions in the case to permit certain types of discovery).

152 *See, e.g.*, Daniel A. Farber & Anne J. O'Connell, *The Lost World of Administrative Law*, 92 Tex. L. Rev. 1137, 1137 (2014); Emily Hammond & David L. Markell, *Administrative Proxies for Judicial Review: Building Legitimacy from the Inside-Out*, 37 Harv. Envtl. L. Rev. 313, 316 (2013); Miriam Seifter, *Second-Order Participation in Administrative Law*, 63 UCLA L. Rev. 1300, 1302 (2016).

153 *See* Heinzerling, *supra* note 87 at 952.

154 *Id.*

155 *See id.* at 958.

CHAPTER 8. REPRODUCTIVE GENETIC INNOVATION, SUBTERRANEAN REGULATION, AND WAYS TO REDUCE POLITICAL INFLUENCE ON REPRODUCTION

1 *About Us*, Human Fertilisation & Embryology Auth., www.hfea.gov.uk.

2 Human Fertilisation and Embryology Act, 1990, c. 37, § 5 (Eng.); *Human Fertilisation and Embryology Authority Access to Anonymised Data*, Human Fertilisation & Embryology Auth. (Nov. 23, 2011), https://data.gov.uk.

3 Myrisha S. Lewis, *The American Democratic Deficit in Assisted Reproductive Technology Innovation*, 45 Am. J. L. & Med. 130 (2019).

4 Jaime King, *Predicting Probability: Regulating the Future of Preimplantation Genetic Screening*, 8 Yale J. Health Pol'y & Ethics 283, 288 at n.20 (2008); Yaniv Heled, *The Regulation of Genetic Aspects of Donated Reproductive Tissue—the Need for Federal Regulation*, 11 Colum. Sci. & Tech. L. 243 (2010); Neroli Sawyer, *Who's Keeping Count? The Need for Regulation Is a Relative Matter*, 92 Fertility & Sterility 1811 (2009); Naomi Cahn, *Necessary Subjects: The Need for a Mandatory National Donor Gamete Databank*, 12 DePaul J. Health Care L. 203, 217–18 (Winter 2009).

5 OvaScience, Inc., *Annual Report (Form 10-K)*, at 15 (Mar. 16, 2015), www.sec.gov ("We are focusing our commercialization efforts for the AUGMENT treatment in countries in which we believe it does not not require pre-review and approval of an application for marketing authorization by the relevant regulatory authorities").

6 OvaScience, Inc., *supra* note 5 at 27.

7 *Id.*

8 Emily Mullin, *FDA Cracks Down on Pioneering Doctor Who Created a Three-Parent Baby*, MIT Tech. Rev. (Aug. 7, 2017), www.technologyreview.com.

9 OvaScience, Inc., *supra* note 5 at 31 ("We could be subject to negative publicity, political action and additional regulation because of the nature of our potential fertility treatments. These factors could increase our development and commercialization costs. . . . Product liability lawsuits against us could cause us to incur

substantial liabilities and to limit commercialization of any potential fertility treatments that we may develop").

10 *See, e.g.*, Paul D. Clement & Laurence H. Tribe, *Laboratory Testing Services, as the Practice of Medicine, Cannot Be Regulated as Medical Devices*, AMER. CLIN. LAB. ASSOC. (2015), www.acla.com/wp-content/uploads/2015/01/Tribe-Clement-White-Paper-1-6-15.pdf.

11 Transcript of Center for Biologics Evaluation and Research, Food and Drug Administration, Cellular, Tissue, and Gene Therapies Advisory Committee Meeting #59 (Feb. 25, 2014), at 13, https://wayback.archive-it.org.

12 *See id.* at 17–18.

13 *Human Cloning: Must We Sacrifice Medical Research in the Name of a Total Ban?*, Hearing Before the Senate Judiciary Committee, 107th Congress, 2d Session (Feb. 5, 2002), HRG-2002-SJS-0045, at 62.

14 *Id.* at 65.

15 *Id.* at 66 ("Questions submitted to Professor Greely by Senator Feinstein").

16 Anna Louise Sussman, *I Froze My Eggs in Europe to Save Money. Then, the Pandemic Hit*, ELLE (Nov. 23, 2020), www.elle.com; *Covid Restrictions Postpone Woman's IVF Treatments Abroad*, BBC NEWS (Nov. 3, 2020), www.bbc.com.

17 *See Medical Science and Bioethics: Attack of the Clones?*, Hearing Before the House Subcommittee on Criminal Justice, Drug Policy, and Human Resources (May 15, 2002), at 506–14.

18 *See* Charlotte Pritchard, *The Girl with Three Biological Parents*, BBC NEWS (Sept. 1, 2014), www.bbc.com; Rachel Nolan, *Behind the Cover Story: Kim Tingley on the Promise and Problems of Three-Parent I.V.F.*, N.Y. TIMES (June 30, 2014, 5:00 AM), http://6thfloor.blogs.nytimes.com; *see also* Transcript of Center for Biologics Evaluation and Research, Food and Drug Administration, Biological Response Modifiers Advisory Committee Open Session Meeting #32, 123–24 (May 9, 2002, 8:00 AM), www.fda.gov.

19 Yeganeh Torbati, *How a Renowned Fertility Doctor Profits from an Unproven Supplement*, WASH. POST. (July 30, 2023), www.washingtonpost.com.

20 *Id.*

21 *Id.*

22 *See, e.g.*, Katarina Lee, *An Ethical and Legal Analysis of OvaScience—A Publicly Traded Fertility Company and Its Lead Product AUGMENT*, 44 AMER. J. LAW & MED. 508, 522 (2018); Karen Weintraub, *Rejuvenating the Chance of Motherhood?*, MIT TECHNOLOGY REVIEW (Dec. 9, 2016), www.technologyreview.com.

23 Torbati, *supra* note 19.

24 The Ethics Comm. of the Am. Soc'y for Reprod. Med., *Disparities in Access to Effective Treatment for Infertility in the United States: An Ethics Committee Opinion*, 116 FERTILITY & STERILITY 52, 54 (2021).

25 *See* Myrisha S. Lewis, *Reproductive Innovation and Reproductive Exceptionalism: How Private Health Insurance Coverage of Fertility Treatment Complements Hostile*

Governmental Action and Expands Access to Assisted Reproduction in the United States, in HEALTH LAW AS PRIVATE LAW (I. Glenn Cohen, Christopher Robertson, Wendy Netter Epstein, Carmel Shacher & Susannah Baruch eds.) (Cambridge University Press 2025).

26 Anthony Kolodny, *How FDA Failures Contributed to the Opioid Crisis*, 22 AMA J. OF ETHICS 743, 744 (2020); Shannon Brownlee & Jeanne Lenzer, *What's Wrong with the FDA?*, WASHINGTON MONTHLY (Jan. 20, 2022); Thomas Tiedt, *The Drug Safety System Conundrum*, 62 FOOD & DRUG L. J. 547, 547–48 (2007).

27 *See* Daniel G. Aaron, *The Fall of FDA Review*, 22 YALE J. OF HEALTH POL'Y, L., & ETHICS 95, 175 (2023) (citing Rebecca S. Eisenberg, *The Role of FDA in Innovation Policy*, 13 MICH. TELECOMM. & TECH. L. REV. 345, 367 (2007)).

28 *Drug Safety: Improvement Needed in FDA's Postmarket Decision-Making and Oversight Process*, U.S. GOV'T ACCOUNTABILITY OFF. (2006), 5, GAO-06-402, www.gao.gov.

29 Wyeth v. Levine, 555 U.S. 555, 578–79 (2009).

30 *State of the Fertility Sector 2021/22*, HUMAN FERTILISATION & EMBRYOLOGY AUTHORITY (Oct. 2022), www.hfea.gov.uk.

31 Robert K. Naviaux & Keshav K. Singh, *Need for public Debate about Fertility Treatments*, 413 NATURE 347 (Sept. 27, 2001).

32 *See generally* Myrisha S. Lewis, *Segmented Innovation in the Legalization of Mitochondrial Transfer: Lessons from Australia and the United Kingdom*, 22 HOUSTON J. OF HEALTH L. & POL'Y 317 (2022); Myrisha S. Lewis, *The American Democratic Deficit in Assisted Reproductive Technology Innovation*, 45 AMER. J. OF L. & MED. 130 (2019).

33 *See* Françoise Baylis, ALTERED INHERITANCE: CRISPR AND THE ETHICS OF HUMAN GENOME EDITING (Harvard University Press 2019), 8 (arguing for societal consensus); Francis Collins, *Experts Conclude Heritable Human Genome Editing Not Ready for Clinical Applications*, NIH DIRECTOR'S BLOG (Sept. 17, 2020), https://directorsblog.nih.gov; Mary Todd Bergman, *Perspectives on Gene Editing*, HARVARD GAZETTE (Jan. 9, 2019), https://news.harvard.edu.

34 John P. Holdren, *A Note on Genome Editing*, THE WHITE HOUSE: PRESIDENT BARACK OBAMA (May 26, 2015, 10:40 AM), https://obamawhitehouse.archives.gov/.

35 The Nat'l Acads. of Sci., Eng'g & Med., MITOCHONDRIAL REPLACEMENT TECHNIQUES: ETHICAL, SOCIAL, AND POLICY CONSIDERATIONS (National Academies Press 2016).

36 *See* discussion in Chapter 5 *supra* (citing Hong Ma et al., *Germline Transmission of Donor, Maternal and Paternal mtDNA in Primates*, 36 HUM. REPROD. 493, 493 (2021), doi: 10.1093/humrep/deaa308P).

37 *The Science and Ethics of Genetically Engineered Human DNA*, Hearing Before the Subcommittee on Rsch. & Tech. of the H. Comm. on Sci., Space, and Tech., 114th Cong. (2015).

38 Jocelyn Kaiser, *Update: House Spending Panel Restores U.S. Ban on Gene-Edited Babies*, AM. ASS'N FOR THE ADVANCEMENT OF SCI. (June 4, 2019), www.science.org.

39 *Id.*
40 *Id.*
41 *Id.*
42 Myrisha S. Lewis, *Normalizing Reproductive Genetic Innovation*, 74 ADMIN. L. REV. 481, 485 (2022).
43 Paul Berg, *Asilomar and Recombinant DNA*, THE NOBEL PRIZE (Aug. 26, 2004), www.nobelprize.org.
44 *Id.*
45 *Id.*
46 *Id.*
47 *Id.*
48 Emily Moskal, *Nobel Prize Winner and Recombinant DNA Pioneer Paul Berg Dies*, Press Release, STANFORD MEDICINE (Feb. 17, 2023), https://med.stanford.edu.
49 *Centers for Disease Control and Prevention Awards Charles River Analytics Grant to Design a Tool for Fertility Clinics to Help Manage Pregnancy Outcomes*, CHARLES RIVER ANALYTICS (Sep. 27, 2022), https://cra.com.
50 *Id.*
51 *See About SBIR and STTR*, SBIR.GOV, www.sbir.gov.
52 Richard Harris, *U.S. Funding of Health Research Stalls as Other Nations Rev Up*, NPR (Jan. 13, 2015), www.npr.org.
53 *Development of Superactive Analogs of FSH for Human Infertility*, SMALL BUSINESS INNOVATION RESEARCH (2011), www.sbir.gov.
54 Todd Kuiken, *U.S. Trends in Synthetic Biology Research Funding*, WILSON CENTER (September 15, 2015), www.wilsoncenter.org/publication/us-trends-synthetic-biology-research-funding.
55 James R. Clapper, *Worldwide Threat Assessment of the US Intelligence Community: Statement for the Record to the Senate Armed Services Committee*, OFF. DIR. NAT'L INTEL. (Feb. 9, 2016), at 6–9, www.dni.gov.
56 Mohamed M. M. Kotb et al., *Does Dehydroepiandrosterone Improve Pregnancy Rate in Women Undergoing IVF/ICSI with Expected Poor Ovarian Response According to the Bologna Criteria? A Randomized Controlled Trial*, 200 EUR. J. OF OBSTETRICS, GYNECOLOGY, & REPRODUCTIVE BIOLOGY 11 (2016), doi:10.1016/j.ejogrb.2016.02.009; Tracy Wing Yee Yeung et al., *A Randomized, Controlled, Pilot Trial on the Effect of Dehydroepiandrosterone on Ovarian Response Markers, Ovarian Response, and In Vitro Fertilization Outcomes in Poor Responders*, 102 FERTILITY & STERILITY 108 (2014); A. Wiser et al., *Addition of Dehydroepiandrosterone (DHEA) for Poor-Responder Patients Before and During IVF Treatment Improves the Pregnancy Rate: A Randomized Prospective Study*, 25 HUMAN REPRODUCTION 2496 (2010).
57 C. Joseph Ross Daval et al., *Association of Advisory Committee Votes with US Food and Drug Administration Decision-Making on Prescription Drugs, 2010–2021*, 4 J. OF AMER. MED. ASSOC. HEALTH FORUM e231718. (2023), https://doi.org/10.1001/jamahealthforum.2023.1718.

58 Eva Heims & Sophie Moxon, *Mechanisms of Regulatory Capture: Testing Claims of Industry Influence in the Case of Vioxx*, 18 REGUL. & GOV. 139 (2023); Sandor Demeter, *The Dangers of 'Political Capture' for Clinicians and Scientists*, HEALTHY DEBATE (June 15, 2022), https://healthydebate.ca; *see* Aaron, *supra* note 27 at 95, 163–65.

59 Sarah Kliff & Azeen Ghorayshi, *Botched I.V.F. Liquid Destroyed Embryos, Lawsuits Claim*, N.Y. TIMES, Feb. 15, 2024, www.nytimes.com.

60 Elpiniki Chronopoulou & Joyce C. Harper, *IVF Culture Media: Past, Present and Future*, 21 HUMAN REPRODUCTION UPDATE 39–55 (Jan.–Feb. 2015), https://doi.org/10.1093/humupd/dmu040.

61 *See* Richard J. Paulson & Eli Y. Adashi, *The Unbearable Ignorance of the Composition of IVF Culture Media*, REPROD. BIOMEDICINE ONLINE (Oct. 26, 2023), https://doi.org/10.1016/j.rbmo.2023.103645; Lizzy Lawrence, *IVF Doctors Demand Full Details on Fluid That Grows Embryos amid CooperSurgical Lawsuits*, STAT NEWS (Mar. 8, 2024), www.statnews.com.

62 *Medical Science and Bioethics: Attack of the Clones?*, *supra* note 17 at 17; *id.* at 23. *See also* Myrisha S. Lewis, *How Analogizing Socio-Legal Responses to Organ Transplantation Can Further the Legalization of Reproductive Genetic Innovation*, 74 SMU L. REV. 665 (2021).

63 *Medical and Social Choices for Infertile Couples and the Federal Role in Prevention and Treatment*, Hearing Before a Subcommittee on the Committee on Government Operations, House of Representatives, 100th Congress (July 14, 1988), at 195.

64 Benten v. Kessler, 799 F. Supp. 281, 290 (E.D.N.Y. 1992).

65 Mary Warnock, *Moral Thinking and Government Policy: The Warnock Committee on Human Embryology*, 63 MILBANK MEMORIAL FUND QUARTERLY 504, 505 (1985).

CONCLUSION

1 James Barragan, *In Roe Decision, Justice Clarence Thomas Invites New Legal Challenges to Contraception and Same-Sex Marriage Rights*, TEX. TRIB. (June 24, 2022), www.texastribune.org; Christina Pazzanese, *Clarence Thomas Isn't Kidding*, HARV. GAZETTE (June 27, 2022), https://news.harvard.edu; Sheryl Gay Stolberg, *Thomas's Concurring Opinion Raises Questions About What Rights Might Be Next*, N.Y. TIMES (June 24, 2022), www.nytimes.com.

2 *See* Myrisha S. Lewis, *Personhood, Politics, Assisted Reproduction, and the Law Post-Dobbs*, 45 PACE L. REV. 83 (2024).

3 *Compare* Roe v. Wade, 410 U.S. 113 (1973) and Dobbs v. Jackson Women's Health Organization, 597 U.S. 215 (2022). *See also* discussion in Chapter 4 *supra*.

4 *See* Myrisha S. Lewis, *Normalizing Reproductive Genetic Innovation*, 74 ADMIN. L. REV. 493 (2022).

5 *See* Lauren Geisser, *INSIGHT: Employer-Subsidized Egg Freezing Benefits—Who Really Pays?*, BLOOMBERG L. (Dec. 21, 2018, 7:00 AM), https://news.bloomberglaw.com.

6 Tolga B. Mesen et al., *Optimal Timing for Elective Egg Freezing*, 103 Fertility & Sterility 1551 (2015).

7 *See, e.g.*, Anna Louie Sussman, *Tinder Drove Me to Freeze My Eggs*, The Economist (Feb. 14, 2022); Amanda Duberman, *"I Felt Liberated": How Freezing Their Eggs Changed These Women's Dating Lives for the Better*, HuffPost (Dec. 18, 2018), www.huffpost.com.

8 Mesen et al., *supra* note 6.

9 Seema Mody & Harriet Taylor, *Egg Freezing Has Become the Go-To for Delayed Parenthood—and Companies Are Popping Up to Provide More Cost-Effective Solutions*, CNBC (May 10, 2019, 3:28 PM), www.cnbc.com.

10 I. Glenn Cohen, George Q. Daley & Eli Y. Adashi, *Disruptive Reproductive Technologies*, 9 Sci. Translational Med. 1, 3 (2017); Sonia M. Suter, *In Vitro Gametogenesis: Just Another Way to Have a Baby?*, 3 J. L. & Biosciences 87 (2015).

11 Cohen, Daley, & Adashi, *supra* note 10 at 3; Jeremy Thompson, *The New Fertility Technology IVG Is Supposed to Change Everything. Don't Count On It Yet*, STAT News, First Opinion (Oct. 2, 2023), www.statnews.com.

12 Nat'l Acads. of Scis., Eng'g, and Med., In Vitro–Derived Human Gametes as a Reproductive Technology: Scientific, Ethical, and Regulatory Implications: Proceedings of a Workshop (National Academies Press 2023), 44 (noting that the FDA has not stated whether it interprets the congressional budget rider barring the agency from using its funds on an application for a clinical trial "in which a human embryo is intentionally created or modified to include a heritable genetic modification" applies to in vitro gametogenesis); *id.* at 48, 90–91.

13 *Id.* at 92.

14 Megan Molteni, *Meet the Fetal Surgeon Forging CRISPR's Next Frontier: Curing Diseases in the Womb*, STAT News (Feb. 21, 2024), www.statnews.com.

APPENDIX A

1 *Letter to Sponsors / Researchers—Human Cells Used in Therapy Involving the Transfer of Genetic Material by Means Other than the Union of Gamete Nuclei*, FDA (July 6, 2001) (on file with author).

APPENDIX B

1 *Letter About Cloning, Clinical Trials and Human Subject Protection*, FDA (Oct. 26, 1998), www.fda.gov/ScienceResearch/SpecialTopics/RunningClinicalTrials/ucm150508.htm (last visited July 13, 2016).

INDEX

Page numbers in *italics* indicate Tables.

Aaron, Daniel G., 142, 157
AARTs. *See* advanced assisted reproductive technologies
abbreviated new drug applications (ANDAs), 102
abortifacients, 10, 145. *See also* mifepristone; misoprostol
abortion, 201 at n. 45; advocacy groups against, 203 at n. 85; Dickey-Wicker Amendment and, 20–21, 70, 102, 131; *Dobbs v. Jackson Women's Health Organization* and, 16, 76–78, 83, 114, 146, 160–61; FDA and, 121–45; federal funding for, 19–20; genetic testing and, 85; Hyde Amendment on, 20, 70, 72, 130, 131–32; IVF for stem cell research and, 7; lobbyists against, 114; Medicaid and, 70; medical practice for, 16; municipal laws and, 16; PGT and, 90; religion and, 12, 64–83, 129–31; reproductive genetic innovation and, 129–31; *Roe v. Wade* and, 76, 82–83, 114, 161; states on, 76–80, 149; surgical centers for, 203 at n. 84
Abortion Funding Restriction Act, 224 at n. 82
Abram (Abraham), 2
abstinence-only, 202 at n. 64
ACOG. *See* American College of Obstetricians and Gynecologists
ACT. *See* Advanced Cell Technology
Adams, Jacqueline, 40–41
Adashi, Eli, 117
administrative agencies, 18–19. *See also specific agencies*
Administrative Conference of the United States, 139
Administrative Procedure Act, 82
adoption, 56–57, 67, 195 at n. 73; Snowflakes Frozen Embryo Adoption Program, 7, 69
adultery, 46–47, 51, 193 at n. 29
advanced assisted reproductive technologies (AARTs), 29, 37, 38–46, 95–96, 151–52; hands-off regime for, 146–59; parentage with, 49–50; subterranean regulation of, 47, 120, 143, 153. *See also* cytoplasmic transfer; mitochondrial transfer
Advanced Cell Technology (ACT), 69, 128–29
advisory committees, 113–14, 157
Affordable Care Act. *See* Patient Protection and Affordable Care Act
AIDS, 69, 105
Alabama, 112, 204 at n. 93, 206 at n. 125; *Dobbs v. Jackson Women's Health Organization* in, 16, 76–78, 83, 114, 146, 160–61; *LePage v. Center for Reproductive Medicine* in, 48, 75, 83
Alan Guttmacher Institute, 80
Alliance for Hippocratic Medicine, 121–22
Alphabet, 175 at n. 42
Alzheimer's disease, 69
AMA. *See* American Medical Association
Amato, Paula, 42, 96

Amazon, 80
American College of Obstetricians and Gynecologists (ACOG), 67, 132
American Fertility Society, 67
American Medical Association (AMA), 100, 132
American Society for Reproductive Medicine (ASRM), 23, 72–73, 107, 158
ANDAs. *See* abbreviated new drug applications
Andrews, Lori, 63, 74
animals, genetically altered, 94–95
Annas, George, 74
anonymous donation, 3
Antinori, Severino, 103
Apple, 8
APRICOT. *See* ART Provider and Patient Resources to Improve Communication about Outcomes and Treatment
Arizona, 57
Arsenault, Trent, 54
ART. *See* assisted reproductive technology
artificial insemination, 2–3, 30–31, 62, 130; as adultery, 46–47, 51, 193 at n. 29; health insurance for, 80, 82; parentage with, 50–52. *See also* intrauterine insemination; traditional surrogacy
ART Provider and Patient Resources to Improve Communication about Outcomes and Treatment (APRICOT), 156
Asilomar Conference, 12, 88–89, 116–17, 155
ASRM. *See* American Society for Reproductive Medicine
assisted reproductive technology (ART), 1, 5–6, 8, 10–11, 15–27, 82, 151–52; commercialization of, 52–55; in COVID-19 pandemic, 150; defined, 30, 184 at n. 15; demographics of, 37–38; development of, 28–47; ethical issues with, 36–38; for eugenics, 39; evolving legal issues with, 48–63; federal funding for, 19–20; funding restrictions for, 70–73; genetic revolution in, 84–97; hands-off regime for, 14, 146–59; health insurance for, 23–27, 152; intellectual property in, 157; laws of medicine and, 3–4; LGBTQ+ and, 38; marriage and, 47, 74; medical practice and, 153; parentage with, 49–50; patents for, 99–102; religion and, 64–83, 153–55; self-regulation of, 12–13, 22–23; societal discourse on, 153–55; in UK, 11, 32, 146; in Uniform Parentage Act, 184 at n. 14; in US, 28–29, 149–50, 156. *See also specific technologies*
AUGMENT, 13–14, 44, 138–39, 190 at n. 135, 228 at n. 5
Australia, 31, 46, 146, 190 at n. 143

Baby God, 63
Baby M, 7, 55–57
Balkin, Jack, 126
Baltimore, David, 89
Baulieu, Étienne-Émile, 123
Baylis, Francoise, 153
Becoming (Obama, M.), 1
Belfast Trust, 32
Benten, Leona, 121–22
Berg, Paul, 12, 86, 87, 88, 89, 100–101, 110, 155
bioethics, 85; on human cloning, 103–5; religion and, 73–76; on stem cell research, 110
biologic license applications (BLAs), 102
Boisselier, Brigitte, 103, 128
Boston Globe, 128–29
Boyer, Herbert W., 86–87, 89
A Brave New World (Huxley), 109
breast cancer, 61
Bridges, Khiara, 85
Brown, Louise Joy, 31, 41, 59–60, 66, 82, 92, 157
Brown & Williamson Tobacco v. FDA, 99, 141, 143
Buddhism, 79
Burroughs Wellcome Fund, 96

Burruss-Tucker, Kandi, 1
Bush, George W., 7, 22, 63–64, 108–11, 113
Buster, John, 100

California, 48, 53, 57, 59
California Institute for Regenerative Medicine (CIRM), 21, 106, 113
campaign contributions, 114
Campbell, Keith, 96
Canada, 45
cancer, 35, 61, 69, 87, 88, 93, 105
Canterbury v. Spense, 40
Cantwell, Maria, 129
Capron, Alexander, 69, 200 at n. 32
Carpenter, Dan, 142
Carr, Elizabeth Jordan, 31, 41, 59–60, 66–67, 71, 81, 85, 92
case law, 4
Casgevy, 92
Catholic Church, 47, 75, 112, 123
CBER. *See* Center for Biologics Evaluation and Research
CBS News, 40–41
CDC. *See* Centers for Disease Control and Prevention
CDER. *See* Center for Drug Evaluation and Research
Center for Biologics Evaluation and Research (CBER), 137
Center for Drug Evaluation and Research (CDER), 137
Centers for Disease Control and Prevention (CDC), 18, 29, 30, 177 at n. 20; APRICOT and, 156; in COVID-19 pandemic, 142; Fertility Clinic Success Rate Act and, 59, 130; IVF Success Estimator of, 59
CHAMPVA, 81
Charles River Analytics, 155
Charo, R. Alta, 108
Charpentier, Emmanuelle, 92
Chicago Tribune, 106
child custody laws, 21
Child Welfare Act, 21
chimpanzees, 94
China, 38, 53, 84, 118
Christianity, 73, 75–76, 78, 79, 202 at n. 64. *See also* Catholic Church
CIRM. *See* California Institute for Regenerative Medicine
Citizens United, 114
Clapper, James, 156
Clinton, Hillary, 79
Clonaid, 103
cloning: of animals, 91, 96, 102–6. *See also* human cloning
Cohen, Andy, 1
Cohen, Jacques, 5, 40–41
Cohen, Stanley N., 86–87, 89
Collins, Francis, 110, 111–12, 153
Colorado, 50
Columbia University, 42
Commerce Clause, 17, 22
commodification, 57
common law, 4
Common Rule, 115
Congressional Record, 106
Connecticut, 57
consent: for artificial insemination, 51; of children, 39–40
contraception: federal funding for, 19–20; Plan B, 120, 132–34, 145, 149, 158, 161; in PPACA, 69, 71; subterranean regulation on, 10
Cooper, Anderson, 1
CooperSurgical, 157
COVID-19 pandemic, 3, 8, 54, 142, 145, 150
Cowan, Bryan, 72–73, 107, 158
CRISPR-Cas9, 85; in China, 84, 118; FDA on, 92, 118; federal funding for, 156; in fertility clinics, 94; for germline gene editing, 92–94; Jiankui and, 12–13; patents for, 18
cryobanks, 52, 53–54
"Cryogenetics of Human Preimplantation Embryos" (Soupart), 66

cryopreservation (egg/gamete/embryo freezing), 2, 8–9, 16; for artificial insemination, 30; costs of, 161–62; disputes over use of, 7, 58; freezer failures with, 7, 35; health insurance for, 35; IVF and, 28–29, 34–35, 48; personhood of, 204 at n. 93; PGT and, 35; in US, 29
cytogenetics, 85
cytoplasmic transfer, 5, 40–42, 135, 146, 149

Daley, George Q., 38–39, 111
Danco Laboratories, 124
DARPA. *See* Defense Advanced Research Projects Agency
Davies, Sally, 96
Davis v. Davis, 58, 111–12
Defense Advanced Research Projects Agency (DARPA), 156
dehydroepiandrosterone (DHEA), 156
Delaware, 57
Department of Defense (DoD), 25–27, 82, 151–52
Department of Energy, 93
Department of Health, Education, and Welfare, 65, 71
Department of Health and Human Services (HHS), 9, 66; Common Law and, 115; EAB and, 158; embryo adoption and, 69; on Plan B, 132–33. *See also* Centers for Disease Control and Prevention; Food and Drug Administration; National Institutes of Health
Department of Veterans Affairs (VA), 25–27, 68, 152
designer babies, 39, 75
DHEA. *See* dehydroepiandrosterone
diabetes, 69, 87, 105
Diamond v. Chakrabarty, 86
Dickey-Wicker Amendment, 20–21, 70, 102, 131
Dion, Céline, 1
Dipp, Michelle, 139
disabilities, 37, 68, 74, 90
divorce: artificial insemination as adultery and, 46–47, 193 at n. 29; IVF and, 48
Dobbs v. Jackson Women's Health Organization, 16, 76–78, 83, 114, 146, 160–61
DoD. *See* Department of Defense
Dolly the sheep, 91, 96, 102–6
Doudna, Jennifer, 92, 93
doulas, 16
Down syndrome, 90
drugs: approval of, 177 at n. 13; cost of, 8; health insurance for, 81; safety and effectiveness of, 17–19. *See also* Food and Drug Administration; *specific drugs and drug types*

EAB. *See* Ethics Advisory Board
Eastern Virginia Medical School, 81
Edwards, Robert G., 31, 36
egg donors. *See* gamete donation
egg freezing. *See* cryopreservation
Egypt, 156
Ellis, Gary B., 72
embryo adoption, 69
embryo destruction, 102; in Alabama, 75; in ART, 38; in fertility clinics, 48, 58; human cloning and, 103–4; with IVF, 68
embryo freezing. *See* cryopreservation
Emmanuel, Ezekiel, 65
Employment Retirement Income Security Act of 1974, 24
England: ART in, 11; IVF in, 27, 31, 46; NHS in, 33; stem cell research in, 111
Ethics Advisory Board (EAB), 65–66, 72, 158, 201 at n. 56
eugenics, 39, 74, 90
Évin, Claude, 124
executive branch, 20–21. *See also* presidents

Facebook, 8, 54
family law, 16, 22, 179 at n. 46, 193 at n. 36
Family Smoking Prevention and Tobacco Control Act, 141

FDA. *See* Food and Drug Administration
FDA v. Alliance for Hippocratic Medicine, 121–22
FDCA. *See* Federal Food, Drug, and Cosmetic Act of 1938
FD&C Act, 227 at n. 136
Federal Advisory Committee Act, 114
Federal Criminal Code, 119
federal employees, 80–81
Federal Food, Drug, and Cosmetic Act of 1938 (FDCA), 105, 119, 127, 137, 144; Amendments of 1962 to, 17; jurisdiction of, 17–18
federalism, 15–18, 176 at n. 1
Federal Register, 66, 131
federal regulation. *See specific agencies, laws, and topics*
Federal Trade Commission (FTC), 18–19, 60
Feinstein, Dianne, 102, 107, 150
fertility clinics: in California, 59; CDC on, 18, 29; CRISPR-Cas9 in, 94; cryopreservation at, 35, 58; embryo destruction in, 48, 58; mix-ups in, 7; in New York, 59; shared risk programs in, 8; in states, 6; in Texas, 59; in US, 28; wrongful deaths in, 48
Fertility Clinic Success Rate Act of 1992, 30, 59, 62, 130; APRICOT and, 156; NBAC and, 105
fertility service, 29
Fifth Amendment, 82
Final Rule, 131
Finding Your Roots, 28
First Amendment, 73
"First do no harm," 36
Florida, 57
Food and Drug Administration (FDA), 4, 60; abortion and, 121–45; advisory committees of, 113–14; ART and, 13; artificial insemination and, 130; at-home kit for intravaginal insemination and, 31; on AUGMENT, 44–45; budget rider barring use of funds, 233 at n. 12; Common Law and, 115; in COVID-19 pandemic, 142; on CRISPR-Cas9, 92, 118; on cytoplasmic transfer, 5, 42, 135, 149; FTC and, 18–19; on gene editing, 117; on gene therapy, 92, 160; on germline gene editing, 5, 154; on GMOs, 95; heritable genetic modification and, 45, 154; Human Cellular and Tissue-Based Rule of, 138; human cloning and, 105–6, 125–29, 134–35, 223 at n. 61; IVF and, 130; jurisdiction of, 17–18; limited resources of, 152–53; on mitochondrial transfer, 5, 42, 44–45, 154; Office of Women's Health at, 133; patents and, 102; on Plan B, 132–34, 149, 161; premarket approval from, 61, 147; product approval system of, 227 at n. 136; reproductive genetic innovation and, 6, 160, 162–63; RU-486 and, 158; on stem cell research, 141–42; tobacco and, 99, 141; transparency at, 149, 158, 161. *See also* investigational new drug application; subterranean regulation
foods, genetically altered, 94–95
Fourteenth Amendment, 78
France, 123–24
Freedom of Information Act (FOIA), 13, 44, 122, 127
Fried, Marlene Gerber, 20
FTC. *See* Federal Trade Commission
Fuller, Lon L., 119–20

gamete donation: commercialization of, 52–55; fraudulent donor profiles for, 7; genetic databases for, 84; in Georgia, 198 at n. 121; lack of regulation of, 196 at n. 97; legitimate children from, 198 at n. 121; temporal storage limitations for, 32; in Uniform Parentage Act, 184 at n. 14; VA and, 25; for Washington, K., 28
gamete freezing. *See* cryopreservation
GAO. *See* Government Accounting Office

Gates, Henry Louis, Jr., 28
Gelsinger, Jesse, 91–92, 210 at n. 73
gene cloning, 91
gene editing, 117–18. *See also* CRISPR-Cas9; gene therapy; germline gene editing
Genentech, 86–87
gene therapy, 91; FDA on, 92, 160; IVF and, 96; at Pennsylvania Medical Center, 210 at n. 73
genetically modified organisms (GMOs), 95, 162
genetic counseling, 25, 85
genetic databases: for artificial insemination, 2–3; for gamete donation, 54, 84; genetic testing and, 54
genetic testing, 63, 74; abortion and, 85; cytogenetics and, 85; *Dobbs v. Jackson Women's Health Organization* and, 78; genetic databases and, 54; Hyde Amendment and, 131–32; IVF and, 90. *See also* preimplantation genetic testing
genome sequencing, 89–90
Georgia, 62, 198 at n. 121
germline gene editing, 85, 92–94; child's autonomy and, 40; in China, 38; ethical issues with, 37; FDA on, 5, 154; NBAC and, 105; NIH and, 70; as reproductive genetic innovation, 5; slippery slope of, 39; subterranean regulation of, 47, 143, 153
Gestational Age Act, in Mississippi, 77
gestational surrogate, 31, 57, 185 at n. 24
Gilbert, Walter, 12, 86
Gleicher, Norbert, 18–19, 151
Global Gag Rule, 20
GMOs. *See* genetically modified organisms
gonorrhea, 50
Google, 8, 175 at n. 42
Gordon Conference on Nucleic Acids, 87–88
Gordy, Kyle, 54
Gore, Albert, Jr., 67, 100
Government Accounting Office (GAO), 133–34, 152
Greece, 45–46
Greenwood, James C., 215 at n. 37
Grifo, James, 5, 24, 119, 140
Grobstein, Clifford, 84–85

Hagar, 2, 7
Hamburg, Margaret, 132
hands-off regime: for ART, 14, 146–59; subterranean regulation and, 151–53
Harkin, Tom, 109, 111
Harris, Kamala, 83
Harris v. McRae, 131
Hart, H. L. A., 119–20
Harvard University, 111, 177 at n. 21
Hatch, Orrin, 107, 217 at n. 77
health insurance: for ART, 23–27, 152; for artificial insemination, 80; for cryopreservation, 35; employer-provided, 24–25; fertility services in, 29; for IVF, 7–8, 24, 25, 80–82; patents and, 101; state mandates for, 24–25, 36, 181 at n. 81
Heinzerling, Lisa, 133, 144
He Jiankui, 12–13, 94, 118
Helms, Jesse (Helms Amendment), 131
heritable genetic modification, 45, 154
HFEA. *See* Human Fertilisation and Embryology Authority
HHS. *See* Department of Health and Human Services
Hilton, Paris, 48
Hinduism, 79
Hippocratic oath, 36
HIV, 94
Hodgen, Gary D., 41, 71–72, 74
Hoescht AG, 124
Hong Kong, 156
Hong Ma, 96
Höög, Christer, 36
Human Cellular and Tissue-Based Rule, 138

human cloning, 90–91, 102–6; FDA and, 105–6, 125–29, 134–35, 223 at n. 61; fringe group support for, 215 at n. 37; IVF and, 112; mitochondrial transfer and, 125; patents for, 99; religion and, 104–5; slippery slope of, 108; states on, 126; stem cell research and, 69–70, 107, 108–9; subterranean regulation on, 128–29
Human Fertilisation and Embryology Authority (HFEA), 32, 41, 45, 68, 147–48
Human Fertility and Embryology Act of 1990, 147
Human Reproduction, 96
Huxley, Aldous, 109
Hyde, Henry, 72, 121–22
Hyde Amendment, 20, 70, 72, 130, 131–32

ICB. *See* Integrated Care Board
ICSI. *See* intracytoplasmic sperm injection
Illinois, 57, 58, 193 at n. 29
incest, 54
IND. *See* investigational new drug application
Indian Child Welfare Act, 21
Indian Health Service, 81
infertility: expense reimbursement for, 206 at n. 113; from gonorrhea, 50; medically induced, 35; VA and, 25
Infertility Center of New York, 194 at n. 58
Institute of Life Clinic, 45–46
institutional review boards (IRBs), 23, 115–16, 134–35
Integrated Care Board (ICB), 33
intellectual property, 99, 157. *See also* patents
International Human Gene Editing Summit, 12–13
International Summit on Human Gene Editing, 94
intracervical insemination, 30, 184 at n. 14
intracytoplasmic sperm injection (ICSI): AUGMENT and, 138; in Uniform Parentage Act, 184 at n. 14
intrauterine insemination, 29, 51–52; cost of, 30–31; health insurance for, 82; in Uniform Parentage Act, 184 at n. 14
intravaginal insemination, 31
investigational new drug application (IND), 102, 190 at n. 135; for AUGMENT, 13–14, 190 at n. 135; for human cloning, 126, 135; for spindle transfer, 137
in vitro fertilization (IVF), 1–2; in Alabama, 78, 83, 112, 160–61; in Australia, 146; Catholic Church and, 75, 112; CDC on, 29; celebrity stories of, 1, 48; Christianity and, 75–76; commercialization of, 52; cost of, 7–8; cryopreservation and, 28–29, 34–35, 48; with cytoplasmic transfer, 5; designer babies from, 39, 75; divorce and, 48; EAB and, 65–66, 72, 158, 201 at n. 56; early history of, 31; embryo destruction in, 38, 68; in England, 27, 146; ethical issues with, 36; FDA and, 130; federal employees and, 80–81; funding restrictions for, 70–73, 80; gene therapy and, 96; with genetic modification or substitution, 29; genetic testing and, 90; health insurance for, 7–8, 24, 25, 80–82; human cloning and, 112; legal restrictions on, 31–32; liability for damage or death of embryo, 206 at n. 125; marriage and, 37; maternal age and, 35; multiple cycles of, 8; multiples with, 35–36; NHS and, 33; NIH and, 65–66, 70–73, 80, 98; number of infants born from, 29; octuplets from, 7, 23; openness to, 2–3; patents and, 100, 101; path dependence and, 65–69; personhood and, 78, 161, 204 at n. 92; regulation of, 67; religion and, 65–69, 112; self-regulation of, 23; shared risk programs for, 8; solution viability in, 157; stem cell research and, 7, 68–69, 109; success rate of, 35; test tube babies from, 31, 36; total children born from, 1; Trump and, 83; in UK, 33, 152; in Uniform Parentage Act, 184 at n. 14; in US, 33–36, 146

in vitro gametogenesis (IVG), 93, 162
IRBs. *See* institutional review boards
Islam, 79
Israel, 156
Ivey, Kay, 83
IVF. *See* in vitro fertilization
IVF Success Estimator, 59
IVG. *See* in vitro gametogenesis

Jackson, Sheila, 105
Japan, 45
Jones, Georgeanna, 71, 81
Jones, Howard, 71, 81, 85
Jones Institute for Reproductive Medicine, 41, 81, 136–37
Judaism, 79

Kaiser Family Foundation (KFF), 29
Kamrava, Michael, 23
Kardashian, Kim, 1, 48
Kass, Leon, 110
Kavanaugh, Brett, 77–78
Kenney, Daniel J., 139
KFF. *See* Kaiser Family Foundation
King v. Burwell, 140, 141
Kymriah, 92

The Lancet, 41
The Language of God (Collins), 111
Lanham Act, 17
laws of medicine, 3–4
Leeuwenhoek, Antonie van, 30
Leigh syndrome, 43
LePage v. Center for Reproductive Medicine, 48, 75, 83
letters as assertions of wrongdoing, in subterranean regulation, 134–35
LGBTQ+, 38
Liu, David, 92–93
lobbyists, 113–14
Loeb, Nick, 48
Louisiana, 48, 57
Lulu, 13, 94

Maeve's Law, 46
Mammoth Biosciences, 93
marriage: ART and, 47, 74; cryopreservation and, 161; *Davis v. Davis* and, 58, 111–12; IVF and, 37; in nuclear families, 2; presumption of, in states, 192 at n. 7; same-sex, 25. *See also* divorce
Maryland, 80–81
Massachusetts: ACT in, 69, 128–29. *See also* OvaScience
Massachusetts General Hospital, 156, 177 at n. 21
Massachusetts Institute of Technology, 92
Masterson, Byron, 224 at n. 82
maternal age, 8, 28, 35
Medicaid, 70, 81, 131
medical malpractice, 22, 61, 153
medical practice, 61; for abortions, 16; ART and, 153
medical research, 61
medical tourism, 111, 149–50
Medical World, 51
Medicare, 81
Mertz, Janet, 100–101
Metzger, Gillian, 19–20
Mexico, 43, 45–46, 145, 148
Mexico City Policy, 20
Michigan, 57
midwives, 16
mifepristone (Mifeprex), 121, 124, 161
Millendo Therapeutics, 45, 139
minimum essential health benefits, 24
misoprostol, 121, 123
Mississippi, 77
Mitalipov, Shoukhrat, 42, 93–96
mitochondrial replacement therapy (MRT), 96
mitochondrial transfer, 42–46, 95–96; in AUGMENT, 13–14, 44, 138–39, 190 at n. 135, 228 at n. 5; in Australia, 46, 190 at n. 143; ethical issues with, 46; FDA on, 5, 44–45, 154; HFEA on, 147–48; human cloning and, 125; slippery slope

of, 39; subterranean regulation of, 153–54; in UK, 95, 96, 190 at n. 143
morality. *See* bioethics; religion
Morrison, Sean, 112–13
Mosher, Jack, 113
MRT. *See* mitochondrial replacement therapy
multiples, 7, 23, 35–36
municipal laws, 16

Nana, 13, 94
National Academy of Sciences, 87–88
National Bioethics Advisory Commission (NBAC), 104–5
National Commission for the Protection of Human Subjects of Biomedical Research, 65
National Conference of Catholic Bishops, 79
National Health Service (NHS), 2, 32–33
National Infertility Awareness Week, 60
National Institute of Medicine, 87–88
National Institutes of Health (NIH), 19; advisory committees of, 113–14; creation of, 177 at n. 20; EAB of, 65–66, 72, 158, 201 at n. 56; germline gene editing and, 70; IVF and, 65–66, 70–73, 80, 98; MRT and, 96; RAC at, 86, 117; recombinant DNA and, 88–89, 116–17; on RU-486, 130; Somatic Cell Genome Editing Consortium at, 162; stem cell research and, 7, 110, 113
National Research Act, 115
National Research Foundation of Korea, 96
National Right to Life, 114
National Science Foundation, 88–89, 156
National Society of Genetic Counselors, 24
Natl' Inst. of Family & Life v. Becerra, 202 at n. 64
NBAC. *See* National Bioethics Advisory Commission
Nevada, 57
Newcastle University, 45
The New England Journal of Medicine, 61
New Hampshire, 57
New Hope Fertility Clinic, 43
New Jersey, 40–41, 56, 57
New York, 42–44, 57, 122, 193 at n. 29
The New Yorker, 123
The New York Times, 48, 52
NHS. *See* National Health Service
NIH. *See* National Institutes of Health
90-Day Fiancé, 54
Nobel Prize in Chemistry, 12, 84, 86, 89, 92, 110, 155
Nobel Prize in Physiology, 36, 89
North Dakota, 57
Northern Ireland, 32
nuclear families, 2
nuclear transplant, 102, 104, 107, 150, 217 at n. 77
nucleic acids, 12, 87–88

Obama, Barack, 113, 132
Obama, Michelle, 1, 7, 25
Obergefell v. Hodges, 22
obfuscation of the evidence of agency action, in subterranean regulation, 136
octuplets, 7, 23
Office of Technology Assessment, 72, 81
Office of Women's Health, 133
Oklahoma, 57
oral contraceptive pill, 123
Oregon Health Sciences University, 42, 95–96
ornithine transcarbamylase (OTC), 91–92
Ott, Emma, 41
Ott, Maureen, 41
Ott, Michael, 41
Our Father, 63
out-of-wedlock births, 49
OvaScience, 18, 138–39, 148, 177 at n. 21, 228 at n. 9. *See also* AUGMENT

Pancoast, William, 30, 51
parentage: with adoption, 56–57; with artificial insemination, 50–52; legal recognition of, 49–50; Social Security Administration and, 16; state laws on, 21–22; UPA and, 6, 30, 50, 62, 184 at n. 14
parental autonomy, 7, 39, 74, 85, 147
Parental Kidnapping and Prevention Act, 21
Parker, Tom, 75
Parkinson's disease, 69
Parrillo, Nicholas R., 139–40
patents: for ART, 99–102; for CRISPR-Cas9, 18; for human cloning, 99; laws on, 99–102; of OvaScience, 18, 177 at n. 21; for recombinant DNA, 86–87, 100–101; for reproductive genetic innovation, 99–102
path dependence, 10, 65–69, 101
Patient Protection and Affordable Care Act (PPACA, Affordable Care Act), 24, 69, 71, 82, 140
Pedersen, Roger, 111
Peduzzi-Nelson, Jean, 111
Pelosi, Nancy, 158
Pennsylvania Medical Center, 210 at n. 73
personhood, 204 at n. 93; IVF and, 78, 161, 204 at n. 92; religion and, 73–76; reproductive cloning and, 98
PGD. *See* preimplantation genetic diagnosis
PGS. *See* preimplantation genetic screening
PGT. *See* preimplantation genetic testing
Pincus, Gregory, 123
Plaisier, Melinda K., 126–27
Plan B, 120, 132–34, 145, 149, 158, 161
Planned Parenthood, 124
Population Council, 124
PPACA. *See* Patient Protection and Affordable Care Act
practice-products, 3, 4
preimplantation genetic diagnosis (PGD), 37, 90, 187 at n. 87
preimplantation genetic screening (PGS), 37, 90, 187 at n. 87
preimplantation genetic testing (PGT), 11, 35, 36–38, 89–90, 187 at n. 87
presidents: executive orders of, 4. *See also specific presidents*
Preyerk, Richardson, 112
Proceedings of the National Academies of Sciences, 88–89
ProPublica, 114
Public Health Service Act, 119, 127, 131, 135, 137, 144
Purdy, Jean, 31

RAC. *See* Recombinant DNA Advisory Committee
Raelians, 103, 135
Reagan, Nancy, 110, 113
recombinant DNA, 84, 85; Berg and, 12; NBAC and, 105; NIH on, 116–17; patents for, 86–87, 100–101; as reproductive genetic innovation, 10; self-regulation of, 23, 86, 87–89, 116–17; stem cell research and, 105
Recombinant DNA Advisory Committee (RAC), 86, 117
Reed, Candice, 31
Reeve, Christopher, 110
Reinventing American Healthcare, 65
religion: abortion and, 12, 64–83, 129–31; ART and, 64–83, 153–55; bioethics and, 73–76; human cloning and, 104–5; IVF and, 65–69, 112; makeup of, 78; personhood and, 73–76; reproductive rights and, 64–83; stem cell research and, 69–70; in US, 11–12, 46–47. *See also* Christianity
reproductive autonomy, 39, 74, 123, 148
reproductive cloning, 91, 98, 106–7, 125, 126
reproductive genetic innovation: AARTs as, 38–46; abortion and, 129–31; in ART, 4–9; FDA and, 6, 160, 162–63; federalism and, 15–16; funding restrictions

for, 70–73; germline gene editing as, 5; patents for, 99–102; politics and ethics of, 6–9; recombinant DNA as, 10; subterranean regulation on, 134–37, 146–59. *See also specific technologies*
reproductive rights: municipal laws on, 16; religion and, 64–83; in states, 14; transparency in, 14
Robertson, John A., 74
Roche, 87
Roe v. Wade, 76, 82–83, 114, 161
Roussel-Uclaf, 123–24
RU-486, 121–24, 130, 158

Saint Barnabas Medical Center, 40–41
same-sex marriages, 25
sanctuary cities, 16
Sanger, Carol, 55
Sanger, Frederick, 12, 86
SART. *See* Society for Assisted Reproductive Technologies
Savulescu, Julian, 39
Schlafly, Phyllis, 107
Schumer, Amy, 1
Science, 71, 88
Scotland, 33
Sebelius, Kathleen, 132–33, 134
SEC. *See* Securities and Exchange Commission
Securities Act of 1933, 17
Securities and Exchange Commission (SEC), 138–39, 148
selective reduction/termination, 85
self-regulation, 98–120; of ART, 12–13, 22–23; of recombinant DNA, 86, 87–89, 116–17; in research and medicine, 115–17
separation of powers, federalism and, 15, 176 at n. 1
Sharkey, Catherine, 139
Sherman Antitrust Act, 17
Shields, Brooke, 1
Sims, J. Marion, 30, 50
Singer, Maxine, 88
slippery slope, 39, 69, 108
Snowflakes Frozen Embryo Adoption Program, 7, 69
Social Security Administration, 16
Society for Assisted Reproductive Technologies (SART), 23
Soll, Dieter, 88
Somatic Cell Genome Editing Consortium, 162
somatic cell nuclear transplantation, 102, 104, 107, 150, 217 at n. 77
Souder, Mark, 103–4, 107, 126–29
Soupart, Pierre, 66
Southern Baptist Convention, 75–76
Spain, 8, 45
sperm donors. *See* gamete donation
spindle transfer, 43, 137
Stanford University, 86–87, 101
Starbucks, 80
states, 3–4; on abortion, 76–80, 149; ART in, 6, 10; cryobanks in, 53–54; doulas and, 16; family law in, 16, 22, 179 at n. 46; federalism and, 15–18, 176 at n. 1; fertility clinics in, 6; health insurance mandates by, 24–25, 36, 181 at n. 81; on human cloning, 126; human embryo research in, 196 at n. 92; marital presumption in, 192 at n. 7; medical malpractice and, 22; midwives and, 16; parentage laws of, 21–22; Parental Kidnapping and Prevention Act and, 21; reproductive rights in, 14; on stem cell research, 21; surrogacy in, 57; UPA in, 50. *See also specific states*
stem cell research: bioethics on, 110; in England, 111; FDA and, 141–42; federal funding for, 19–20; human cloning and, 69–70, 107, 108–9; IVF and, 7, 68–69, 109; NIH and, 7, 110, 113; politics of, 7; recombinant DNA and, 105; religion and, 69–70; slippery slope of, 69; states on, 21; therapeutic cloning for, 91

Steptoe, Patrick, 31
Stern, Elizabeth, 55–57
Stern, William, 55–57, 194 at n. 58
Stevens, John Paul, 152
subterranean regulation, 4, 13–14, 98, 119; of AARTs, 47, 120, 143, 153; on abortifacients, 10; chilling effects of, 136–37; of contraception, 10; criticism of, 139–44; disadvantages of, 151–53; of germline gene editing, 47, 153; on human cloning, 128–29; lack of jurisdiction and, 135–36; letters as assertions of wrongdoing in, 134–35; of mitochondrial transfer, 153–54; obfuscation of the evidence of agency action in, 136; on reproductive genetic innovation, 134–37, 146–59
Suleman, Nadya, 7, 23
surgical centers, 77, 203 at n. 84
surrogacy. *See* gestational surrogate; traditional surrogacy
Surrogacy Parenting Agreement, 194 at n. 58
syphilis, 65

targeted regulation of abortion providers (TRAP laws), 76–77
Tay-Sachs disease, 85, 90
techno-anxiety, 36, 120
Teigen, Chrissy, 48
Tennessee, 58, 111–12
test tube babies, 31, 36
Texas, 57, 59, 203 at n. 84
therapeutic cloning, 91, 106–7, 125
Thompson, Jamie, 109
Thompson, Tommy, 126
TMZ, 48
tobacco, 99, 114, 141
Tober, Diane, 53
tort law, 152–53
traditional surrogacy: Baby M and, 7, 55–56; contract unenforceability of, 32; IVF with, 1
transparency, 120; of advisory committees, 157; at FDA, 149, 158, 161; from hands-off regime, 150; in reproductive rights, 14
TRAP laws. *See* targeted regulation of abortion providers
TRICARE, 25, 81–82
Troxel v. Granville, 22
Trump, Donald, 19, 79, 83
Turkey, 45
turkey basters, 51–52
Turner syndrome, 42
Tuskegee syphilis experiment, 65
21st Century Cures Act of 2016, 160

UCSF. *See* University of California at San Francisco
UK. *See* United Kingdom
Ukraine, 46
Uniform Parentage Act of 2017 (UPA), 6, 30, 50, 62, 184 at n. 14
United Kingdom (UK): ART in, 11, 32, 146; cryopreservation in, 8; cytoplasmic transfer in, 41, 42; gamete donation in, 54; HFEA of, 32, 41, 45, 68, 147–48; IVF in, 31–32, 33, 152; mitochondrial transfer in, 45, 95, 96, 190 at n. 143; NHS in, 2, 32–33; Warnock Committee/Report in, 32, 38, 48–49, 68, 200 at n. 32. *See also* England
United States (US): administrative agencies in, 18–19; ART in, 28–29, 58–61, 149–50, 156; cryopreservation in, 8, 29, 34; cytoplasmic transfer in, 40–42, 146; executive branch in, 20–21; federalism in, 15–18, 176 at n. 1; fertility clinics in, 28; historical reactions to ART in, 11; IVF in, 7–8, 31, 33–36, 46, 146; mitochondrial transfer in, 42; opposition to ART in, 11–12; regulation in, 151–52; religion in, 11–12, 46–47; reproductive autonomy in, 148; research funding in, 19–20; RU-486 in, 124. *See also specific agencies, laws, and topics*

University of California at Berkeley, 92
University of California at San Francisco (UCSF), 86, 101, 111
University of Michigan, 112–13
University of Mississippi, 107
University of Missouri, 99
University of Pennsylvania, 91–92
UPA. *See* Uniform Parentage Act of 2017
US. *See* United States
US Department of Agriculture (USDA), 95
US Patent and Trademark Office, 18, 86, 99
U.S. v. Regenerative Sciences, 142
U.S. v. Rutherford, 17
Utah, 57

VA. *See* Department of Veterans Affairs
Vanderbilt University, 65–66
Vergara, Sofia, 7, 48
Vermont, 95
Veterans' Administration, 206 at n. 117
Virginia, 57
The Virginian-Pilot, 41

Wadlington, Walter, 62
Walden, Guy, 130
Waldman, Lois, 79–80
Wales, 32–33
Warnock, Mary, 32, 37, 158–59
Warnock Committee/Report, 32, 38, 48–49, 68, 200 at n. 32
Washington (state), 57
Washington, Earl, 28
Washington, Kerry, 28
Washington Post, 18–19, 151
Wasserman Schultz, Debbie, 154
Waxman, Henry, 130
Weissman, Irving, 105
Welsh Health Specialised Services Committee (WHSSC), 32–33
West, Michael, 129
West Virginia, 57
West Virginia v. EPA, 141
Whitehead, Mary Beth, 55–57, 60, 194 at n. 58
Whitehead, Richard, 194 at n. 58
WHSSC. *See* Welsh Health Specialised Services Committee
Wicker, Roger, 106, 109. *See also* Dickey-Wicker Amendment
Williams, Brian, 34
Williams, Jo Beth, 60
Woodcock, Janet, 142
Wrongful Death of a Minor Act, 161
Wyden, Ron, 122, 130
Wyeth v. Levine, 152

Yale University, 88

Zamboni, Luciano, 66
Zavos, Panayiotis (Panos), 103, 107–8
Zhang, John, 42–44, 137, 145, 148
Zoon, Kathryn, 126, 129, 135